Controlled Drugs

Law and Practice

Controlled Drugs
Law and Practice

Richard Lord MA(Cantab)
Barrister-at-Law

Consulting Editor

Christopher Sumner MA(Cantab)
Barrister-at-Law

London
Butterworths
1984

England	Butterworth & Co (Publishers) Ltd, 88 Kingsway, LONDON WC2B 6AB
Australia	Butterworths Pty Ltd, SYDNEY, MELBOURNE, BRISBANE, ADELAIDE, PERTH, CANBERRA and HOBART
Canada	Butterworth & Co (Canada) Ltd, TORONTO and VANCOUVER
New Zealand	Butterworths of New Zealand Ltd, WELLINGTON and AUCKLAND
Singapore	Butterworth & Co (Asia) Pte Ltd, SINGAPORE
South Africa	Butterworth Publishers (Pty) Ltd, DURBAN and PRETORIA
USA	Butterworth Legal Publishers, ST PAUL, Minnesota, SEATTLE, Washington, BOSTON, Massachusetts, AUSTIN, Texas and D & S Publishers, CLEARWATER, Florida

© Butterworths & Co (Publishers) Ltd 1984

British Library Cataloguing in Publication Data

Lord, Richard D.
    Controlled drugs: law and practice.
    1. Drug abuse _____ Law and
    legislation _____ Great Britain
    I. Title
    344.104'4233   KD3460

    ISBN 0-406-01610-0

Photoset by Butterworths Litho Preparation Department
Printed and bound in Great Britain by Biddles Ltd, Guildford, Surrey

Foreword

by Rt Hon Lord Rawlinson of Ewell QC

This is a timely and important book. It should become a part of the library of every judge, practitioner, or official who works in the Criminal Courts. But this book is also of much interest to a wider public. For the use of drugs and the offences arising from their importation, possession, and use are nowadays very widespread. Nevertheless many remain very ignorant not only of the modern scale of drug use but also of the vast financial rewards that can come from the traffic in drugs. Behind many crimes and many family tragedies lies this modern scourge.

The book itself provides much important information for the layman as well as the lawyer. It gives a useful summary of the history of the use of drugs; it identifies those parts of the world from which the main categories of commonly used drugs emanate; it describes the customary method of administration of each drug, and, broadly, their effects; and it calculates the profits earned from each link along the chain from producer to consumer. A comparison of street value with production cost demonstrates vividly why this traffic is now 'big business' and why it attracts the close attention of sinister organisations.

As the author concludes, 'many of society's attitudes to drugs and drug use are based on inaccurate information'. This book should do much to remedy this, for it also provides some general information on counselling and rehabilitation centres, while yet giving full discussions of the leading decisions of the Courts over what constitutes 'being knowingly concerned' in importation, and possession.

Mr Lord is to be congratulated on producing so useful a work of general as well as of technical character which should play a significant part in helping to reduce the level of ignorance about one of the most disturbing influences of our times.

PETER RAWLINSON

Preface

The purpose of this book can be very simply expressed. It is to provide a self-contained guide to the law and practice concerning controlled drugs. It is the aim of the author that anyone whose work involves him in the legal aspect of the misuse of drugs will find in this work the information which he or she requires. The principal Statutes, Regulations and cases in this field are described and in addition there are sections on the history and policy of the law and on the effects, prices and other properties of the drugs themselves. These sections have been included in the belief that it is essential for those working in this area to have some knowledge not only of the law, but of the subject of drugs and drug use generally.

The book is written mainly with the legal practitioner in mind, but it is hoped that it will be of use and interest to many others, such as members of the judiciary, magistrates, the police and customs, probation officers, students and interested laymen.

In writing this book I have received much assistance from various sources. In particular I would like to thank the Institute for the Study of Drug Dependence for providing a great deal of essential information with unfailing enthusiasm, Roger Lewis, Christine Johnson, the Home Office, the Oxford Drug Squad and the library staff at Christchurch, Oxford, Warwick University and the Inner Temple. Finally I would also like to thank Messrs Wright, Hassall and Co for providing me with wordprocessing facilities.

I have endeavoured to state the law as it stands at 1 June 1984.

RICHARD LORD
Leamington Spa,
Warwickshire

Contents

Foreword   v
Preface   vii
Table of Legislation   xi
Table of Cases   xvii
Abbreviations   xxii

Part I Introduction

1 History and Policy of the Legislation   3
2 The Advisory Council   7
3 Some Commonly Abused Drugs   9

Part II Procedure

4 Introduction   23
5 Powers of the Police and Customs   25
6 Procedure   34

Part III Substantive Offences

7 Importation and Exportation   41
8 Production and Supply   47
9 Possession   51
10 Cultivation of Cannabis   68
11 Misuse of Drugs Act 1971, section 8   71
12 Misuse of Drugs Act 1971, section 9   75
13 Misuse of Drugs Act 1971, section 20   78
14 Miscellaneous Offences   79
15 Conspiracy and Attempt   82
16 Misuse of Drugs Act 1971, section 28   86

Part IV Sentencing

17 Sentencing   91
18 Forfeiture   99

Part V Lawful Use

19 Lawful Use   105

Appendices

1 Misuse of Drugs Act 1971   117
2 Other Statutory Provisions   151
3 Regulations   174
4 Specimen Indictments, Search Warrant and Licence to
  Produce, Supply and Possess   204
5 Sentencing Table   208
6 Selected Statistics   209
7 Profits at Various Stages of the Supply Chain   217
8 Further Information   218

INDEX   221

Table of Legislation

References in this Table to *Statutes* are to Halsbury's Statutes of England (Third Edition) showing the volume and page at which the annotated text of the Act will be found. Page references printed in bold type indicate where the Act is set out in part or in full.

PAGE

Attendance of Witnesses Act 1854 (12 *Statutes* 823) 143
Courts Act 1971 (41 *Statutes* 285) s 57 99
Criminal Attempts Act 1981 (51 *Statutes* 734)
s 1 84
5 . . . . **84**
Criminal Justice Act 1948 (8 *Statutes* 337)
s 1 (1) 172
Criminal Justice Act 1967 (8 *Statutes* 583)
s 91 81
Criminal Law Act 1967 (8 *Statutes* 552) 29
s 2 . . . . 26, **172**
(4) 26
Criminal Law Act 1977 (47 *Statutes* 142, 692, 762) 29, 61
s 1 . . . . 82, **173**
(1) 84, 85, 205
25 (3) 161
28 168
52 . . . . 60, 174
61 (1) 168
Customs and Excise Act 1952 (9 *Statutes* 55) 34, 174
s 45 125
(1) 131
56 125
(2) 131
304 . . . . . . 43, 44, 83, 125
Customs and Excise Management Act 1979 (49 *Statutes* 290) . . 28, 36, 44, 80, 100
s 5 . . . . **151**
16 . . . . 29, 30, 151
27, 28 . . . . 29, **152**

PAGE

Customs and Excise Management Act 1979—*contd*
s 29 . . . . **152**
34 29
35 . . . . 152, 153
37 151
43 168
49 . . . . **153**
(1) 101
50 . . . . 35, 41, 82, **154**
68 . . . . 35, 41, 82, **155**
78, 82 29
88, 89 . . . . **156**
138 . . . . 29, 156
139 . . . . . . 29, 101, **157**
140 . . . . 29, 101
141 . . . . . . 29, 101, **158**
142 . . . . . . 29, 101, **158**
(1) **101**
143 . . . . 29, **159**
144 . . . . 29, **160**
145 . . . . 37, **160**
(1), (5) 37
146 . . . . 37, **160**
(1), (2) 37
147 . . . . 37, 161
(1) 37
(2), (3) 38
148 . . . . . . 37, 38, **162**
(1), (2) 38
149, 150 . . . . . 37, 38, **162**
151–153 . . . . . . 37, **163**
154 . . . . . . 37, 38, **163**
(1), (2) 38
155 . . . . **164**
161 . . . . 28, **165**
163 . . . . **28**, **165**
(2) 28
164 . . . . 29, **166**

PAGE

Customs and Excise Management
Act 1979—*contd*
s 170 . . 35, 43, 45, 46, 49, 83, **166**
    (2) . . . 41, 43, 44, 45, 48, 205
  171 . . . . **167**
    (2) 35
  Sch 1 . . . . 35, 168
  Sch 3 . . . . .101, 102, **169**
Dangerous Drugs Act 1920 . . .4 , 75
Dangerous Drugs 1965 (21
  Statutes 952) . . 4, 5, 72, 125, 188
  s 2, 3 149
    4 (3) 36
    5 . . . . 36, 73, 74
    6 (1) 187
    8 36
  10, 11 149
  18 85
Dangerous Drugs Act 1967 (21
  Statutes 971)
  s 1 (1), (2) 149
  2, 3 149
  Schedule 149
Dangerous Drugs and Poisons
  (Amendment) Act 1923 . . . 4
Dentists Act 1957 (21 *Statutes*
  712) 137
Documentary Evidence Act 1868
  (12 *Statutes* 841) 163
Drugs (Prevention of Misuse) Act
  1964 (21 *Statutes* 942) . 5, 7, 188
  s 5 149
Extradition Act 1870 (13 *Statutes*
  249)
  Sch 1 . . . . 36, 136
Extradition Act 1932 (13 *Statutes*
  275)
  s 1 36
Food and Drugs Act 1955 (14
  Statutes 15) 184
  s 89 . . . . 177, 178
Food and Drugs (Scotland) Act
  1956 184
  s 27 . . . . 177, 178
Government of Ireland Act 1920
  (23 *Statutes* 843)
  s 6 138
Health Services Act (Northern
  Ireland) 1971. 174
Hovercraft Act 1968 (31 *Statutes*
  725) 30, 132
Interpretation Act 1889 (32 *Statutes*
  434) 175, 192, 195, 197
  s 26 135

PAGE

Interpretation Act 1978 (48 *Statutes*
  1296)
  s 5 79
  38 (2) 149
  Sch 1 79
Interpretation Act (Northern Ireland) 1954
  s 41 (6) 123, 136
Magistrates' Courts Act 1952
  (21 *Statutes* 181)
  s 114 163
Magistrates' Courts Act 1980
  (50 (2) *Statutes* 1433)
  s 18–21 34
  127 (1) 37
Matrimonial Proceedings (Magistrates' Courts) Act 1960 (17
  Statutes 241)
  s 16 (1) 136
Medical Act 1956 (21 *Statutes*
  624) 137
Medical Act 1969 (21 *Statutes*
  836) 137
Medicines Act 1968 (21 *Statutes*
  981) 129, 175, 184, 192
  s 69 137
  75, 80 125
  Sch 3 . . . . 177, 178
Medicines, Pharmacy and Poisons
  Act (Northern Ireland) 1945 . 138
Mental Health Act 1959 (25 *Stat-
  utes* 42) 192, 194
Merchant Shipping Act 1894 (31
  Statutes 57) 174
Merchant Shipping (Oil Pollution)
  Act 1971 (41 *Statutes* 1345) . . 174
Metropolitan Police Act 1839
  s 66 26
Midwives Act 1951 (21 *Statutes*
  599) 180
  s 17 181
Midwives (Scotland) Act 1951 . . 180
  s 18 181
Mineral Workings (Offshore In-
  stallations) Act 1971 (41 *Statutes* 940) 174, 180
Misuse of Drugs Act 1971 (41
  Statutes 878): 4, 5, 80, 169, 174 192
  s 1 . . . . 7, **118**
    (2) 7
  2 . . . . 41, **119**
    (5) 8
  3 . . . . . .68, 82, 105, 108, **120**,
    154, 155, 167

PAGE

Misuse of Drugs Act 1971—*contd*
s 3 (1) 41, 82, 83, 175, 205
  4 . . . 47, 48, 51, 68, 69, 105, **120**
  (1) **47**, 48, 51, 66, 71, 176,
                177, 178, 179, 180
  (2) **47**, 48, 86, 91
  (3) 48, 50, 86
  5 . . . . . . 42, **51**, 68, 105, 121
  (1) 175, 176, 179, 180
  (2) **42**, 50, 65, 86, 204
  (3) 50, 67, 86, 204
  (4) **65**
  6 . . . **68**, 69, 105, 109, **122**, 181
  (2) 86
  7 . . . . 47, 51, 65, 68, 75, 105,
              109, 112, **122**
  (3) 066, 105
  (4) 202
  8 . . . . 48, **71**, 72, 73, 74, 76,
              109, **123**, 181
  (a) 69, 74, 204
  (b) 74
  9 . . . . . 34, 57, 75, **76**, 86, **123**
  10 . . . . 75, 105, 112, **124**
  (2) 113, 114
  11 . . . . 105, 112, **124**
  (1), (2), (4), (6) 112
  12 . . . . 105, 112, **125**
  (2) 192
  13 . . . . 105, 112, **125**
  (1) 113, 196
  (2) 113
  (3) 113, 196
  14 . . . 112, 113, 114, **126**, 196, 197
  (1) 197, 201
  (2) 197
  (7) 201
  15 . . . . 105, 112, 113, 114, **127**
  (6) 201
  16 . . 105, 112, 113, 114, **129**, 196
  (2), (3) 114
  17 . . . . . 105, 112, 114, **129**
  (3) 34, 114
  (4) 114
  18 . . . . 114, **130**
  (1) 113, 114
  19 . . . . 82, 84, **131**, 196
  20 . . . . 78, 94, 131
  21 . . . . 36, 79, **131**
  22 . . . . **131**
  23 . . . . . 25, 30, 31, **131**, 207
  (1) 30, 32
  (2) 30, 31
  (3) 31, 32, 206
  (4) 30, 32

PAGE

Misuse of Drugs Act 1971—*contd*
s 24 . . . . . 25, 26, 30, 31, **32**, **123**
  25 . . . . 100, **133**, 196
  (1)–(3) 34
  (4) 34, 37
  (5), (6) 34
  26 . . . . 35, 43
  27 . . . . **99**, 100, **134**
  28 . . . 47, 51, 54, 65, 68, 69, 70,
            76, 84, 86, 87, 88, **134**
  (1) 86
  (2) 68, 76, 86, 87, 88
  (3) 244, 86, 87, 88
  29 . . . . 36, **134**
  30 . . . . 109, **135**
  31 . . . . 8, **135**
  (3) 8
  32 . . . . **136**
  33 . . . . **36**, 136
  34, 35 . . . . **136**
  36 . . . . **136**
  (1), (2) 78
  37 . . . . 69, **136**
  (1) 47, 48, 54, 60,
                61, 62, 69, 75
  (3) 53
  38 . . . . **138**
  39 . . . . **138**
  (2) 188
  40 . . . . **138**
  Sch 1 . . . . . . 8, **139**, 175, 196
  Sch 2 . . . . 8, 60, 62, 63, **139**
  Pt I 62, 63
    IV 61
  Sch 3 . . . 108, 114, **142**, 197, 202
  Pt I 112
  Sch 4 . . . . . 34, 100, **144**, 196
  Sch 5 . . . . **149**
  Sch 6 . . . . **150**, 188
National Health Service Act 1946
  (23 *Statutes* 9) . . . 174, 177, 178,
                          184, 194
National Health Service (Isle of
  Man) Act 1948 174
National Health Service Re-
  organisation Act 1973 (43 *Stat-
  utes* 764) . . . 174, 177, 178, 184
National Health Service (Scotland)
  Act 1947 . . . 174, 177, 178, 184
National Health Service (Scotland)
  Act 1972 (43 *Statutes* 758) . . 182
Offences against the Person Act
  1861 (8 *Statutes* 147)
  s 22 . . . . 80, **172**
  23 . . . . 49, 80, **172**

PAGE

Offences against the Person Act
    1861—*contd*
    24 . . . . 80, **172**
Penal Servitude Act 1891 (25 *Stat-
    utes* 816)
    s 1 (1) 172
Pharmacy Act 1868   4
Pharmacy and Poisons Act 1933
    (21 *Statutes* 860)
    s 8–10 138
    25 . . . . 177, 179
Policy (Property) Act 1897 (25
    Statutes 280) 158
Powers of Criminal Courts Act
    1973 (43 *Statutes* 288)
    s 43 99

PAGE

Public Health Act 1936 (26 *Statutes*
    189) 192, 194
Road Traffic Act 1972 (42 *Statutes*
    1633)
    s 5   80
    159   26
Supreme Court of Judicature
    (Consolidation) Act 1925
    s 49 143
Trade Union and Labour Relations
    Act 1974 173
Tribunals and Inquiries Act 1971
    (41 *Statutes* 248) 108
Veterinary Surgeons Act 1966 (21
    Statutes 143)
    s 2, 8 137

Statutory Instruments

PAGE

Dangerous Drugs Regulations
    (Northern Ireland) 1965, SI
    1965 No 30 (NI) 149
Dangerous Drugs (Notification to
    Addicts) Regulations 1968, SI
    1968/136 196
Dangerous Drugs (Supply to
    Addicts) Regulations 1968, SI
    1968/416 196
    reg 1 196
Dangerous Drugs (No 2) Regu-
    lations 1964, SI 1964/1811 . . 149,
                                187, 188
    reg 26 188
Defence of the Realm Regulations
    1916 No. 22
    reg 40, 40B   4
Indictment Rules 1971, SI 1971/
    1253 35
    r 4, 6 . . . . **35**
    7 . . . . **35** , 36
Misuse of Drugs (Amendment)
    Regulations 1974, SI 1974/402: 106
Misuse of Drugs (Amendment)
    Regulations 1975, SI 1975/499: 106
Misuse of Drugs (Amendment)
    (No 2) Regulation 1975, SI
    1975/1623 106

PAGE

Misuse of Drugs (Amendment)
    Regulation 1977, SI 1977/
    1380 106
Misuse of Drugs (Amendment)
    Regulations 1979, SI 1979/326: 106
Misuse of Drugs (Designation)
    Order 1977, SI 1977/1379
    r 1 . . . . **202**
Misuse of Drugs (Notification of
    and Supply to Addicts) Regu-
    lations 1973, SI 1973/799 . 106, 113
    reg 1 . . . . **194**
    2 . . . . **194**
    (2) 111
    3, 4 . . . . 111, **195**
    Schedule **196**
Misuse of Drugs (Notification of
    and Supply to Addicts)
    (Amendment) Regulations
    1983, SI 1983/1909 111
Misuse of Drugs Regulations 1973,
    SI 1973/797 106
    reg 1 . . . . 106, **174**
    2 . . . . 107, **174**
    3 . . . . **175**
    4 . . . . **175**
    (1), (2) 108
    5 . . . . 109, 176

PAGE

Misuse of Drugs Regulations 1973
—*contd*
reg 6 . . . . .107, 176
 7 . . . . .108, **176**
 (1)–(3) 108
 8 . . . . . . .107, 108, **176**
 (1) 108
 (2) 107, 108
 9 . . . . . . .107, 108, **178**
 (1) 108
 (2) 107, 108
 10 . . . . .107, **179**
 (2) 107
 11 . . . . . .107, 108, **180**
 12, 13 . . . . . . .109, 181
 14 . . . . .109, 181
 (2)–(6) 109
 15 . . . . .110, **183**
 16 . . . . 110, **184**
 17, 18 184
 19, 20 . . . . . .110, **185**
 21–23 . . . . . .110, **186**
 24 . . . . . .110, **187**, 207
 25 . . . . 110, **187**
Sch 1 . . . . .106, 108, **188**, 194
Sch 2 . . . . .106, 107, 108, **189**
Sch 3 . . . . .106, 107, 108, **190**
Sch 4   . . . . .106, 109, **191**

PAGE

Misuse of Drugs (Safe Custody)
 Regulations 1973, SI 1973/798: 106
reg 1, 2 191
 3 . . . . . . .110, 111, **192**
 4 . . . . .111, **192**
 5 . . . . .111, **193**
Sch 1 . . . . **194**
Sch 2 111
Misuse of Drugs Tribunal (England
 and Wales) Rules 1974, SI
 1974/85 112
reg 1–4 . . . . **197**
 5–7 . . . . **198**
 8–11 . . . . **199**
 12–15 . . . . **200**
 16–18 . . . . **201**
 19–21 . . . . **202**
Offshore Installations (Logbooks
 and Registration of Death)
 Regulations 1972, SI 1972/
 1542 186
Tribunals and Inquiries (Misuse of
 Drugs Tribunals) Order 1973,
 SI 1973/1600 108
Weights and Measures (Equivalents for dealing with drugs)
 Regulations 1970, SI 1970/
 1897 175

Table of Cases

Cases are listed under the name of the accused whenever the usual method of citation would cause them to be preceded by the abbreviation "R v" signifying that the prosecution was undertaken by the Crown.

A
                                                                    PAGE

Abbott v Smith [1965] 3 QB 662n, [1964] 3 All ER 762 73
Airton v Scott (1909) 100 LT 393, 73 JP 148 76
Alderson v Booth [1969] 2 QB 216, 53 Cr App Rep 301, CA . . . 27
Anderson [1981] Crim LR 270, CA 95
Anderson v Reid (1902) 86 LT 713, 66 JP 564, DC 29
Aramah (1983) 76 Cr App Rep 190, [1983] Crim LR 271, CA . . 92, 94, 208
Ardalan [1972] 2 All ER 257, 56 Cr App Rep 320, CA . . . 44, 45, 83
Armstrong v Clark [1957] 2 QB 391, [1957] 1 All ER 433 81
Ashdown (1974) 59 Cr App Rep 193, CA 73
Ashton-Rickardt [1978] 1 All ER 173, 65 Cr App Rep 67, CA . . 53, 88
Atkinson [1978] Crim LR 307, CA 32
A-G v Hunter [1949] 2 KB 111, [1949] 1 All ER 1006 101
A-G v Robson (1850) 5 Exch 790 73
A-G's Reference (No. 1 of 1981) [1982] QB 848, 75 Cr App Rep 45, CA . 46

B

Bayliss and Oliver [1978] Crim LR 361, OC 59
Beard [1974] 1 WLR 1549, [1975] Crim LR 92 99
Best (1979) 70 Cr App Rep 21, [1979] Crim LR 787, CA . . . 63, 64
Bibi [1980] Crim LR 732 94
Bird v Adams [1972] Crim LR 174, DC 64
Blake and O'Connor (1978) 68 Cr App Rep 1 50
Bocking v Roberts [1974] QB 307, [1973] Crim LR 517, DC . . 58, 59
Bott (1979) 1 Cr App Rep 218 208
Boyesen [1982] AC 768, 75 Cr App Rep 51, HL 58
Brocey v Read [1963] Ch 88, [1962] 3 All ER 472 72
Brazil v Chief Constable of Surrey [1983] 3 All ER 537, 77 Cr App Rep 237, DC 26, 31
Brown (1976) 64 Cr App Rep 231, [1977] Crim LR 291, CA . . 26, 27
Buckley (1979) 69 Cr App Rep 371, [1979] Crim LR 664, CA . . 49
Bushwell [1972] 1 All ER 75, [1972] 1 WLR 64, CA 66

C

Campbell [1982] Crim LR 595 72
Carr Briant [1943] KB 607, 29 Cr App Rep 76, CCA 87
Carver [1978] QB 472, 67 Cr App Rep 352, CA 58, 59
Cato [1976] 1 All ER 260, 62 Cr App Rep 41 80
Cavendish [1961] 2 All ER 856, 45 Cr App Rep 374, CCA . . . 53
Champ (1981) 73 Cr App Rep 367, [1982] Crim LR 108, CA . . 69
Chatwood [1980] 1 All ER 467, 70 Cr App Rep 39, CA . . . 64
Chic Fashions (West Wales) Ltd v Jones [1968] 2 QB 299, [1968] 1 All ER 229, CA 27

PAGE

Christie v Leachinsky [1947] AC 573, [1947] 1 All ER 567, HL . . . 27
Clark v R (1884) 14 QBD 92, 52 LT 136 76
Collins v Wilcox (1984) Times, 17 April, DC 26
Colyer [1974] Crim LR 243 59
Courtie [1984] 1 All ER 740, [1984] 2 WLR 330, HL 43
Cowlairs Co-operative Society Ltd v Glasgow Corpn 1957 SLT 288 . . 72
Cramp (1880) 5 QBD 307, 39 LJ MC 44 80
Cross (1857) 1 H&N 651, 26 LJ MC 28 76
Customs and Excise Comrs v Jack Bradley (Accrington) Ltd [1959] 1 QB
219, [1958] Crim LR 786 101
Customs and Excise Comrs v Sokolow's Trustee [1954] 2 QB 336, [1954]
2 All ER 5 37
Cuthbertson [1980] 2 All ER 401, 71 Cr App Rep 148 100

D

Dallaway (1983) 7 October, (unreported), CA 67
Davies and Marshall-Price (1982) 4 Cr App Rep (S) 302, [1983] Crim
LR 46, CA 94
Delgado [1984] 1 All ER 449, [1984] 1 WLR 89, CA 49, 50
Denton v John Lister Ltd [1971] 3 All ER 669, [1971] 1 WLR 1426, DC . 101, 169
Dhulipala Kameswara Rao v Wyles [1949] 2 All ER 685, 113 JP 516 . . 107, 111
DPP v Brooks [1974] AC 862, 59 Cr App Rep 185, PC 52
DPP v Doot [1973] AC 807, 57 Cr App Rep 600, HL 45, 83
DPP v Goodchild [1978] 2 All ER 161, 6 Cr App Rep 56, HL . . . 48
DPP v Majewski [1977] AC 443, [1977] Crim LR 532 88
DPP v Nock and Alsford [1978] AC 979, 67 Cr App Rep 116 . . . 83, 84
Donnelly v Jackman [1970] 1 All ER 987, 54 Cr App Rep 229, DC . . 26
Downes (1984) Times, 13 June, CA 50
Dunbar [1982] 1 All ER 188, 74 Cr App Rep 88, CA 66

E

Ewens [1967] 1 QB 322, 50 Cr App Rep 171, CCA 65

F

Faulkner and Thomas [1977] Crim LR 47 93
Farr [1982] Crim LR 745, CA 48
Farrow v Tunnicliffe [1976] Crim LR 126, DC 31
Fernandez [1970] Crim LR 277, CA 54
Fox v Dingley [1967] 1 All ER 100, [1967] 1 WLR 379, DC 36, 71
Fraser [1967] Crim LR 597 95

G

Garrett v Arthur Churchill (Glass) Ltd [1970] 1 QB 92, [1969] 2 All ER
1141, DC 46
Geen [1982] Crim LR 604, CA 31
Ghani v Jones [1970] 1 QB 693, [1969] 3 All ER 1700, CA 27
Glanvill Enthoven & Co v IRC (1925) 41 TLR 258, HL 73
Goodchild (No 1) [1977] 2 All ER 163, 64 Cr App Rep 100 61
Goodchild (No 2) [1978] 2 All ER 161, 67 Cr App Rep 56, HL . . . 61
Goodchild (No 2) [1978] 1 All ER 649, 65 Cr App Rep 165, CA . . . 61, 62
Gorman v Standen [1964] 1 QB 294, 48 Cr App Rep 30, DC . . . 73
Graham [1969] 2 All ER 1181, [1970] 1 WLR 113, CA 58
Green [1976] QB 985, 62 Cr App Rep 74, CA 44
Greenfield [1983] Crim LR 397, CA 50
Greensmith [1983] 3 All ER 444, 77 Cr App Rep 202, CA 63

H
PAGE

Hambleton v Callinan [1968] 2 QB 427, [1968] 2 All ER 943, DC . . 57, 75
Hancock and Holdgate [1978] Crim LR 174, CA 94
Harris [1968] 2 All ER 49n, 52 Cr App Rep 277, CA 49
Harris [1979] Cr App Rep 122 84
Haughton v Smith [1975] AC 476, 58 Cr App Rep 198 83
Hennah (1877) 13 Cox CC 547 80
Hennessey (1978) 68 Cr App Rep 419, CA 43
Hierowski [1978] Crim LR 563 . . . . . . 58, 59, 64
Holmes v Chief Constable Mersey Police [1976] Crim LR 125, DC . . 48
Hussain [1969] 2 QB 567, 53 Cr App Rep 448, CA 43

I

Inwood [1973] 2 All ER 645, 57 Cr App Rep 529, CA 27
Irala-Prevost [1965] Crim LR 606, CCA 53
Irving [1970] Crim LR 642, CA 54

J

Jacobsohn v Blake (1884) 6 Man & G 919, 13 LJCP 89 101
Jaggard v Dickinson [1981] QB 527, 72 Cr App Rep 33 88
Jagger (1967) 51 Cr App Rep 473, [1967] Crim LR 587, CA . . . 66
Jakeman (1983) 76 Cr App Rep 223, [1983] Crim LR 104, CA . . . 44
Jeffrey v Black [1978] QB 490, [1977] Crim LR 555, DC . . . 28
Jolley [1971] 56 Cr App Rep 217, [1972] Crim LR 193, CA . . . 94
Josephs (1977) 65 Cr App Rep 253, CA 72
Jusoh [1979] Crim LR 191, CA 94

K

Kenlin v Gardiner [1967] 2 QB 510, [1966] 3 All ER 931, DC . . 26
Khan [1982] 3 All ER 969, 4 Cr App Rep 298 99
King [1978] Crim LR 228 . . . . 49, 67
Kyprianou v Reynolds [1969] Crim LR 656, DC 85

L

Lang and Evans [1977] Crim LR 286 64
Lanham v Rickwood (1984) Times, 10th May, DC 81
Lawless [1981] Crim LR 845, DC 94
Lawrence (1981) 3 Cr App Rep 49 208
Lipman [1970] 1 QB 15, 53 Cr App Rep 600, CA 88
Littleford [1978] Crim LR 48 32
Lockyer v Gibb [1967] 2 QB 243, [1966] 2 All ER 653, DC . . . 54, 88

M

Macauley (1967) 52 Cr App Rep 230, [1967] Crim LR 716, CA . . 93
McBean v Parker [1983] LR 399, DC 26, 31
McCulloch (1982) 4 Cr App Rep 98 208
Marais [1981] 2 All ER 833, [1981] 1 WLR 774 80
Marriott [1971] 1 All ER 595, 55 Cr App Rep 82, CA 55
Mehagian and Fenwick (1972) 57 Cr App Rep 488, [1973] Crim LR 250 95
Menocal [1980] AC 598, 69 Cr App Rep 157 . . . . . 83, 99
Metropolitan Water Board v Paine [1907] 1 KB 285, 76 LJKB 151, DC . 72
Mieras v Rees [1975] Crim LR 224, DC 84
Mogford [1970] 1 WLR 988, [1970] Crim LR 402 72
Moore [1979] Crim LR 789 49
Morgan [1977] Crim LR 488, CA 100
Muir v Smith [1978] Crim LR 293, DC 64

N   PAGE

Ng and Dhalan [1978] Crim LR 174, CA 94
Nakhla v R [1976] AC 1, [1975] 2 All ER 138 76
Naylor [1979] Crim LR 532 28
Neal (1983) 77 Cr App Rep 283, CA 45, 49, 83
Neale v RMJE (a minor) (1984) Times, 5 March 81

O

Owen [1973] Crim LR 455, CA 95

P

Palmer [1974] Crim LR 375, CA 93
Peaston (1978) 69 Cr App Rep 203, [1979] Crim LR 183, CA . . . 53
Peevey (1973) 57 Cr App Rep 554, CA 60
Powrie [1973] Crim LR 708, CA 94
Pragliola [1977] Crim LR 612 60

R

R v Chelmsford Justices, ex parte Amos [1973] Crim LR 437, DC . . 85
Ribeiro and Perry [1979] Crim LR 90 52
Rice v Connolly [1966] 2 QB 414, [1966] 2 All ER 649, DC 26
Roote [1981] Crim LR 189, CA 95
Rubinstein and Grandison (1982) 4 Cr App Rep 202 208

S

Sang [1980] AC 402, 69 Cr App Rep 282, HL 26
Searle [1971] Crim LR 592, CA 53, 56
Searle v Randolph [1972] Crim LR 779, DC 54, 56, 88
Secretary of State for Education and Science v Tameside Metropolitan
    Borough Council [1977] AC 1014 108
Smith [1966] Crim LR 558, CCA 52
Smith [1973] QB 924, 57 Crim App Rep 737, CA 42
Spires (1983) 17 November, (unreported) 208
Stearn (1982) 4 Cr App Rep 195 208
Stevens [1981] Crim LR 568, CA 63
Storey (1968) 52 Cr App Rep 334, [1968] Crim LR 387, CA 64
Sweet v Parsley [1970] AC 132, 53 Cr App Rep 221, HL . . . 73, 74, 76

T

Taaffe [1984] 1 All ER 747, [1984] 2 WLR 326, HL 42, 43
Talgarth Justices [1973] Crim LR 756 71
Tansley v Painter [1969] Crim LR 139, DC 56
Tao [1977] QB 141, 63 Cr App Rep 163, CA 72
Taonis (1974) 59 Cr App Rep 160, [1974] Crim LR 332 94
Tarpy v Rickard [1980] Crim LR 375, DC 59
Taylor v Chief Constable of Kent [1981] 1 WLR 606, 72 Cr App Rep 318,
    DC 69
Tesco Supermarkets v Nattrass [1972] AC 153, [1971] 2 All ER 127 . . 79
Thomas (1976) 63 Cr App Rep 65, [1976] Crim LR 517, CA . . . 73
Thomas [1981] Crim LR 496, CA 63
Thomas v Sawkins [1935] 2 KB 249, 104 LJKB 572, DC 27
Tudhope v Robertson 1980 SLT 60 69

V

Vickers [1975] 2 All ER 945, [1975] 1 WLR 811 78
Virgin (1983) 5 Cr App Rep 148 208

W

PAGE

Wall [1974] 2 All ER 245, 59 Cr App Rep 58, CA 44
Ware v Fox [1967] 1 All ER 100, [1967] 1 WLR 379, DC . . . 36, 71
Warner v Metropolitan Police Comr [1969] 2 AC 256, 52 Cr App Rep 373,
  HL 52, 53, 54, 55, 56
Watts [1984] 2 All ER 380, [1984] 1 WLR 757, CA 63
Watts and Stack (1979) 70 Cr App Rep 187, [1980] Crim LR 38, CA . . 45
Webb [1979] Crim LR 462 . . . . . . ` . . . 59
Wells [1976] Crim LR 518, CA 64
West Mersea UDC v Fraser [1950] 2 KB 119, [1950] 1 All ER 990, DC . 72
Whitehead [1982] QB 1272, 75 Cr App Rep 289 82
Wilkins (1861) Le and Ca 89, 31 LJMC 72 80
Williams [1969] Crim LR 497, CA 93
Williams [1971] Crim LR 356 83
Williams [1971] 2 All ER 444, 55 Cr App Rep 275, CA . . . 44, 45
Winter [1973] Crim LR 63, CA 93
Worsell [1969] 2 All ER 1183, 53 Cr App Rep 322, CA . . 57, 58, 60
Wright (1975) 62 Cr App Rep 169, CA 53

Y

Young [1984] 2 All ER 164, [1984] 1 WLR 654 88

Abbreviations

CEA   Customs and Excise Act 1952
CEMA   Customs and Excise Management Act 1979
MDA   Misuse of Drugs Act 1971

Part I
Introduction

1 History and Policy of the Legislation

This section outlines the history of legislation intended to counter the misuse of what are now the controlled drugs, and the general ideas and policies which gave rise to that legislation. No mention will be made of the general Poisons Acts and similar legislation which is concerned with regulating the supply by pharmacists of various medicinal drugs not generally the subject of misuse.

The use of drugs for non-medical purposes is not a new phenomenon. The powers of opium to induce euphoria have been known for hundreds of years and coca leaves have been chewed in South America since before the sixteenth century. Cannabis was described in Chinese literature as early as 2737 BC and the hallucinogenic peyote mushroom has been used in religious ceremonies for many centuries.

In Britain, too, opium, cocaine and cannabis have been known for a long time, although only opium was used to any extent before this century. However, the idea of the problem drug taker, as typified today by the young, socially maladjusted addict was unknown to society until after the 1939–45 war.

Opium was used to an increasing extent throughout the nineteenth century and by the 1870s a vast amount was being consumed as a cheap and effective remedy for a variety of ills including gastric disorders and for the purpose of quietening children. Opium was administered either dissolved in alcohol (laudanum) or in one of the many patent medicines containing it which could be bought over the counter at druggists. Addicts were almost invariably persons who had initially taken the drug for medicinal reasons, and a large percentage were themselves doctors or chemists. The image of the Victorian addict who was normally middle-aged and middle-class, and whose addiction would frequently be unknown to others, is diametrically opposed to that of today's heroin addict.

Cocaine had very little medical use, although it was occasionally administered as a dental anaesthetic. Sigmund Freud was at one time an advocate of its beneficial effects, and in the early part of this century it began to emerge as a 'street drug' used and sold by prostitutes in Soho, and also as a recreational drug for the more bohemian element of the upper classes.

There was, however, a growing national and international awareness of the dangers of opium abuse, and in 1869 the Pharmacy Act placed some minor controls over opium and its preparations. This was a move which had little practical effect and use of opium continued unabated. This was the scene against which was set the Dangerous Drugs Act 1920, the first of a series of statutes which placed an increasing number of substances under (in general) increasingly strict control, culminating in the Misuse of Drugs Act 1971, hereafter referred to in this book as the MDA. The primary purpose of the 1920 Act and subsequent ones was to control the use and supply of drugs considered to be dangerous in order to minimise the risk of abuse and addiction. Awareness and publicity of the dangers of opium and cocaine had been increasing steadily for some time prior to 1920, but two principal factors hastened the passing of the legislation.

Firstly, at the Shanghai Conference in 1909 and the Hague International Opium Convention in 1912, some of the most influential countries of the world (including Britain) had decided to prohibit the use of opium. These conferences were held at the instigation of the United States of America, which itself had a serious opium problem. The second important factor was the 1914–18 war. Morphia (an opium derivative) was used widely as a painkiller in the treatment of the enormous number of appallingly wounded soliders, and addiction from this cause was not uncommon. More importantly, the wartime climate facilitated the passage of regulations which were an infringement of personal liberty, as the public were more inclined to accept such measures as being emergency ones necessary in the national interest. The parts of the drugs legislation which cause the greatest restriction on individual liberty are the provisions making possession for personal consumption a criminal offence, and it was during the war that unauthorised possession of opium and cocaine first became an offence, under the Defence of the Realm Regulations 1916 No. 22.[1] The 1920 Act, although passed in order to implement the terms of international obligations, was to a large extent a codification of the wartime regulations.

After the 1920 Act subsequent legislation was either an extension or modification of the existing restrictions. The number of controlled drugs increased steadily, as did the number of controls and the penalties for their contravention. The 1923 Dangerous Drugs Act gave police investigating drug offences the power to obtain search warrants in certain circumstances, and the 1925 Dangerous Drugs Act extended the controls to include cannabis, after a violent denunciation of the evils of it by the

---

1 Regulations 40 and 40B.

Egyptian delegate to the Second Opium Conference and Geneva Convention in 1925.

For almost forty years after the passing of the 1925 Act the problem of drugtaking appeared to recede. Prosecutions for drugs offences dropped sharply after 1923, and continued to show a general decline in the years up to 1945. There was also a similar decline in the number of known addicts in this same period. Although various statutes were passed between 1925 and 1964 which concerned dangerous drugs (the term controlled drug was introduced only in the 1971 Act), they were of little practical significance, consisting mainly of consolidation of and minor extensions to existing controls.

In the 1960s drugtaking again rose to the forefront of the national consciousness. The decade of the 1960s is recognised as an era of great social change, and an increase in drugtaking was one of the principal manifestations of the alteration in outlook. The use of cannabis, rare before 1950, spread from isolated incidents among the immigrant communities to widespread use by the younger generation at large. Amphetamines, prescribed in large numbers as slimming pills, became extremely popular as a recreational drug for teenagers. In addition a new generation of very powerful synthetic hallucinogens, such as LSD, spread from San Francisco (where they were first used in quantity) to Britain. General improvements in transport and communication made the importation, exportation and distribution of all kinds of drugs very much easier.

It was to counter the growth in amphetamine misuse that the Drugs (Prevention of Misuse) Act 1964 was introduced. This Act introduced controls over the possession of amphetamines and in 1966 it was extended to include LSD. This was the first Act concerning drugs which was passed as a result of domestic initiative rather than in order to fulfil international treaty obligations. In 1965 the Dangerous Drugs Act was passed to consolidate earlier dangerous drugs legislation. However, the law was still in an unsatisfactory state. Legislation was piecemeal and sometimes inconsistent. In particular the 1964 and 1965 Acts did not complement each other well. An offence under one Act relating to drug X might not be an offence under the other Act for drug Y. It was in order to rationalise and combine the various strands of the law on dangerous drugs that the 1971 MDA was passed. In addition, in the House of Commons the Home Secretary gave four other aims of the Act. They were:

Firstly, to distinguish between possession of and trafficking in drugs.

Secondly, to have the power to operate without consulting international bodies.

Thirdly, to stamp out overprescribing.

Fourthly, to set up a statutory Advisory Council on the Misuse of Drugs.

From the report of the Rolleston Committee in 1926, when questions of policy on treatment of drug addiction were first seriously considered, until 1968, doctors were entitled to treat addicts as patients in any way they saw fit, and there was little restraint on their right to prescribe controlled drugs. Despite indications that the system had substantial shortcomings, the First Brain Committee reporting in 1960 made no significant recommendations for change. By the time of the Second Brain Committee's report in 1965 it was clear that a fundamental change of policy was necessary. A tiny minority of weak, elderly or incompetent doctors was being exploited by addicts into overprescribing wildly, creating a black market in surplus drugs which the system was designed to prevent. Of the changes implemented in 1968, the three most important provisions were:

(a) That heroin and cocaine could be prescribed to addicts only by specially licensed doctors. In practice licences were issued only to doctors in special drug clinics attached to hospitals.

(b) That the Home Office was given control over irresponsible doctors who could be banned from prescribing any specified controlled drug.

(c) That doctors had to notify the Home Office when they attended a drug addict. This provision allowed the more effective monitoring of drug addiction.

The success of this policy is hard to assess. The problem of doctors overprescribing has been largely overcome, but there has been an enormous growth in the importation, distribution and consumption of non-pharmaceutical heroin. This is becoming increasingly cheap and plentiful and the number of registered addicts is rising sharply.[2]

An assessment of the success of the broader spectrum of controlled drugs legislation is equally difficult. There is no doubt that the law appears to be almost totally ineffective in preventing those who wish to take drugs from obtaining illicit supplies. More and more 'professional' criminals are turning to drug trafficking as an alternative to traditional crimes such as robbery. It is estimated that no more than 10 per cent of the total of illicit drugs imported into the country or manufactured here are prevented from reaching the consumer.[3] It can only be a matter for speculation as to the effects of either relaxing the controls or increasing the penalties for their contravention.

2 See Appendix 6 for some statistics on addition.
3 This figure is for obvious reasons impossible to obtain with any accuracy and should be regarded only as an approximate indicator.

2 The Advisory Council

Until the 1960s the provisions of the law relating to dangerous drugs reflected to a large extent the measures agreed at international conferences for the control of such drugs, and the initiative for changes in the law usually came from international rather than domestic quarters. When in the early 1960s the government attempted to combat the rapid growth of the abuse of amphetamines in the United Kingdom, the result was a hastily conceived and often criticised Act, namely the Drugs (Prevention of Misuse) Act 1964. When the 1971 MDA was being drafted it was felt that there should be some suitably authoritative body in the United Kingdom which would be charged with keeping the law relating to drugs under review, advising the government and where necessary proposing changes in the law. In this way the law would be able to move quickly and efficiently with the changes in drug problems, and without the need to consult international bodies at every stage. The result of this approach is the Advisory Council on the Misuse of Drugs, established by section 1 of the MDA. By section 1(2) this body (hereafter referred to as 'the Council') has the general duty:

> to keep under review the situation...with respect to drugs which are being or appear likely to be misused...and to give to...Ministers...advice on measures (whether or not involving the alteration of the law) which...ought to be taken for preventing the misuse of such drugs or dealing with social problems connected with their misuse...

There are then listed five specific areas to which the Council should pay particular attention. They are:
  (a) restricting the availability of such drugs or supervising arrangements for their supply;
  (b) enabling problem drug users to obtain advice and treatment;
  (c) promoting co-operation between appropriate bodies concerned with drug abuse;
  (d) educating the public about the danger of drug abuse;
  (e) promoting research into matters relevant to drug abuse.
The relationship between the government and the Council is a two

7

way one. As well as the Council advising the government, the government must consult with the Council on various matters.

By Section 2(5) no alteration may be made to Schedule 2 (listing controlled drugs) except on the recommendation of or after consultation with the Council.

Section 31 makes general provisions as to regulations made under the MDA and by subsection (3) no such regulations may be made except after consultation with the Council. This means that the Council must be involved in any change in the law under the MDA. Of course the government is not bound to put into effect the advice or recommendations of the Council, but the consultation must be genuine and not merely a pretence.

The constitution of the Council and supplementary provisions relating to its workings are set out in Schedule 1. There must be at least twenty members, to be appointed by the Secretary of State after consultation with appropriate bodies, and there must be at least one person on the Council who has wide and recent experience in each of the fields specified in paragraph 1(2).

By paragraph 2 the Council may appoint committees, some of whose members are not Council members, to consider and report on any matter referred to them. The Schedule also deals with the quorum for the Council, which by paragraph 3 is seven, the procedure adopted by the Council, and the payment of remuneration and expenses to its members.

3 Some Commonly Abused Drugs

The social use and abuse of drugs is outside the scope of this book. However, it is vital that a practitioner or member of the judiciary who becomes professionally involved in drugs cases should have some knowledge of the characteristics of the drugs involved.

The MDA and associated legislation deal with a very wide range of drugs which differ enormously in their effects, both physical and psychological, their prices, sources, method of consumption, the type of person who uses them and the danger to such users. Perhaps the only common factor is that they are illegal. Partly because of their illegality, it is difficult for the layman to obtain reliable information on the use and effects of controlled drugs. Reports in the press are frequently sensationalised and inaccurate.

For these reasons the following section has been included. It contains a list of the more commonly abused controlled drugs, and outlines some of their characteristics. Under each broad heading there is a list of the common drugs in that group, followed by their slang names, appearance, price, source and dosage (where appropriate), method of administration and short- and long-term effects, both physical and psychological. In addition, mention will be made of some drugs which are not controlled, but whose abuse and its consequences make their inclusion appropriate.

In this listing there are ten broad categories. The classification is neither scientific nor exhaustive, but most of the relevant drugs fall conveniently into one of these groups.

1 General points about drug abuse

In addition to the specific effects which the various drugs have on the user, some general observations should be made.

1 Means of administration of drugs
Quite apart from the action of the drug taken, serious damage may be done by the act of injection if it is administered in this way. The drugs most commonly injected are the opiates, amphetamines and

barbiturates. The use of non-sterile needles can cause hepatitis, gangrene, skin infections, sores and abscesses. Vein damage may also occur and deposits of the drug can build up under the skin, especially if the drug used is in a form which is insoluble or otherwise unsuitable for injection. In addition, the risk of overdose is increased when a drug is injected.

Smoking, particularly of cannabis resin, can cause respiratory diseases such as asthma and bronchitis.[1]

Long-term sniffing of cocaine can damage nasal membranes and the septum.

2 Mixing of different drugs

The consumption of more than one type of drug within a short period of time can be especially hazardous and have unpredictable consequences. In particular the combination of alcohol with tranquillisers such as barbiturates can depress bodily functions to the point of unconsciousness and death.

3 Impurities

Due to the illicit nature of the drugs market there is no guarantee that the user will be taking what he thinks he is. Supplies of drugs are frequently adulterated. In many cases this is merely a 'dilution' with an inert substance by a seller trying to make larger profits, but sometimes other psychoactive drugs or toxic substances may be added to or substituted for the substance which the user thinks he has, with unpredictable results.

4 Subjective reactions

It is important to note that the effects of a drug on a person will often vary with the personality and mood of the user as well as the properties of the drug itself. Sometimes individuals may have a toxic reaction to a particular drug, or it may simply affect them in a different way from another person taking an identical dose.

5 Indirect damage

The chronic drug abuser or addict will often have a lifestyle which in itself is harmful. Inadequate food, sleep, shelter and cleanliness are common characteristics of such individuals and these will obviously have an adverse effect on their health.

1 Much of the damage caused by smoking cannabis resin is caused by the smoking of the tobacco with which it is usually mixed. Some researchers suggest that smoking herbal cannabis is actually good for asthma.

Finally, it is perhaps worth noting that the majority of users of most types of drugs (with the exception of the opiates and barbiturates) consume these drugs without developing dependence or showing significant adverse effects.[2] Such people may use drugs for a number of years without ever coming to the attention of the police or the medical profession.

2 Controlled drugs

1 Opioids

a Drugs in this category Opium, morphine, heroin, diconal, methadone.

b General information The opioids include both the opiates which are derived from the milk of the opium poppy and also the synthetic drugs with similar properties to those of the opiates. Opium itself contains both morphine and codeine. Morphine can be converted into the more powerful and dangerous drug diamorphine (heroin). Diconal and methadone are synthetic opiates. All the opiates are Class A drugs.

c Slang names Slang names for morphine/heroin include smack, H, horse, Henry, skag.

d Appearance Opium is a brown resin and morphine is a brown powder. Heroin is a powder which may be white, brown, beige or grey in colour.

e Source The routes taken by opiates to their consumers are complex and varied, but the opium poppy is grown in Turkey, Iran, Pakistan, Afghanistan, the Middle East and the Far East (in particular in the golden triangle of Laos, Burma and Thailand). At the time of writing about 80 per cent of the heroin imported into this country is of Pakistani origin.

---

2 Dependence on the opioids is by no means inevitable, but is more likely than with most other drugs. Some casual users never become addicted, and it seems that of those who are addicted many never come to the attention of the police, medical profession or the Home Office. The vast majority of illegal drug use involves cannabis which is generally considered not to be harmful in itself. In addition many users of stimulants and hallucinogens maintain controlled use and a stable lifestyle including normal employment and social activities. The number of users who are convicted of drug offences or required medical treatment is a fraction of the total number estimated to use drugs (see Chapter 4). For further references on this topic, see Plant, *Drugtakers in an English Town*, Tavistock Publications (1975); Zinberg, *Drug, Set and Setting*, Yale University Press (1984); *Drugs and Drug Abuse*, Addiction Research Foundation of Toronto; *The Cannabis Stalemate*, Druglink (Winter 1982).

f Price   The price of opiates in the UK has fallen sharply in recent years. Its current street price is in the region of £60–£80 per gram. (All prices quoted are for 1984.)

g Dosage   An addict with an average habit might be expected to consume 1/4 gram per day.

h Method of administration   Opium may be smoked or dissolved (e.g. in alcohol, producing laudanum) and taken orally. Morphine/heroin may be sniffed, smoked, taken orally or injected.

i Effects: short term   The opiates are all similar in effect. They are analgesics and produce a feeling of relief both from mental anxieties and physical pain, discomfort and hunger. They will also give a feeling of well-being. In small doses these effects are not accompanied by a decrease in awareness or mental impairment. Nausea and vomiting may occur, especially when the drug is used for the first time. Larger doses will cause stupor, coma and even death.

j Effects: long term   A user will develop tolerance, i.e. a larger dose will be required to produce the same effect. With repeated use over a short period of time both physical and psychological dependence will result. Withdrawal from use by an addict will cause physical symptoms which can be extremely unpleasant but which are normally equivalent to a bad dose of flu combined with a severe bout of depression. The psychological dependence or craving is much harder to break and is longer lasting.

2 Cocaine and coca leaf

a Drugs in this category   Coca leaf and cocaine.

b General information   Coca leaf and especially cocaine are powerful stimulants and are both Class A drugs. Cocaine is extracted by a chemical process from the leaf.

c Slang names for cocaine   Coke, C, Charlie, snow, toot.

d Appearance   Cocaine is a white powder.

e Source   The coca plant from which cocaine is obtained grows in South America.

f Price   The price of cocaine in part accounts for its characterisation as the 'champagne of drugs'. Only the well-off can afford the typical price of £75 per gram. However, as the amount of the drug imported increases, the price falls and the use of cocaine appears to be spreading throughout all classes of drug takers.

g Dosage An average dose would be 25 to 50 milligrams. In a day a user might consume up to 1/8 to 1/4 gram although this figure will vary according to the circumstances.

h Methods of administration Cocaine is normally sniffed, but may also be taken orally or injected.

i Effects: short term Cocaine is a powerful stimulant and when taken will give feelings of energy, strength, confidence and euphoria. It may increase sexual desire and enhance the enjoyment of most activities, even apparently mundane or routine ones. The effects are short-lived, lasting perhaps half an hour to an hour, depending on dosage. Large doses, especially if taken at short intervals, can cause irritability, anxiety and agitation.

j Effects: long term Chronic use of cocaine will produce effects including insomnia, lack of appetite, anxiety and irritability, and even paranoia. Physical dependence can occur, although not so readily as with the opiates. Psychological dependence is much more likely.

3 Hallucinogens

a Some drugs in this category Lysergide (LSD), Dimethyltrypt-amine (DMT), Phencyclidine (PCP), MDA, STP. Some naturally occurring hallucinogens are mescaline and the 'magic' mushroom (not illegal[3]) which contains psilocybin.

b General information The hallucinogens are very powerful drugs which can have extremely intense effects on the mind. A number of naturally occurring plants have hallucinogenic properties but the most important members of this group for present purposes are the synthetic ones, of which the most common is LSD. All the hallucinogens are Class A drugs.

c Slang name A common name for LSD is acid.

d Appearance The hallucinogens are so potent that their appearance is governed by that of the medium or matrix in which they are produced. LSD is often taken on blotters (squares of absorbent paper treated with LSD solution) or microdots (tiny tablets containing a mixture of the drug and an inert base).

---

3 But see Chapter 9 where the legality of prepared magic mushrooms is discussed.

e Source   LSD is synthesised and may be produced anywhere. 'Magic' mushrooms grow naturally in many parts of the UK during the autumn, especially in the West Country and Wales.

f Price   About £2 to £2.50 per dose for LSD.

g Dosage   As LSD is so potent, only a very small dose (100–250 micrograms) is needed to produce the desired effect.

h Methods of administration   The hallucinogens are almost invariably taken orally.

i Effects: short term   The hallucinogens have relatively few and insignificant physical effects. Their danger lies in their enormously powerful psychological action. More than with any other group of drugs, the exact effect will depend both on the mood and personality of the taker and on his environment. Reactions will vary between euphoria and terror. Distortion of colour, time and form is common, as is 'cross-over' of the senses (i.e. hearing colour, seeing sound). Mystical-type experiences and loss of the sense of ego may also occur.

j Effects: long term   There is no possibility of physical addiction to LSD or similar substances. Indeed the tolerance which the body develops means that a dose taken within a few days of a previous one will have little or no effect. The danger with LSD is that of psychological disturbance. A regular taker may experience long-term detachment from reality. Users who have psychotic tendencies may be precipitated into actual psychosis. Occasionally 'flashbacks' occur, where the subject re-experiences part of his drug 'trip' weeks or even months after it has finished.

'Magic' mushrooms (psilocybin semilanceata) can be possessed and consumed in their natural state quite legally, and have an effect similar in nature to but less powerful than LSD.

4 Amphetamines

a Some drugs in this category   Amphetamine, dexamphetamine, methylamphetamine.

b General information   The amphetamines are synthetic stimulants. Methylphenidate and phenmetrazine are similar to the amphetamines and similarly are Class B drugs (unless contained in a preparation designed for administration by injection in which case they, like all Class B drugs, become Class A drugs).

c Slang names for the amphetamines These include speed, uppers, blues, bennies, dexies.

d Appearance Amphetamines may occur as a white powder or as tablets or capsules in a variety of shapes and colours.

e Source Amphetamines are manufacturered by a relatively simple chemical process. They are either produced illicitly or licit supplies are misappropriated and misused. This latter source was of particular importance in the 1960s when amphetamines were widely prescribed as slimming pills.

f Price About £10 to £14 per gram in powder form.

g Dosage A user might take 1/4 gram in a day.

h Method of administration Amphetamine powder may be sniffed. Also the drug may be taken orally or injected.

i Effects: short term Amphetamines are stimulants. They will cause in the taker a feeling of excitement, energy and general confidence. As with cocaine, the taker will often become enthusiastic even for mundane tasks, and is likely to be talkative and active. The effects of amphetamine last much longer than those of cocaine. While the effects last he will not feel tired or hungry. However, the drug does not replace the body's need for food and sleep, but merely suppresses it. When the effects wear off after a few hours, the taker will frequently feel exhausted, depressed and hungry.

j Effects: long term Psychological dependence on amphetamines develops much more readily than physical addiction. A user may go on a 'run' of the drug where the adverse effects experienced when the drug wears off are countered by a further dose (which has to be larger because of the body's tolerance). This cycle may go on for days until the user is totally exhausted. The chronic user is likely to develop symptoms such as anxiety, irritability and restlessness, together with paranoia which can cause aggression and hostility. Nausea, weight loss and insomnia are also common complaints of the regular user.

5 Cannabis

a Some drugs in this category This category includes cannabis, cannabis resin and the cannabinol derivatives.

b General information   The most widely used of the controlled drugs, cannabis occurs in two principal forms. These are herbal cannabis, which is the dried leaves and flowering tops of the plant, and cannabis resin, which is a more potent form obtained by scraping the leaves. Cannabis oil, an even more concentrated form of the drug, is occasionally used, but pure tetrahydracannabinol (THC) which is the active ingredient of cannabis is virtually unknown outside research laboratories. Cannabis is a Class B drug, except for the cannabinol derivatives such as THC which are Class A.

c General slang   Pot (rather outdated), dope. For herbal cannabis, marijuana, grass. For resin, hash or shit.

d Appearance   Herbal cannabis, consisting of dried leaves, looks rather like large-leaved tea, and resin, which ranges in colour from reddish brown or gold to black, resembles dried mud, but is less brittle.

e Source   The plant Cannabis sativa grows in any reasonably warm climate. It is widespread throughout the Middle and Far East, South America and Africa. It is increasingly grown in greenhouse type conditions in the UK.

f Price   Cannabis prices vary with type and quality between £30 and £80 per ounce.

g Dosage   1/2 to 3/4 gram would be sufficient to make about two cannabis cigarettes, which would cause two or three people to become midly intoxicated.

h Methods of administration   Cannabis is normally smoked, either in a cigarette or a pipe. It may also be taken orally, for example by dissolution in tea or coffee, or mixed into a cake.

i Effects: short term   These vary depending on the taker's personality and environment, but small doses are likely to cause feelings of relaxation, talkativeness and hilarity. Larger doses usually have a more introspective effect, with distortions of time and space and hallucinations possible. There is normally an enhanced enjoyment of all the senses, together with the 'crossover' effect, where music is seen, etc. The user often feels hungry and thirsty. The feelings are not invariably pleasant, and in particular inexperienced users who take large doses may find the effects frightening or depressing. First-time users often experience no effects at all.

j Effects: long term Cannabis is not physically addictive, although regular users may develop a mild psychological dependence. Much research has been done into the effects of long-term cannabis use, and the results are inconclusive. No long-term ill effects have been proved, although smoking (especially of resin) may cause lung and respiratory problems. The chronic user is likely to become apathetic and unmotivated.[4]

3 Non-controlled drugs

6 Barbitutates

a Some drugs in this category Barbiturates include Nembutal, Thiopental, Seconal and Tuinal.

b General information The abuse of barbiturates can be extremely damaging (see below) but these drugs are not covered by the MDA because at the time of the passing of the Act they were being prescribed in very large numbers as tranquillisers, and it was felt that the MDA was an inappropriate means of control. Barbiturates are also used medically as anaesthetics. They are now prescribed much less widely than in the 1970s.

c Slang names Barbs, downers.

d Appearance Barbiturates are normally produced in the form of coloured tablets or capsules.

e Source Barbiturates are synthetic. Although the prescription of barbiturates has been greatly reduced, the main source of the drugs is still through the diverting of legitimately produced or prescribed drugs for abuse.

f Price £1–£2 per capsule.

g Dosage The strength of the drugs varies with the different brands, but one capsule is often enough to produce a noticeable effect.

h Methods of administration Barbiturates are normally taken orally, but the tablets may be crushed up and injected, a method of administration which is particularly hazardous.

4 It has been suggested that the apathetic attitude of many chronic cannabis users is not attributable to the drug itself, but that an apathetic and unmotivated person is more likely to become a chronic and heavy user.

i Effects: short term   Barbiturates depress the central nervous system in a similar way to alcohol and in many ways their effects are similar too. Small doses produce a feeling of relaxation and sociability. Larger doses will cause lack of motor co-ordination, slurring of speech, and sometimes aggression. The taker will tend to fall asleep. Still larger does will cause coma or death. The effects of barbiturates are compounded by taking them in conjunction with alcohol.

j Effects: long term   The barbiturates are highly addictive, both physically and psychologically. The chronic user is likely to become irritable, nervous and anxious, and may suffer from hallucinations. Withdrawal from high doses can cause various unpleasant effects up to and including convulsions and death. Nausea, faintness and pneumonia are also associated with chronic barbiturate abuse. As tolerance develops, with the body needing a higher dose each time for the same effect, there is little corresponding rise in the lethal dose, so there is a risk of accidental overdose.

7 Minor tranquillisers

a Some drugs in this category   Drugs which can be broadly described as minor tranquillisers include Librium, Valium and Mogadon.

b General information   The drugs in this group, which are not controlled by the MDA, are now mostly commonly prescribed as tranquillisers and sleeping pills, to a large extent replacing the barbiturates, which are much more dangerous (see above).

c Slang names   These include tranx and moggies.

d Appearance   These drugs are produced in the form of tablets in a variety of shapes and colours.

e Use   Because there is little non-medical use of these drugs, there is no significant 'black' market (the fact that they are widely available and not controlled is also relevant). The dose and method of administration (oral) will normally be as prescribed.

f Effects: short term   These drugs have the characteristics that their collective name would suggest, i.e. a relaxing and tranquillising action. In general, they do so without the sleepiness and impairment of mental and bodily function associated with the barbiturates, although some takers suffer these effects.

g Effects: long term There is much less risk of dependence than with barbiturates, but the effect of tolerance means that the drugs become ineffective for their prescribed purpose. Physical and psychological withdrawal symptoms occur, including nausea, anxiety and the feeling of being unable to cope.[5]

8 Minor stimulants
Most of the Class C drugs specified in the MDA are minor stimulants (methaqualone is a sedative). None of these is apparently abused to any extent, and it is not felt necessary to describe them in detail, but merely to point out their existence. Methaqualone, which was a constituent of Mandrax, was abused considerably, but has now been withdrawn from sale by the manufacturers.

9 Alcohol
Alcohol is not, of course, a controlled drug. The only restrictions imposed by English law are on its sale and its consumption by young persons. It is extremely widely used throughout the Western world.

a Effects: short term The short-term effects of alcohol are too well known to merit an extensive description. Its action is that of a central nervous system depressant, causing relaxation, sociability and lack of inhibition. With larger doses this lack of inhibition can lead to aggression, and motor functions and clarity of thought are impaired. Still larger doses cause drowsiness, unconsciousness and death.

b Effects: long term Tolerance to alcohol develops, thus necessitating an increase in dosage for the same effect. Heavy drinking can adversely affect the stomach, the heart, the liver and the brain. Withdrawal symptoms include tremors, sweating, anxiety and hallucinations (delirium tremens). Alcohol is also dangerous taken in conjunction with certain other drugs, particularly other depressants such as barbiturates.

10 Solvents
An increasing practice in the UK is the abuse by inhalation of solvents contained in glue, cleaning fluids and aerosol sprays,

5 There is some debate whether these so-called withdrawal symptoms are a physical reaction or whether they are merely a return of the state which necessitated tranquilliser use in the first place.

particularly among adolescents. This practice is perfectly legal[6] and there is no restriction on the sale or possession of such substances. The solvents are inhaled and absorbed into the blood stream through the lungs. The taker may enhance the effects by placing a plastic bag containing the solvent over the head, which increases the concentration of the vapours (and incidentally the risk of accidental suffocation).

a Effects: short term   The solvents depress certain body functions such as heart rate and breathing. This can cause disorientation, impairment of motor functions and unconsciousness. The taker normally recovers to normal within a short time of the inhalation. While intoxicated he may behave in a bizarre or aggressive manner.

b Effects: long term   Physical dependence is not normally a problem among solvent sniffers, although there may be a general feeling of malaise upon withdrawal from their regular use. Tolerance develops, necessitating larger doses for the same effect. Psychological dependence is also rare, but may affect a minority of users. The results of research into the effects of long-term use are inconclusive, but it appears that such use may cause liver and kidney damage.

6 But see Chapter 14 on miscellaneous offences for attempts to control it. At the time of writing a Bill is being introduced which will make it an offence to sell glue to persons under sixteen in certain circumstances.

Part II
Procedure

4 Introduction

Drugs offences pose some unique problems to the authorities whose responsibility it is to deal with them.

Firstly, there is the sheer size of the problem in numerical terms. It is estimated that some 5 million people presently living in the U.K. have used controlled drugs at one time or another in their lives, and of this number a sizeable proportion use drugs regularly.[1] Only a tiny fraction of the transgressors are ever discovered, let alone prosecuted or convicted, and indeed were the position otherwise the judicial system would be clogged with minor drugs cases. It is likely that drugs offences are second in number only to motoring offences.

Secondly, most drugs offences do not have any direct victims in the normal sense of the word, as murder or theft do. Most offences will never come to the authorities' attention as there is no causal connection between offence and investigation. Unless the offences are reported by zealous citizens or unless they are discovered 'on the street' the majority of offenders will never be noticed. Another aspect of this point is that most drugs offences can be committed quietly, easily and privately away from the eyes of the authorities, thus decreasing the likelihood of detection.

Thirdly, the law of druugs has a considerable technical aspect. Although everybody knows what a robbery or a careless driving offence looks like, the same cannot be said of drugs offences. Although the specialist Customs officers and drug squads are well informed about drugs, the day-to-day patrols and street searches are carried out by officers who are as likely as not to be unable to recognise a blotter of LSD or the smell of cannabis, let alone some of the less common drugs. (Obviously this will be less so in areas which are notorious for drug abuse.) The general public are still

---

1 Such figures are difficult to estimate with accuracy. For a summary of the various surveys, see 'Surveys and Statistics on Drugtaking in Britain' (15DD March 1983). One of the most reliable surveys was commissioned by the BBC, conducted by Triesman and published in 1973 by the Social Research Design Consultancy. Entitled 'Survey to estimate the number of cannabis users in the U.K.', it concluded that 3.8 million people living in the U.K. had used cannabis. If one adds other drugs and takes into account the increase in drug use since 1973, the figure of 5 million may be conservative.

more ignorant. Many a parent has admired their child's green fingers, blissfully unaware that the plant being cultivated is cannabis.

The practical answer to these points is that the police do not attempt indiscriminately to catch as many drug offenders as possible. Their resources will be concentrated on catching producers of and traffickers in drugs. This is partly as a matter of logistics, whereby the limited manpower available must be directed at the most serious offenders, and partly due to recognition of the fact that a person smoking cannabis in private is not in general posing a threat to society. Indeed, recently two police forces have announced that as a matter of policy many first time possessors of cannabis will be cautioned rather than prosecuted.

The responsibility for legal control of drug abuse is split between the police and the Customs and Excise (hereafter referred to as the Customs). The Customs are concerned with preventing the importation (and, of lesser practical importance, the exportation) of controlled drugs. Due to the climate of this country all cocaine and opiates and the vast majority of cannabis consumed in the United Kingdom must be imported, as the appropriate plants do not flourish here. The enormous profits generated from small quantities of drugs (see Appendix 7) make the idea of drug smuggling very tempting for professional criminals. Within each area the relevant police force is responsible for other drugs offences within their area, and most forces have special drugs squads of a few officers (ranging from two or three officers to about thirty for some of the larger forces) to deal with this. The Customs and police obviously liase and assist each other where this is expedient.

Although the importation of drugs into the United Kingdom is increasing, the number of Customs officers on duty at the various ports and airports in this country has decreased in recent years. Millions of law-abiding people and a huge volume of legitimately imported goods enter the country every year, and the task of discovering drugs and drug smugglers is an unenviable one, especially as the modern smuggling gangs are frequently well-organised and well-financed. In these circumstances it can easily be understood why the trafficking of drugs continues to rise despite the heavy sentences passed on those involved.

5 Powers of the Police and Customs

The area of the law concerned with powers of arrest, search and seizure is extremely complicated and in many aspects far from clear. The powers of the police are not always the same as those of Customs officers, and indeed the powers of the police are not always the same in different parts of the country, being dependent in some instances on local statutes. The law is contained in a variety of public and local statutes together with a large body of case law, which is not always mutually consistent and reconcilable. There is presently before Parliament the Police and Criminal Evidence Bill, which if enacted will radically alter the current position and render obsolete much of the existing law.

Although the law of arrest, search and seizure is part of the general criminal and constitutional law rather than specifically part of drugs law, it is felt that this subject deserves mention by way of general summary because it is frequently part of the background to drugs cases, many of which are initially detected by street searches. This chapter section is arranged as follows:

(1) summary of the powers of arrest, search and seizure of the police;
(2) special powers of Customs officers;
(3) provisions of MDA, sections 23 and 24.

1 General powers of arrest, search and seizure

Two general points are worthy of note, both of which arise out of the uncertainty and complexity of the law. Firstly, if the police exceed their powers, they may be liable for trespass, assault or unlawful imprisonment under the civil law. Occasionally they may be subject to criminal proceedings as well. However, if a suspect wrongly believes that the police are exceeding their powers, and he resists accordingly, he is likely to be charged with a relatively serious offence such as assault with intent to resist arrest or assaulting a police officer in the execution of his duty.

Secondly, if the police exceed their powers of search and seizure, the illegality of their action does not prevent anything found or seized being used as evidence against the suspect,[1] which is widely believed to be an unsatisfactory state of affairs.

a Powers of the private citizen   The private citizen has no power of search and seizure, but he may arrest a person where an arrestable offence has been committed, in circumstances specified in section 2 of the Criminal Law Act 1967. Most of the offences under the MDA are arrestable offences so if X discovered that his friend Y was in possession of some cannabis he would be entitled to arrest him.

b Powers of the police   The police are entitled to stop persons in the street in order to ask them questions. How far they are able to go in the way of temporary detention for the purposes of asking such questions is unclear (see *Kenlin v Gardiner*[2] and *Donnelly v Jackman*[3] and *Brown*.[4] Such persons need not answer the questions, but if they give false replies or otherwise hinder the police they will be liable for obstructing the police in the execution of their duty.[5] The police are also entitled to stop motor vehicles under section 159 of the Road Traffic Act 1972, but this power is for the purpose of checking vehicles for defects and should not be abused for other purposes.

The police are entitled to stop and search persons in the street under a wide variety of statutory powers. Some of these statutes are local (e.g. the Metropolitan Police Act 1839, section 66), and some are public, such as the MDA. Grounds for search include a reasonable suspicion that the person is in possession of firearms, stolen goods, drugs or protected birds. The police must state the reasons for the search[6] and a subject should not be searched intimately except in a private place.

The police may arrest in a wide variety of situations. They may of course effect an arrest in pursuance of a warrant or where an arrestable offence has been committed or is reasonably suspected to have been committed.[7] They have numerous other common law and statutory powers of arrest in specific circumstances (e.g. under section 24 of the MDA).

---

1 *Sang* [1980] AC 402, 69 Cr App Rep 282, HL.
2 [1967] 2 QB 510, [1966] 3 All ER 931, DC.
3 [1970] 1 All ER 987, 54 Cr App Rep 229, DC.
4 (1976) 64 Cr App Rep 231, [1977] Crim LR 291, CA. See also *Collins v Wilcock* (1984) Times, 17 April, DC.
5 *Rice v Connolly* [1966] 2 QB 414, [1966] 2 All ER 649, DC.
6 *Brazil v Chief Constable of Surrey* [1983] 3 All ER 537, 77 Cr App Rep 237, DC, and *McBean v Parker* [1983] Crim LR 399, DC.
7 Criminal Law Act 1967, s. 2(4).

As a general rule, unless a person is arrested he is free to go as he pleases.[8] However, the case of *Brown*[9] suggests that although every arrest is a deprivation of liberty, the converse is not always true. Arrest does not require physical touching,[10] but it should be made clear to the person concerned that he is under arrest, and he should be told the reason for his arrest.[11]

The police may enter (by force if necessary) private premises in order to arrest someone for an arrestable offence or in pursuance of a warrant for arrest. Except for these situations, a police officer can otherwise only enter private premises with the consent of the occupier or with a search warrant. The three exceptions to this rule are:

(a) in order to stop or prevent a breach of the peace;[12]
(b) when in 'hot pursuit' of an escaped convict or suspect;
(c) in order to save life, limb or serious damage to property.

The basic rules of seizure are contained in the cases of *Chic Fashions (West Wales) Ltd v Jones*[13] and *Ghani v Jones*[14] and they may be summarised as follows.

(a) There is a power to take goods which are material evidence concerning the crime for which the person is arrested or regarding which the police are searching.
(b) If no person has been arrested or charged, police may only take goods if:
   (i) there are reasonable grounds for believing an offence has been committed; and
   (ii) there are reasonable grounds for believing that the article is either the fruit of the crime or a weapon or material evidence; and
   (iii) the police must not keep it longer than is necessary to complete their investigation or preserve it as evidence; and
   (iv) the lawfulness of the conduct is to be judged at the time when it takes place.

In addition, a right of search will arise when a person is arrested. The scope of this power is uncertain. The police definitely have a power to search a person and any area under his control at the place of arrest. They may not search his premises for a crime unconnected with that for which he was arrested at a place

8 *Inwood* [1973] 2 All ER 645, 57 Cr App Rep 529, CA.
9 *Brown* (1976) 64 Cr App Rep 231, [1977] Crim LR 291, CA.
10 *Alderson v Booth* [1969] 2 QB 216, 53 Cr App Rep 301, DC.
11 *Christie v Leachinsky* [1947] AC 573, [1947] 1 All ER 567, HL.
12 *Thomas v Sawkins* [1935] 2 KB 249, 104 LJKB 572, DC.
13 [1968] 2 QB 299, [1968] 1 All ER 229, CA.
14 [1970] 1 QB 693, [1969] 3 All ER 1700, CA.

different from where he was arrested.[15] The case of *Naylor*[16] suggests that the right of search on arrest is limited to searching for:

(a) objects connected with the crime for which the arrest was made; and

(b) objects which might be used to escape from custody or cause injury.

2 Powers of Customs officers

Customs officers are primarily concerned with preventing the unlawful importation and exportation of dutiable or prohibited goods, such as controlled drugs, and their powers differ from those of the police. The Customs and Excise Management Act 1979 (hereafter referred to as the CEMA) gives a great many powers to Customs officers. Some of them are not directly relevant to the law relating to drugs. These various powers will not be considered in great detail, but the more important ones will be outlined. As a broad generalisation the powers of the Customs in the area of search, seizure and detention are greater than those of the police. The general provisions of particular sections will be explained, and the full text of the sections is listed in Appendix 2.

Search

Section 161 of the CEMA gives a general power to Customs officers who have reasonable grounds for suspecting that controlled drugs may be kept or concealed in any place or building. Provided they hold a writ of assistance[17] they may enter (using force if necessary) such a place in order to search for and seize any such articles. If this is done at night (defined as between 11 p.m. and 5 a.m.) they must be accompanied by a constable. In addition Customs officers may also obtain search warrants in the normal way by application to a magistrate. Section 163 gives power to stop and search any vehicle or vessel where there are reasonable grounds for suspecting that it is carrying controlled drugs. Anybody refusing to stop or permit such a search will be committing an offence under subsection (2), for which the maximum penalty is a fine of £100. A person in contravention of section 163(2) is also likely to be committing the more general and

15 *Jeffrey v Black* [1978] QB 490, [1977] Crim LR 555, DC.
16 [1979] Crim LR 532.
17 A writ of assistance is in effect a kind of permanent search warrant. Its duration is strictly speaking for the reign of the current sovereign plus six months, and these writs are normally held by all appropriate investigating officers.

serious offence under section 16. Section 164 gives a power, subject to certain safeguards, to search persons where there are reasonable grounds for suspicion that they are carrying controlled drugs and if they are in the vicinity of a border, dock or port. A magistrate has no power to inquire into the reasonableness of a search unless it is a mere pretence.[18]

Sections 27 and 28 give powers to Customs officers to board aircraft and ships within the limits of airports and ports. Although the sphere of operation of some of the Customs officers' powers is limited to ports and airports,[19] their effectiveness is not in practice curtailed even when dealing with smugglers who land drugs by ship or aircraft other than at a recognised port or airport, and the general powers of arrest and so on are sufficient for most purposes. By section 34 Customs officers have a power to prevent the unauthorised taking off of aircraft. By section 82 they have the right to moor a Customs vessel anywhere, and to patrol any shore, riverbank, railway or airport boundary (unless the property in question is a garden or pleasure ground. The exact scope of the term 'pleasure ground' is uncertain but not of great practical significance.)

Arrest and detention
Section 138 gives Customs officers and members of the armed forces the power to detain any person if he has committed an offence under the Act, or if there are reasonable grounds for suspecting that he has done so. This power may only be exercised within three years of the commission of the offence. However, if it was not practical to detain the person at the time of the commission of the offence, or if he has been detained and subsequently escaped, then he may be detained at any time, and the date of the commission of the offence is deemed to be the time of detention. The powers under section 138 are in addition to general powers to arrest for arrestable offences. As drug offences under the Act will almost invariably be arrestable offences, the provisions of the Criminal Law Act 1967 for these offences may be more powerfful.

Forfeiture
Sections 139–144 deal with forfeiture. There are wide powers of forfeiture under the Act and these are considered under the section on forfeiture.

18 *Anderson v Reid* (1902) 86 LT 713, 66 JP 564, DC.
19 See, for example, the specific power to inspect baggage in CEMA, s. 78, which relates to persons leaving or entering the UK.

Obstruction

Section 16 lists a number of activities which can be conveniently summarised as obstructing a Customs officer in the exercise of any powers conferred by the Act or in the execution of his duty. A person guilty of an offence under the section is liable to a penalty of two years' imprisonment if convicted on indictment. Any person committing an offence or aiding or abetting the commission of an offence under the section may be detained (if there are are reasonable grounds for thinking an offence is being committed, but if there are not, then the detention is, on the wording of the section, apparently unlawful). The numerous cases on the meaning of obstruction in the context of obstructing the police will be useful guidelines to the scope of the section.

3 MDA, sections 23 and 24

These two sections give the police extra powers in the specific context of drugs offences. Section 23 is concerned with powers of search and section 24 with powers of arrest.

Section 23

Section 23(1) gives power for a constable or other authorised person to enter the premises of a person carrying on the business of producing or supplying controlled drugs, and to demand to inspect any books or documents or stocks of drugs. Obstruction of a person in the exercise of this power, or concealment of any of these items or failure to produce them without reasonable excuse, is an offence under subsection (4).

The most important part of section 23 is subsection (2), which gives the police a general power to search a person, vehicles or vessels if there is reasonable cause to suspect that the person is in possession of a controlled drug, or that a controlled drug may be found on the vehicle or vessel. Ancillary to this power is the power to detain the person or stop the vehicle or vessel for the purpose of conducting the search. The term 'vessel' includes a hovercraft within the meaning of the Hovercraft Act 1968. The section does not authorise a constable to enter premises to conduct such a search, although in most cases he will have such a power anyway as reasonable suspicion that somebody is in possession of a controlled drug is equivalent to having reasonable suspicion that he is committing the (arrestable) offence of possession.

No statistics are kept regarding the total number of searches of the public, but it seems that it is under this section that a large proportion of 'street searches' are carried out. The police policy in conducting such searches has been subject to criticism from a number of quarters[20] and has caused much tension and hostility towards the police, especially in areas with a high proportion of ethnic minorities. Records from the years 1972 to 1978 of searches carried out under section 23(2) show a success rate (i.e. when drugs are found) of 25–30 per cent. Much of the controversy revolves around the interpretation of the terms 'reasonable suspicion'. Suspects searched have complained that long hair, unconventional dress, or being Rastafarian should not of itself constitute reasonable grounds for suspicion. The requirements of reasonable suspicion must be satisfied at the time of the search, and an illegal search cannot be retrospectively justified by anything found during the course of it, although, of course, anything found will still be admissible as evidence.

Various cases have explored the scope of section 23 and certain rules have emerged from them. It is now clear that a person stopped and searched under the power in section 23(2) must be told the reason why he is being searched.[1] An intimate search should not be carried out in public or by a police officer of the opposite sex to the suspect. The power to search given by section 23(2)(a) is coupled with a power to detain for this purpose. Such a detention is not an arrest, but may include taking the suspect to a police station for a thorough search. In *Farrow v Tunnicliffe*[2] D and X were stopped by the police on suspicion of selling cannabis oil. A superficial search was made, but the police wished to do a more thorough one at the police station. On the way D threw or pretended to throw something out of the window and told X to run. He was convicted of obstructing a police officer in the execution of his duty. The court said that section 23(2) was clearly intended to operate parallel with section 24. There was no requirement to arrest before search and the police were therefore acting legally in taking D to the police station without arresting him.

Although section 23(2)(a) gives a right to detain for the purpose of searching, it does not give a right to detain for questioning. However, the case of *Geen*[3] suggests that the right to detain for search implies a right to detain for questioning prior to or incidental to a search.

The power in section 23(3)(b) to search a vehicle or vessel is coupled with a requirement of suspicion that a person is in

20 See the Scarman report on the Brixton disorders (Cmnd 8427) and various Release publications.
1 *Brazil v Chief Constable of Surrey* [1983] 3 All ER 537, 77 Cr App Rep 237, DC, and *McBean v Parker* [1983] Crim LR 399, DC.
2 [1976] Crim LR 126, DC.
3 [1982] Crim LR 604, CA.

possession of a controlled drug. In *Littleford*[4] a police constable suspected that a car was stolen. He did a computer check and discovered that it was suspected of being involved with controlled drugs. The court held that there was no power to search such a vehicle when it was the vehicle which was suspected, as opposed to a particular person.

Subsection (3) makes provisions concerning the issue and execution of search warrants. The warrant is valid only for the premises named therein, as is illustrated by the case of *Atkinson*.[5] D lived at flat number 30. The police wished to search it, and assumed that it was flat number 45 as it was next to flat 46. They obtained a warrant naming flat 45. When they arrived D bolted the door and flushed some tablets down the lavatory. He was acquitted of obstruction under section 23(4), as the police were not in the execution of their duty. The warrant authorised them to enter flat 45, not flat 30. However, the court did suggest that a trivial misdescription or misspelling would not invalidate a warrant.

Section 23(4) creates three offences of obstruction of a person who is exercising his powers under the section. They are:

(a) obstruction of such a person;
(b) concealing any books, documents or stocks referred to in section 23(1);
(c) failing without reasonable excuse to produce on demand such books, documents or stocks.

Section 24
Most offences under the MDA are arrestable offences, and a police officer may arrest without warrant any person whom, with reasonable cause, he suspects of having committed such an offence. In addition to these powers, section 24 confers on a constable the power to arrest without warrant if he with reasonable cause suspects a person of having committed an offence under the Act and:

(a) he with reasonable cause believes that the person will abscond unless arrested; or
(b) the name and address of the person are unknown to, and cannot be ascertained by him; or
(c) he is not satisfied that a name and address furnished by that person as his name and address are true.

This section is self-explanatory. The main point of interest is the difference in wording between subsections (1)(a) and (1)(c).

4 [1978] Crim LR 48.
5 [1976] Crim LR 307, CA.

Subsection (a) uses the phrase 'with reasonable cause believes', implying an objective test, whereas subsection (c) is expressed as 'not satisfied', implying a subjective test (i.e. the police officer need have no reasonable grounds for being not satisfied).

6 Procedure

The law of controlled drugs is a particular branch of the general criminal law and the normal rules of criminal procedure and evidence apply to it from the moment a suspect is charged up to the end of the trial and/or sentence. There are, however, provisions peculiar to this branch of the law which are worthy of some comment.

Mode of trial

The MDA, section 25(1)–(3), specifies that Schedule 4 of the Act lays down the mode of trial and maximum penalties for the various offences under the Act, and further continues to explain the format of Schedule 4. It can be seen from this Schedule that all the MDA offences except for that under section 17(3)[1] are triable either way, that is to say on indictment or summarily. Sections 18 to 21 of the Magistrates' Courts Act 1980 apply to these offences, and their effect is that D must be told of his right to elect for trial by jury, and that he can only be tried summarily with his consent.

Section 25(4) of the MDA provides that any MDA offence may be tried summarily under an information laid within twelve months of the commission of the offence, as opposed to the normal limit of six months. Sections 25(5) and 25(6) contain the corresponding provision in respect of Scottish and Northern Irish courts.

Maximum penalties

The scheme of maximum penalties is quite clear from Schedule IV and need not be repeated here. The penalties are in line with the general philosophy that Class A drugs are more dangerous than Class B drugs, which are in turn more dangerous than Class C drugs (indeed this is the basis of the classification), and that producers and suppliers of drugs are to be penalised more severely than simple possessors (see Chapter 17 on sentencing). The only anomaly is in the maximum penalties for section 9 offences.

The general scheme of the Customs and Excise Act 1952 and the offences under it was designed mainly with legitimate but dutiable

1 Failure to comply with a requirement to give information regarding drugs supplied.

goods in mind. The maximum penalties provided for under the 1952 Act were considered insufficient in the context of controlled drugs offences, and for this reason section 26 of the MDA provided for increased penalties under the CEA where drugs were involved. This provision has now been repealed and re-enacted with certain amendments by a combination of sections 50, 68 and 170 and Schedule 1 of the 1979 Act. The maximum penalties are now, for a Class A or B drug:

(a) on summary conviction, a penalty of the prescribed sum or three times the value of the goods, whichever is the greater, or to imprisonment for a term not exceeding six months, or both;

(b) on conviction on indictment, to a penalty of any amount, or to imprisonment for a term not exceeding fourteen years, or to both.

For a class C drug, they are:

(a) on summary conviction in Great Britain, to a penalty of three times the value of the goods or £500, whichever is the greater, or to imprisonment for a term not exceeding three months, or to both;

(b) on summary conviction in Northern Ireland, to a penalty of three times the value of the goods or £100, whichever is the greater, or to imprisonment for a term not exceeding 6 months, or to both;

(c) on conviction on indictment, to a penalty of any amount, or to imprisonment for a term not exceeding five years, or to both.

The prescribed sum is specified by section 171(2) to be £1,000.

Drafting of indictments
Care must be taken when drafting indictments that the provisions of the Indictment Rules 1971[2] are complied with. Three rules of particular interest are:

(a) Rule 4: this states that no more than one offence shall be contained in each count (the rule against duplicity).

(b) Rule 6 (which applies to statutory offences): this states that the statement of offence shall refer to the relevant section, paragraph or schedule of the Act and the particulars shall disclose the essential elements of the offence.

(c) Rule 7: this provides that where an offence is couched in the alternative then it may be charged in the alternative.

It is obviously important to distinguish provisions which create two or more separate offences from those which create one

2 SI 1971/1253.

chargeable in the alternative. There is much case law on the subject but the most helpful authority for present purposes is *Fox v Dingley, Ware v Fox.*[3] This authority consists of two cases, both reported together, both concerned with section 5 of the Dangerous Drugs Act 1965, the relevant part of which reads:

> If a person—
> (a) being the occupier of any premises, permits those premises to be used for the purpose of smoking cannabis...or of dealing in cannabis...he shall be guilty of an offence...

In *Ware v Fox* D was charged with permitting premises to be used for smoking cannabis *or* dealing in cannabis. In *Fox v Dingley* D was charged with permitting premises to be used for smoking cannabis *and* dealing in cannabis. In both cases the counts were held bad for duplicity. Lord Parker CJ said that although the alternative offences were contained in the same sentence of the same section of the Act, nevertheless the activities necessary for the offences were different and they were therefore separate offences.

In view of this approach it would seem, for example, that section 4(3)(a) creates two separate offences. It is not obvious how many separate offences are created by section 8, although certainly paragraphs (a) to (d) all involve different activities and there must therefore be at least four separate offences. An example of an offence couched in the alternative within the meaning of rule 7 is that under section 21, where the terms 'consent, connivance or...neglect' all create one offence. For some examples of indictments see Appendix 4.

Service of notices

The formal requirements of the service of any notice which may have to be served under the provisions of the MDA are set out in section 29.

Extradition

By section 1 of the Extradition Act 1932, the Schedule to the Extradition Act 1870 is amended to include 'offences against any enactment for the time being in force relating to dangerous drugs, and any attempt to commit such offences'. Both the CEMA 1979 and the MDA are such enactments, and so offences under them are covered by the Extradition Acts. Section 33 of the MDA further amended the 1870 Act Schedule to insert the offence of conspiracy to commit such offences. The Extradition Acts apply in

3 [1967] 1 All ER 100, [1967] 1 WLR 379, D.C

the main to Commonwealth countries. The procedure for extraditing fugitive offenders from other countries is governed by bilateral treaties existing between them. In the absence of any such treaty no extradition is possible. This is in practice the effect where Spain is concerned, because although there is a treaty between the United Kingdom and Spain it has not been ratified.

General procedure under the Customs and Excise Management Act 1979

This Act provides for certain procedures to be followed prior to and during prosecution of offences under it. These provisions are contained in sections 145–154 of the Act. These sections are reproduced in full in Appendix 2. As much of the material is self-explanatory, with little case law to qualify it, the effect of these provisions will be described here only in outline.

Institution of proceedings

By section 145(1) it is provided that proceedings under the Act may only be instituted by order of the commissioners. Subsection (5) preserves the right of the Attorney-General to institute proceedings in appropriate cases. Any proceedings in a court of summary jurisdiction must be commenced in the name of an officer. Failure to comply with the provisions of the section will not invalidate those proceedings.

Service of process

This is covered by section 146. Subsection (1) lists valid means by which a summons or other process for the purpose of proceedings under the Act may be served on persons or corporations. Subsection (2) provides that personal service of such summons or notice by a Customs officer is valid. The section does not apply in relation to proceedings in the High Court (or Court of Session of Scotland).

Proceedings for offences

By section 147(1), except where otherwise provided in the Act, proceedings may be commenced not later than three years after the offence has been committed. Where the proceedings are summary this provision overrides section 127(1) of the Magistrates' Courts Act 1980 which sets a six months' limit. Contrast section 25(4) of the MDA. It was held in a case[4] under this Act

---

4 *Customs and Excise Comrs v Sokolow's Trustee* [1954] 2 QB 336, [1954] 2 All ER 5.

that civil proceedings for forfeiture or condemnation do not fall within this section. Subsection (2) provides that examining justices shall not try a case summarily without the consent of the commissioners (or the Attorney-General if he instituted proceedings). By subsection (3) the prosecution have a right to appeal from any decision of the magistrates' court to the crown court, as well as a right to require the statement of a case for the opinion of the High Court.

Place of trial of offences

Section 148 confers wide geographical jurisdiction on the courts to try offences under the Act, in addition to such jurisdiction as they may already have. Section 148(1) specifies three alternative places of trial for offences under the Act, namely:

    (a) the place where the person charged resides or is found;

    (b) the place where anything detained or seized in connection with the offence was so detained or seized or found or condemned as forfeited;

    (c) any court having jurisdiction in the part of the United Kingdom (England and Wales, Scotland or Northern Ireland) where the offence was committed.

By subsection (2), if the offence was committed outside the jurisdiction (which is no bar to liability under various offences), the place of commission is deemed to be any place in the UK where the offender is found or to which he is first brought after the commission of the offence.

Miscellaneous provisions

Section 149 limits the magistrates' powers to order imprisonment in respect of non-payment of penalties in certain circumstances. By section 150, where liability under the Act is incurred by two or more persons jointly, the liability is in effect provided to be joint and several, such that the commissioners may proceed against any one of those persons for the full amount.

    Section 154 deals with the method of proof of certain relevant matters and formalities in proceedings under the Act. Subsection (1) provides that an averment shall be, unless the contrary is proved, sufficient evidence of the matter in question, for those matters listed. These include the fact that a person is a Customs officer, and that a ship is a British ship. Subsection (2) places the · burden of proof in various matters on the party against whom the proceedings were brought. The standard of proof is that of balance of probabilities. The matters listed include whether goods were subject to a prohibition on importation and exportation, and whether any duty has been paid or secured in respect of any goods.

Part III
Substantive Offences

7 Importation and Exportation

Offences involving the importation of drugs are very common and the law relating to importation is therefore of considerable practical significance. Three of the most commonly abused drugs in the United Kingdom are obtained from plants which do not readily grow in this country (cannabis, cocaine and heroin) and it follows that the overwhelming bulk of these drugs which are consumed here are at some stage imported. When one also considers that importation is normally effected by persons with a financial motive, rather than by those who wish to consume the drugs themselves, it can be readily understood why the importation of controlled drugs is severely penalised by the courts.

Section 3(1) of the MDA reads as follows:

Subject to subsection 2 below—
   (a) the importation of a controlled drug; and
   (b) the exportation of a controlled drug are hereby prohibited.

Because the section merely prohibits the importation and exportation of controlled drugs, but does not create a specific offence of importation or exportation, cases involving importation are normally dealt with in one of two ways.

Firstly, where more than one person is involved in some agreement or plan to import controlled drugs the participants may be charged with conspiracy to evade the prohibition created by section 3(1). This is often appropriate as the importation of controlled drugs frequently necessitates much planning and organisation by several persons. The law on this aspect of importation is dealt with in the chapter on conspiracy.

Secondly, an importer may be charged under section 170(2) of the Customs and Excise Management Acts 1979 with the offence of 'being knowingly concerned in the fraudulent evasion of the prohibition on the importation of controlled drugs'. (Specific offences of importation and exportation are provided for in sections 50 and 68 respectively of the CEMA 1979, but these are narrower in scope than the section 170(2) offence and are rarely charged.)

Importation

At what stage are goods imported or exported? Section 5 of the CEMA lays down rules which have effect for the purposes of the Act, although they clearly will be important guidelines in cases brought under the MDA. Section 5(2) reads as follows:

> Subject to subsections (3) and (6) below, the time of importation of any goods shall be deemed to be—
> (a) where the goods are brought by sea, the time when the ship carrying them comes within the limit of a port;
> (b) where the goods are brought by air, the time when the aircraft carrying them lands in the United Kingdom or the time when the goods are unloaded in the United Kingdom, whichever is the earlier;
> (c) where the goods are brought by land, the time when the goods are brought across the boundary into Northern Ireland.

Presumably if D swims ashore with controlled drugs, or if a ship lands elsewhere than at a port, the time of importation is when the person or ship actually lands.

In the case of *Smith*[1] D wished to send cannabis from Kenya to Bermuda. The journey involved changing planes at London. In response to D's defence that there was no importation, it was held that the importation took place as soon as the plane from Kenya landed, and was exported when loaded on to the plane to Bermuda. Although importation clearly takes place at a particular instant, being concerned with the importation is a continuing act (see below).

Knowingly concerned

What amounts to being 'knowingly concerned...in a fraudulent evasion of the prohibition'? Clearly there must be an importation. There is, however, some doubt concerning the extent of D's knowledge of the exact nature of the goods and of the importation itself which is required to bring him within the section. In the recent case of *Taaffe*[2] the House of Lords considered the law in the context of the following facts: (a) D was enlisted to smuggle a prohibited substance into England; (b) the substance was in fact cannabis; (c) D believed it to be money; (d) money was not a prohibited substance; (e) D thought that it was. The House of Lords in dismissing an appeal by the Crown from the Court of Appeal approved a passage in the Lord Chief Justice's judgment where he said:

---

1 [1973] QB 924, 57 Cr App Rep 737, CA.
2 [1984] 1 All ER 747, [1984] 2 WLR 326, HL.

he is to be judged against the facts as he believed them to be...Had this indeed been currency and not cannabis no offence would have been committed...the respondent's mistake of law could not convert the importation of currency into a criminal offence...'

This appears to be a logical and correct conclusion. However, during the course of his rather short speech in the House, Lord Scarman suggested in passing that although the case of *Hussain*[3] was correctly decided, the validity of the decision in *Hennessey*[4] might have to be reconsidered in the light of the House of Lords decision in *Courtie*.[5] This comment was technically *obiter* but has raised some problems. To demonstrate why requires some explanation. The case of *Hussain* was one under section 304 of the Customs and Excise Act 1952 (the forerunner of section 170 of the 1979 Act) in which the illegal importation of dutiable or prohibited goods was one single offence. It was said in that case that D need not know the precise nature of the goods imported and if he thought they were bottles of brandy (dutiable) but they were in fact drugs (prohibited) he would still fall within the section. It was also said that he need not know their exact nature if he knows that they are prohibited. It was this reasoning which was presumably approved in *Taaffe*. In 1971, section 26 of the MDA created different penalties for contravention of the section when drugs were involved from those when other prohibited goods were involved. Also the 1979 Act created two separate offences of importation of dutiable goods and importation of prohibited goods. In the case of *Hennessey*, D imported goods which he thought were pornographic films (prohibited) but were in fact drugs (also prohibited). It was held that for liability to attach to him, D must only know that the goods were prohibited, and need not know what sort of prohibited goods they were. This was the state of the law until *Taaffe*. In the case of *Courtie* the House of Lords held that where there are different penalties for different ways of committing an apparently single offence, in fact two separate offences exist. The significance of Lord Scarman's remarks in *Taaffe* may now become apparent. According to the *Courtie* doctrine the offence of importing prohibited goods is in reality two offences (one where drugs are involved, carrying higher penalties, and the other where goods other than drugs are involved). Thus it would appear that in order to satisfy the requirement of knowledge in section 170(2) D must know that it is drugs as opposed to other prohibited goods which are being imported. There are, however, considerable logical difficulties

3 [1969] 2 QB 567, 53 Cr App Rep 448, CA.
4 (1978) 68 Cr App Rep 419, CA.
5 [1984] 1 All ER 740, [1984] 2 WLR 330, HL.

arising from this approach, and until the point is fully considered by a court of appellate jurisdiction, some difficulties arise which will need further clarification.[6]

Concerned

Once these requirements of knowledge are satisfied, the very broad interpretation of the expression by the courts means that all those involved with any aspect of the importation at any stage will be caught by it. For example, acts done entirely abroad can amount to being concerned in an importation. In *Wall*,[7] D's part was limited to handling some cannabis abroad preparatory to its shipment to the UK and he was held to be within the scope of section 304 of the CEA 1952 (the predecessor of the 1979 Act, section 170(2)). The broad approach has in recent years become broader still. In *Williams*,[8] it was agreed that D would sell cannabis which X would import from India. D was convicted although he became involved directly only after the importation (cf. *Ardalan*[9]). Another case which in the purists' view stretches the meaning of the phrase 'concerned in' is *Green*.[10] A crate arrived at Southampton for which D completed Customs clearance forms. It was opened by Customs officers who discovered cannabis inside for which they substituted peat. The crate was collected by D and taken to a warehouse. D was held to be within section 304 of CEA 1952. It was stated that being knowingly concerned was a continuing offence which did not cease when the cannabis was replaced by peat, and the liability of D was unaffected whether or not he became concerned after the substitution. Another recent case is that of *Jakeman*[11] where D booked two cases containing cannabis on to a flight to London via Rome from Ghana. The flight was diverted to Paris where the cases were not collected. Officials sent them on to London where again they were not collected. D claimed that she abandoned the intention to import

---

6 The logical extension of this approach leads to some interesting results. Not only are the penalties for drugs and 'non-drugs' different, but so are those for Class C drugs and Class A and B drugs. This implies that if D thinks he is importing a Class A drug but it is in fact a Class C drug then he has a defence. It is unlikely that the House of Lords intended such a result, and indeed it would make the position under the Customs and Excise Management Act 1979 different from that under the MDA. The MDA, by section 28(3)(a), expressly provides that it is no defence under the Act for D to say that he believed the substance to be controlled drug X when it was in fact controlled drug Y. This suggests that a person charged under section 170(2) might have a defence open to him not available to a person charged under the MDA.

7 [1974] 2 All ER 245, 59 Cr App Rep 58, CA.

8 [1971] 2 All ER 444, 55 Cr App Rep 275, CA.

9 [1972] 2 All ER 257, 56 Cr App Rep 320, CA.

10 [1976] QB 985, 62 Cr App Rep 74, CA.

11 (1983) 76 Cr App Rep 223, [1983] Crim LR 104, CA.

the cases before they reached London. This was held to be no defence as at the time of booking D had a guilty mind and the actual importation was effected by innocent agents.

It is now clear from the case of *Neal*[12] that this very broad approach to the phrase 'concerned in' is the correct one. In this case a large quantity of of cannabis was found at D's farmhouse. There was no evidence as to how it got there although D admitted he knew it had been imported. On these facts the Court of Appeal held that D had been rightly convicted under CEMA 1979, section 170(2). In a passage of his judgment which must now be taken to represent the law, Griffiths LJ said:

> the question was whether the statutory provision was directed only to case where the accused was part of or connected with the actual smuggling operation, or whether it included cases where the goods came into the possession of the accused who had not been involved with the act of importation as such. The weight of authority is in favour of the latter construction. The statutory forerunners of section 170 have been consistently viewed as long-stop or catch all sections – see, for example, Lord Salmon's judgment in *DPP v Doot* [1973] AC 807, 57 Cr App Rep 600, HL. Moreover on the authorities it is clear that offences under section 170 could be committed after the importation by persons not directly involved with the importation...see *Williams*...and *Ardalan*...

It is arguable that this decision has in practice extended the section 170(2) offence to 'being knowingly concerned with controlled drugs which have been imported'. This poses questions as to how far D must be removed from the importation before he escapes liability under the section. If A imports drugs which B sells to C who sells it to D who consumes it, which of A, B, C and D fall within the section? Certainly A, and according to *Neal*, B will be liable. Whether C or D are remains an open question. On the one hand it is clear from the judgment that liability is not limited to those involved in the importing operation (whether as organiser, actual importer, storekeeper or in any other capacity). On the other hand, it was said in the case that not every transaction involving drugs (which must have been imported) falls within the section. It is not easy to propound a test to show where the line should be drawn, and perhaps the best way to approach the law is to say that each case must be looked at to see whether in the circumstances there was sufficient knowledge or intention to fall within the very wide limits of the offence.

In the case of *Watts and Stack*[13] the Court of Appeal declined to take this approach to its extreme logical limit. The defendants were charged with being concerned in the importation of cocaine

12 (1983) 77 Cr App Rep 283, CA.
13 (1979) 70 Cr App Rep 187, [1980] Crim LR 38, CA.

but the prosecution called no evidence to show that there had been an importation. The Crown's argument that where a drug such as cocaine (which does not grow here) is involved the onus falls on D to disprove importation was rejected. The court held that the prosecution must show a link between the *actus reus* of the offence and a particular importation.

Some confusion has been caused by the scope of the word 'fraudulent' in the context of section 170. In *A-G's Reference (No. 1 of 1981)*[14] it was held that the term fraudulent did not require any lies or deceit towards Customs, but simply meant the deliberate evasion or attempted evasion of the prohibition. In the light of this decision it appears that the word 'fraudulent' adds nothing to the section.

Finally, in the context of exportation, activities which could amount to being concerned in exportation are not limited to those done at the actual time of exportation but could include handing over goods for export.[15]

14 [1982] QB 848, 75 Cr App Rep 45, CA.
15 *Garrett v Arthur Churchill (Glass) Ltd* [1970] 1 QB 92, [1969] 2 All ER 1141, DC.

8 Production and Supply

Section 4 of the MDA creates two offences which may briefly be described as the production of and the supply of controlled drugs. These two offences are entirely different in kind. Although a producer of controlled drugs will almost always also become a supplier of the drugs he has produced, the converse is not always true. The two offences will be dealt with separately.

Production of controlled drugs

Section 4(1) of the MDA commences as follows:

> Subject to any regulations under section 7 of this Act for the time being in force, it shall not be lawful for a person—
> (a) to produce a controlled drug...

Section 4(2) reads as follows:

> Subject to section 28 of this Act it is an offence for a person—
> (a) to produce a controlled drug in contravention of subsection 4(1) above;
> (b) to be concerned in the production of such a drug in contravention of that subsection by another.

In section 37(1) the meaning of the word produce is expanded by means of examples of production which are specifically to be included. The relevant part reads as follows:

> 'produce' where the reference is to producing a controlled drug means producing it by manufacture, cultivation or any other method, and 'production' has a corresponding meaning.

This expression is therefore drawn very widely and covers any process by which a controlled drug comes into existence. If before the process in question a particular controlled drug does not exist and afterwards it does, then that act or process amounts to production. In practice some drugs such as LSD or amphetamine are only capable of being produced by chemical synthesis. Others such as cannabis, whose definition includes the plant in its natural state, may be produced by cultivation. Cannabis resin is produced by a refining or extracting process. Whether this falls under the heading of manufacture or other method is an academic argument which need not be pursued here. Production includes preparation where before the production the substance contains a controlled drug but did not amount to that drug because it was a substance in its natural state.[1]

A person assisting in the production of a controlled drug may of course be committing an offence under section 4(2)(a) by the normal rules of principals and accessories. Quite apart from such liability, section 4(2)(b) creates the separate offence of being concerned in the production of a controlled drug by another. This section is largely self-explanatory and the main point of interest is the meaning of the term 'concerned in' (contrast the wording of section 170(2) of the Customs and Excise Management Act 1979). In *Farr*,[2] D was an addict who allowed A and C to use his kitchen knowing that they were producing pink heroin. The Court of Appeal held that D was not liable under the section as there had to be 'an identifiable participation' in the production. (N.B. Sections 4 and 8 are not mutually exclusive and D would have had no defence to a charge under section 8.) If a number of persons are all involved in a venture to produce drugs, and if some are charged under section 4(2)(b), at least one must be charged under section 4(2)(a) as the person doing the actual producing which the remainder are concerned in.

Supply of controlled drugs
Section 4(1) prohibits the supply of and the offer to supply a controlled drug and section 4(3) creates three separate offences involving a contravention of this prohibition. It seems that sections 4(3)(b) and 4(3)(c) are drafted as separate sections merely because of the grammatical difficulty of combining them in the way they are combined in sections 4(1)(b) and 4(3)(a). The meaning of the word supply is specifically defined to include distributing by section 37(1). The precise differences between 'supply' and 'distribution' are not obvious, but it appears that whereas supply implies a transfer of title or possession, distribution is the physical act of splitting a quantity of a substance and transferring possession of the smaller quantities to another. While not every act of supply will be one of distribution, a distribution will normally be a number of acts of supply.

In *Holmes v Chief Constable Merseyside Police*,[3] D held controlled drugs for himself and others. He was convicted of possession with intent to supply. The conviction was upheld on the

---

1 As in *DPP v Goodchild* [1978] 2 All ER 161, 6 Cr App Rep 56, HL.
2 [1982] Crim LR 745, CA. It is not clear from the report whether the charge was under s.4(2)(a) or 4(2)(b), but the latter seems most likely.
3 [1976] Crim LR 125, DC.

basis that as a supply included distribution, someone who purchased for himself and as an agent for others was intending to distribute and therefore supply it.[4] This approach cannot, however, be taken too far, and some restriction is placed on it by the case of *King*.[5] In this case D, if visited by friends, would make a joint (cannabis cigarette) from his supply of cannabis and then pass it round to his friends, each of whom would take a puff and pass it on to the next. This technically amounts to a distribution. The court held firstly that there must be a real and not merely a constructive intent to supply and secondly that supply must be given its everyday ordinary meaning. Passing a joint around did not amount to supply. There is only supply if initially D has material in his possession and afterwards it has passed into the possession of another. Presumably if one of the friends extinguished the joint, half-finished and pocketed it, with D's knowledge and consent, this would be a supply.

The rationale of the decision is, it appears, that provision of drugs for consumption in itself is not equivalent to supply if the consumer is never in possession of them. This must be correct if, for example, the drugs are placed in a large pipe in the centre of the room and everyone takes a puff at it. It is arguable, however, that when a joint is actually passed round, the current holder has sufficient control over the drugs in the joint at that instant to be in possession of it.

In the case of *Moore*[6] the court declined to follow *King*. D persuaded two girls to leave a pub and 'go for a smoke'. He was caught making a joint and was charged with possession with intent to supply. His defence that this was only an offer to supply the smoke and not the cannabis was rejected. The court held that an offer of consumption could be equated an offer to supply and that D was therefore guilty of the offence. In *Harris*[7] D injected X with X's own heroin. This was held not to constitute a supply, but it did amount to the offence of administering a noxious thing contrary to section 23 of the Offences against the Person Act 1861. (It is not clear whether the fact that a substance is a controlled drug renders it *ipso facto* a noxious substance.) It is possible that this case is no longer good law in the light of *Delgado*.[8] If the heroin had been D's the position is not clear but it would seem that as X would never be in possession of the heroin there would be no supply. Just as the case of *Neal*[9] has given section 170 of the CEMA a 'catch all'

4 Cf. *Buckley* (1979) 69 Cr App Rep 371, [1979] Crim LR 664, CA.
5 [1978] Crim LR 228.
6 [1979] Crim LR 789.
7 [1968] 2 All ER 49, 52 Cr App Rep 277, CA.
8 [1984] 1 All ER 449, [1984] 1 WLR 89, CA.
9 (1983) 77 Cr App Rep 283, CA.

interpretation, the recent Court of Appeal decision in *Delgado* has broadened the scope of the word 'supply' to its limit. In this case D claimed that a quantity of cannabis found in a taxi in which he was riding was being kept by him for a friend, to whom he was going to return it. He was charged with possession with intent to supply, the supply being the return of the drugs to their owner. The Court of Appeal held that such an act would amount to a supply and that D was therefore liable. Skinner J, delivering the judgment of the court, said (at 92):

> Thus we are driven back to considering the word supply in its context. The judge himself relied on the dictionary definition which is a fairly wide one. The court has been referred to the *Shorter Oxford English Dictionary*, which gives a large number of definitions of the word 'supply' but they have a common feature, viz.: that in the word supply is inherent the furnishing or providing of something which is wanted. In the judgment of this court, the word supply in section 5(3) of the Act of 1971 covers a similarly wide range of transactions. A feature common to all of those transactions is a transfer of physical control of a drug from one person to another. In our judgment questions of the transfer of ownership or legal possession of those drugs are irrelevant to the issue whether or not there was intent to supply.[10]

A final point on the intention aspect of the offence of possession with intent to supply is that the intention must be that of the supplier, and not of a third party. So if D is in possession of some cannabis with the intention that X should supply it to others, he does not fall within the scope of section 5(3),[11] although normally of course D will have to supply it to X before X can supply it to third parties. It has recently been decided by the Court of Appeal that even if D is in joint possession of the drugs with the person who intends to supply it, and even if D knows that that person intends to supply it, he (D) is not within the scope of section 5(3).[12]

---

10 *Delgado* is a case on section 5(3) but the meaning of supply must be the same as that in section 4(3). It is arguable that the case (in theory at least) enables a person to be guilty of supply even when the limited nature of his physical control over the drug would not amount in law to possession for the purposes of a section 5(2) offence. For a case of offering to supply from a distance, see *Blake and O'Connor* (1978) 68 Cr App Rep 1, where D was charged under section 4(3)(c).

11 *Greenfield* [1983] Crim LR 397, CA.

12 *Downes* (1984) Times, 13 June, CA.

9 Possession

Offences of possession of controlled drugs are the most common contraventions of the drugs legislation. Although a producer, importer or supplier of controlled drugs will normally, of course, also be in possession of the drugs, this chapter, covering principally section 5 of the MDA, is concerned with the simple possessor and end user of controlled drugs.

Section 5 commences as follows:

5.(1) Subject to any regulations under section 7 of this Act for the time being in force, it shall not be lawful for a person to have a controlled drug in his possession.

(2) Subject to section 28 of this Act and to subsection 4 below, it is an offence for a person to have a controlled drug in his possession in contravention of subsection (1) above.

(3) Subject to section 28 of this Act, it is an offence for a person to have a controlled drug in his possession, whether lawfully or not, with intent to supply it to another in contravention of section 4(1) of this Act.

(Section 7 is concerned in general with making lawful the possession of certain controlled drugs by persons such as doctors, dentists, etc. Section 28 provides a general defence of mistake of fact. Both these sections will be dealt with more fully at a later stage.)

Section 5 creates two separate but related offences. Subsection (2) is the basic possession offence under which possessors of small quantities of controlled drugs for their own use will be charged. Subsection 3 creates the more serious offence of possession with intent to supply, which is designed to catch the potential supplier of controlled drugs.

The cases in section 5 fall broadly into two groups, those concerned with the meaning of possession and those interpreting the definitions of 'controlled drug'. Cases in the latter category are also of relevance to offences under other sections of the MDA.

The meaning of possession

Most people have a basic understanding of the concept of possession, but defining it in the context of section 5 is no easy task. The exact ingredients of possession will vary according to the circumstances. In the words of Lord Morris in *Warner v Metropolitan Police Comr.*[1] 'The word possession though much to be found in the vocabulary of the law, cannot always be given the same meaning in all its divers contexts.' In many situations the best approach in determining whether or not D is in possession of a controlled drug is one of common sense, taking into account all the relevant circumstances. Lord Morris, also in *Warner v Metropolitan Police Comr.*, stated that the term possession 'must be given a sensible and reasonable meaning in its context'.

Similarly in the case of *DPP v Brooks*,[2] the Privy Council opined that the technical doctrines of the civil law on possession have no application in the law of possession of controlled drugs.

Although it must be emphasised that possession and its elements may differ greatly from one situation to another, there are nevertheless many cases offering rules and guidelines as to the meaning of possession in various circumstances. Ribeiro and Perry list no less than eight different kinds of possession,[3] and their basic classification is respectfully adopted in the following paragraphs.

Ideal possession
The most straightforward or 'ideal' kind of possession is described by Lord Wilberforce in *Warner v Metropolitan Police Comr.*[4]

> Ideally a possessor of a thing has complete physical control over it, he has knowledge of its existence, its situation and its qualities – he has received it from a person who intends to confer possession of it and he has himself the intention to possess it exclusively of others.

This type of possession is 'ideal' from the prosecution's point of view, and there are no avenues of escape by which D can argue that he was not in possession. Lord Wilberforce's definition contains the two key elements of any kind of possession, the *actus reus* of physical custody or control and the *mens rea* of knowledge and intention.

Illustrations of the meaning of possession
The following cases give some illustrations of these requirements:

In *Smith*,[5] the judge in summing up to the jury implied that if D lived in or had an interest in a room she controlled everything in it.

1 [1969] 2 AC 256, 52 Cr App Rep 373, HL.
2 [1974] AC 862, 59 Cr App Rep 185, PC.
3 [1979] Crim LR 90. The eight types of possession listed in the article are 'ideal possession', 'strict possession', 'possession of a container's contents', 'joint possession', 'possession through an innocent agent', 'unconscious custody', 'possession of traces' and 'consumed drugs'. The text of this work does not follow exactly the structure of the article.
4 [1969] 2 AC 256, 52 Cr App Rep 373, HL.
5 [1966] Crim LR 558, CCA.

On appeal it was held that the judge had misdirected the jury – the correct test was whether D knew of the drug within the room and if so whether she had possession of it within the meaning of the Dangerous Drugs Act. It is clear that although knowledge is an essential ingredient of possession,[6] mere knowledge of the presence of a drug does not of itself amount to possession.[7]

The case of *Cavendish*[8] is actually concerned with stolen goods but throws light on the scope of possession. In this case stolen goods were found on D's premises. It was held that if D was absent when they were delivered, it must be proved that he became aware of their presence and exercised some control over them to be in possession of them. Similarly, if delivery of goods is made to an employee, his employer is not in possession of them unless he gave the employee instructions and authority to take the goods.

In *Peaston*,[9] D lived in a bedsitter in a house where mail was delivered downstairs. A parcel addressed to him was taken upstairs by the police and handed to D, who was in bed. He opened it, saw that it contained amphetamine and handed it back to the police. In holding that D was guilty of possessing the drug the court said that this was not a *Warner v Metropolitan Police Comr.*[10] type of case. D had admitted asking for the package to be sent and was therefore in possession of it as soon as it came through the letter box.

In *Wright*,[11] D was a passenger in a car being followed by the police. He was handed a tin by a fellow passenger and asked to throw it out of the window, which he duly did. It subsequently transpired that the tin contained cannabis. D admitted that when he was handed the tin it occurred to him that it might contain cannabis. It was held following *Warner v Metropolitan Police Comr.*[12] that the facts did not amount to possession of the cannabis and that there was a distinction to be drawn between physical custody and possession.

MDA, section 37(3)

It is worth noting that by section 37(3) of the MDA the notion of possession is extended to include the situation whe.ᴄ ᴅ is in control of a thing in the custody of another. Thus if D places a controlled drug in a safe deposit box at his bank and retains a key

6 *Ashton-Rickardt* [1978] 1 All ER 173, 65 Cr App Rep 67, CA.
7 *Searle* [1971] Crim LR 592, CA, and *Irala-Prevost* [1965] Crim LR 606, CCA.
8 [1961] 2 All ER 856, 45 Cr App Rep 374, CCA.
9 (1978) 69 Cr App Rep 203, [1979] Crim LR 183, CA.
10 [1969] 2 AC 256, 52 Cr App Rep 373, HL.
11 (1975) 62 Cr App Rep 169, CA.
12 [1969] 2 AC 256, 52 Cr App Rep 373, HL.

to it or if he instructs his employee to keep it in his sandwich box then D is deemed to be in possession by section 37(3). The bank and its employee will also be in possession of the drug (if they know about it).

Possession and knowledge

Clearly D must have some knowledge of a thing before he can possess it. If he is totally unaware of its existence, then this ignorance negates possession. If a controlled drug is slipped secretly into D's pocket he is not in possession of it.[13] Similarly if a controlled drug is placed into the hand of a sleeping man he is not in possession of it. Such a situation may be described as unconscious custody and does not amount to possession.

If D knows that he possesses something but is not sure exactly what it is the situation is more difficult. A lack of certain knowledge will not negate possession where a man is suspicious of the nature of a substance but deliberately avoids ascertaining it. In *Fernandez*[14] a seaman was held to be in possession of cannabis contained in a cigarette in a package that broke open. He was not sure what the contents were, but thought that they might be cannabis. The fact that he was suspicious but did not inquire was enough to impute to him possession.[15]

In *Irving*,[16] D was acquitted of possessing a heroin tablet. It was found in a bottle of his stomach pills and his defence was that his wife, for whom heroin tablets had been prescribed, must have put it there. The ratio of this decision is apparently that as D was not aware of the presence of the heroin tablet he could not be in possession of it. Although this result is probably a sensible and practical one, it causes considerable difficulties. In particular it is hard to reconcile with the 'strict possession' and the 'container' cases below and it is submitted that *Irving* was wrongly decided. In any event if Mr Irving were prosecuted today on the same facts he would have a defence under section 28.

Strict possession

If D knows that he possesses something but not that it is or contains a controlled drug, the doctrine of strict possession may impute to him the possession of the controlled drug.[17] In *Searle v Randolph*,[18] D picked up a number of cigarette ends from the floor of his tent which had been used by others. Unknown to him, one

13 *Lockyer v Gibb* [1967] 2 QB 243, [1966] 2 All ER 653, DC.
14 [1970] Crim LR 277, CA.
15 Cf. *Warner v Metropoliton Police Comr.* and the package cases, above.
16 [1970] Crim LR 642, CA.
17 *Lockyer v Gibb* [1967] 2 QB 243, [1966] 2 All ER 653, DC.
18 [1972] Crim LR 779, DC.

of them contained cannabis. He was found guilty on the basis that
the offence of possession was an offence of strict liability. The fact
that the cigarette end was a cannabis one and not an ordinary one
as he thought afforded D no defence. A slightly different situation
arose in *Marriott*.[19] Here D was in possession of a penknife, to the
blade of which was adhering a small piece of cannabis. The judge
directed the jury that if D possessed the penknife then he
possessed the cannabis. This was held to be a misdirection.
Although if D knew there was some foreign matter on the blade it
might be that he possessed the cannabis, mere possession of the
knife did not imply possession of the cannabis. These two cases are
authority for the proposition that where D knowingly has custody
or control of a thing but is mistaken as to its quality (as opposed to
a more fundamental mistake as to its nature or kind) he is in
possession of it. If, for example, in *Marriott* D had not noticed the
foreign matter at all, as he claimed, but had believed himself to be
in possession of a clean penknife he would not have been in
possession of the cannabis because a penknife is fundamentally
different in kind from a piece of cannabis. It can be seen that this
rule of strict possession may operate harshly and it was partly to
alleviate this that section 28 was inserted in the MDA (giving a
general defence of mistake of fact).

Possession of a container's contents

A different set of rules applies where the controlled drug of which
possession is alleged is concealed from direct perception by some
package, box or other container. The leading case on this and
indeed many other aspects of possession is *Warner v Metropolitan
Police Comr*[20] where D's appeal against conviction for possession
of a controlled drug was allowed by the House of Lords. The facts
of the case were simple. D collected a package from a public house
which he thought contained scent. In fact it contained 20,000
amphetamine tablets. It was held that D was not in possession of
them. The ratio of the case is not easy to divine as their Lordships'
speeches were not all along the same lines, but the case produced
many important dicta on the general law of possession as well as
being authority for the following propositions in respect of
'container' cases.

Firstly the prosecution must prove that
(a) D had custody or control of the container, and
(b) D knew that he had custody or control, and
(c) D knew that the container contained something,

These can be combined and summarised by saying that the
prosecution must show that D possessed a container which he

19 [1971] 1 All ER 595, 55 Cr App Rep 82, CA.
20 [1969] 2 AC 256, 52 Cr App Rep 373, HL.

knew contained something. Once this is done there is a *prima facie* inference that D possessed the contents, and an evidential burden falls on D. He must adduce evidence that:

(i)   he had no opportunity or authority to open the container, and

(ii) he had no reason to suspect that the contents were illicit, and

(iii) he honestly believed that the contents were different in kind (and not merely in quality) from the actual contents.

(This last requirement presupposes that D turned his thought to the contents of the container at all.) If D does adduce such evidence, then the prosecution have the legal burden of disproving it.

The case of *Warner v Metropolitan Police Comr.* provides a workable solution to the problem of container cases, but questions remain unresolved. What constitutes a container? Was the cigarette in *Searle v Randolph* a container? Was Mr Irving's bottle of pills a container? It is suggested that *Irving* is incorrect. Another difficulty arising from *Warner v Metropolitan Police Comr.* is that of distinguishing differences of kind from differences of quality. There can be no hard and fast rule and it is submitted that esoteric metaphysical arguments should be avoided. The kind/quality distinction will simply be a question of fact in each case.

Joint possession

Questions of law can arise where D1 and D2 are jointly charged with possession of a controlled drug. Two different situations may occur. The first is where D1 is involved in possession or other offences relating to controlled drugs and D2 is alleged to have been involved or assisted in the enterprise. The normal rules on principals and accessories apply here. In *Tansley v Painter*[1] D1 and D2 were sitting together in a car. D1 was selling cannabis from the car. D2 claimed that he know nothing of this. Although the court disbelieved him he was acquitted of possesing the amphetamine on the grounds that to show joint possession it is insufficient to show D2's knowledge of another's possession. There must be some sort of joint enterprise before D2 can be convicted of possession. The case is an application of the general rule that possession is more than mere knowledge (if D2 had been acting as lookout he would have had no defence).

The second situation is where a controlled drug is found in a room, house or car jointly occupied by a number of people. In *Searle*[2] D and some friends were on holiday together in a van in

1 [1969] Crim LR 139, DC.
2 [1971] Crim LR 592, CA.

which controlled drugs were found. No particular drugs were attributable to any one defendant. The judge directed the jury that in this situation knowledge of the presence of the drug was enough to amount to possession. On appeal this was held to be a misdirection. The court again emphasised the point that possession was more than mere knowledge and held that in order to establish joint possession it must be shown that there was some sort of joint enterprise involved or that there was a common pool of drugs from which any one of the defendants could draw. This ruling, although it makes the task of the prosecution very difficult, is, it is submitted, the correct and logical approach.

Possession after consumption

An entirely different question arose in the case of *Hambleton v Callinan*.[3] A urine sample from D was found to contain amphetamine and he was charged with possession of it. He was acquitted of the charge on the grounds that when the amphetamine had been consumed its character had changed and it was impossible to say that it was in D's possession. It is not clear from the report in this case exactly how the amphetamine had 'changed in character'. On the basis that it was still amphetamine and not a by-product, the change must have been physical and not chemical (i.e. it was in solution in D's urine rather than in powder or tablet form). It is submitted that on this assumption the true *ratio* of the case is that D has consumed the drug and not that it had undergone a physical change. If D dissolves a controlled drug in his morning cup of tea and is arrested before he can drink it, it is submitted that he is in possession of it. In the present case D would have had no defence to a charge of past possession whether the drug had undergone a physical or a chemical change.

It is interesting to note that for the purposes of section 9, opium is defined to include any residue (remaining after the drug has been smoked). This is a very wide definition, because in the process of combustion the opium ceases to exist as such (although traces of unburnt drug will no doubt remain).

Possession of minute quantities

There have been many cases concerned with whether D can properly be held to be in possession of very small quantities of a controlled drug. In *Worsell*,[4] D was in possession of a tube which contained microscopic droplets of heroin. They were too small to

3 [1968] 2 QB 427, [1968] 2 All ER 943, DC.
4 [1969] 2 All ER 1183, 53 Cr App Rep 322, CA.

see, pour out or measure. D was acquitted on the grounds that the tube in reality contained nothing. The court did however suggest (*obiter*) that the droplets would have been evidence of past possession, to which charge D would have had no defence. Following and applying *Worsell* but narrowing its scope was the case of *Graham*,[5] where it was said that if amounts of a controlled drug were capable of being weighed and measured then they could not be said to amount to nothing.

An important case regarding minute quantities of controlled drugs was *Bocking v Roberts*.[6] D had a hookah pipe containing traces of cannabis which were too small to be weighed or measured. However, it could be inferred that there were at least 20 micrograms of cannabis because the test only gave a positive reaction to amounts of at least that quantity. In dismissing D's appeal against conviction for possession the Court of Appeal said that the 'de minimis' principle had no application in the law of controlled drugs. However, before convicting the tribunal must be satisfied that the quantity was sufficient to justify the charge and was not just slight traces indicating possession on a previous occasion. In the present case there were at least 20 micrograms which was enough to justify the charge.

Bocking v Roberts laid down the correct approach in law and also found on the facts that the charge was justified. In *Hierowski*[7] roaches (butt ends) containing 20 micrograms of cannabis were found in D's possession. Expert evidence was adduced to the effect that the burning of any part of the cannabis plant would by distillation produce minute traces of cannabis such as these. It was held in this case that the traces in reality amounted to nothing and that there was no case to answer.

Quite separate from the *Bocking v Roberts* principle was the (now discarded) 'usability' test. Although this doctrine is no longer applicable it was only recently held to be so and it is worth mentioning to avoid confusion. The 'usability' test on which the leading case was *Carver*[8] stated that a person was not guilty of possession of a controlled drug if the amount involved was too small to be usable (i.e. to produce an effect on the user). This test was developed in order to counter what were considered to be frivolous prosecutions for minute quantities of controlled drugs, but it is submitted that the reasoning on which it is based is fallacious and in any event *Carver* has been overruled by the House of Lords in *Boyesen*[9] where it was held that the usability or

5 [1969] 2 All ER 1181, [1970] 1 WLR 113, CA.
6 [1974] QB 307, [1973] Crim LR 517, DC.
7 [1978] Crim LR 563.
8 [1978] QB 472, 67 Cr App Rep 352, CA.
9 [1982] AC 768, 75 Cr App Rep 51, HL.

otherwise of a quantity of a controlled drug is irrelevant for the purposes of determining whether it is in D's possession.[10]

An alternative approach to the issue of minute quantities is to apply the maxim that knowledge is a necessary ingredient of possession. If the amount of a drug involved is very small it may be invisible and it is arguable that D may not know of its existence (cf. *Colyer*[11]). On the other hand, the fact that a trace is invisible does not itself mean that D will be ignorant of its existence, as he may well realise that smoking of certain drugs leaves traces.

Possession and duplicity

Where several small and separate amounts of a controlled drug are found in D's possession the question arises whether the prosecution may include all the amounts in one count or whether such a count is bad for duplicity. In *Bayliss and Oliver*[12] D had one piece of one sort of cannabis (0.083 grams) and one piece of another sort (0.011 grams) in his room. It was held that the Crown could not be permitted to join the two amounts, giving one count alleging possession of 0.094 grams. Such a count was bad for duplicity. In *Webb*,[13] however, D was charged in count 1 with possession of 26.4 milligrams of cannabis consisting of several pieces found in various articles in D's room. It was held that there was no need to sever the different counts for the various pieces because not more than one offence of possession was disclosed.[14]

10 Although the approaches of *Carver* and *Bocking v Roberts* are different it is arguable that the end result is the same from both points of view. When is a trace so small that the charge cannot be justified? Although traces of cannabis are weighable and measurable long before they are usable, the same is not necessarily true of other drugs. If the droplets in Mr Worsell's tube had been LSD solution would the result have been the same? Perhaps the true test should be that traces must be immeasurable, unweighable and unusable before D is not in possession of them. With the *Hierowski* approach still be valid if the traces produced by distillation are measurable and usable?
11 [1974] Crim LR 243.
12 [1978] Crim LR 361, DC.
13 [1979] Crim LR 462.
14 The precise facts of *Bayliss and Oliver* are not clear from the report of the case. However, it does appear that the two pieces of cannabis involved were of different origins. The case is perfectly consistent with *Webb* if one states the true test as follows: if the drugs are all identical, from the same source and obtained at the same time, then no matter how they are split up or stored (by the same possessor) then possession of all of them may properly be included in one count. If these criteria are not met then more than one offence of possession is disclosed and the counts must be severed. Also on this subject see *Tarpy v Rickard* [1980] Crim LR 375, DC.

Miscellaneous points on possession

A different issue arose in the case of *Peevey*[15] where 6 dexadrine tablets were found in D's wallet and 92 similar ones under the driving seat of his car. In his summing up the judge told the jury that the question was whether all or any of the tablets were in D's possession. He did not tell the jury that they were entitled to say in respect of which tablets they found him guilty of possession. In dismissing D's appeal the Court of Appeal held that there was no misdirection and that the judge's omission was not wrong in law. There was no danger of a partial verdict being returned – this was a separate issue which could only occur in a case where the jury were entitled to bring in a verdict of guilty of a lesser offence.

The case of *Pragliola*[16] illustrates one final point on the law of possession. D had been convicted in 1974 of possession of cannabis. During the investigation into the offence a pair of scales and a pipe had been removed by the police. No charge was made in relation to the pipe which contained minute traces of cannabis and it was returned to D in 1975. Subsequently D was charged with possessing the traces from the date of the return of the pipe in 1975. The court held that the charge and the extension back in time were oppressive. The charge would only have been justified if the possession of cannabis in the extension back related to the moment when police took possession of the pipe and if the extension back was of limited duration and if the offence charged was in effect recent possession of the drug.[17]

Definition of controlled drug

The list of controlled drugs is contained in Schedule 2 of the MDA. This list can be amended by the Home Secretary. The vast majority of controlled drugs are described by a scientific name which connotes a precise chemical formula. In cases involving such drugs the prosecution will normally adduce expert evidence that the sample in respect of which possession is alleged is of that particular formula. However, some of the more commonly abused drugs which occur naturally are described in their natural state by their common name, and two drugs, namely cannabis (and cannabis resin) and opium are further defined by section 37(1) of the MDA.

By this section, as amended by the Criminal Law Act 1977, section 52, cannabis is defined as:

> Any plant of the genus cannabis or any part of such a plant (by whatever name designated) except that it does not include cannabis

15 (1973) 57 Cr App Rep 554, CA.
16 [1977] Crim LR 612.
17 Cf. *Worsell* [1969] 2 All ER 1183, 53 Cr App Rep 322, CA.

resin or any of the following products after separation from the rest of the plant—

(a) Mature stalk of any such plant;

(b) Fibre produced from mature stalk of any such plant;

(c) Seed of any such plant.

Cannabis resin is defined as:

the separated resin, whether crude or purified, obtained from any plant of the genus cannabis.

Opium itself is not defined by the Act, but by section 37(1):

prepared opium means opium prepared for smoking and includes dross and any other residue remaining after opium has been smoked

and by Part IV of Schedule 2:

'medicinal opium' means raw opium which has undergone the process necessary to adapt it for medicinal use in accordance with the requirements of the British Pharmacopoeia, whether it is in the form of powder or is granulated or is in any other form, and whether or not it is mixed with neutral substances.

The case of *Goodchild*

The Criminal Law Act amendment was necessary to reverse in part the result of the prosecution of Kevin Goodchild.[18] Despite this, the case of *Goodchild* (*No. 2*) is still of relevance to the law regarding definition of controlled drugs. The facts of the case were simple. Goodchild was in possession of 4 ounces of leaf and stalk of a cannabis plant. At that time the definition of cannabis included only the flowering and fruiting tops of the plant. D was charged *inter alia* with:

(a) possessing cannabis (count 1);

(b) possessing cannabis resin (being contained in the leaves and stalk – count 3);

(c) possessing a cannabinol derivative (being contained in the stalk and leaves – count 5).

18 [1978] 2 All ER 161, 67 Cr App Rep 56, HL. The Goodchild saga is rather convoluted. At the first trial D pleaded guilty on count 1, was acquitted on the direction of the judge on count 3, and count 5 lay on the file. After the count 1 conviction was quashed by the Court of Appeal (sub nom. *Goodchild* (*No. 1*) [1977] 2 All ER 163, 64 Cr App Rep 100), the prosecution was given leave to proceed with count 5, which it did in a second trial, at which D pleaded guilty after a ruling by the judge. D appealed against this conviction, and it was the hearing of this appeal which is *DPP v Goodchild* and to which the above references correspond. The other relevant part of *Goodchild* (*No. 2*) is the hearing in the Court of Appeal by way of A-G's reference of the challenge by the Crown of the ruling on count 3 at the first trial ([1978] 1 All ER 649, 65 Cr App Rep 165). It was the result of *Goodchild* (*No. 1*) in the Court of Appeal which was reversed by the CLA 1977 amendment.

On appeal to the House of Lords against his conviction on count 5, D's appeal was allowed on the grounds that possession of a controlled drug is not established by possession of a naturally occurring substance containing it. In the case in the Court of Appeal[19] one of the questions referred by means of the Attorney-General's reference to the Court of Appeal was 'Could possession of leaves and stalk only amount to possession of cannabis resin?' The court answered in the negative on the grounds that the preparation contemplated by section 37(1) was 'a serious and deliberate removal of the resin of the plant by whatever process was available'. (N.B. Since the 1977 amendment D would have been convicted on count (a).)

Different forms of controlled drugs

The three parts of Schedule 2, corresponding to Class A, B and C drugs, are each split into a number of separate paragraphs. Paragraph 1 lists a number of controlled drugs and the other paragraphs describe generically drugs which are chemicals extremely closely related to those in paragraph 1, such as their salts or isomers.[20] For example, for Class A drugs, paragraphs 2 to 4 of Part I of the Schedule provide respectively for stereoisomers of those in paragraph 1, esters or ethers of those in paragraph 1, and salts of those in paragraphs 1 or 2. Paragraph 5 describes any product or preparation containing a paragraph 1 drug. Paragraph 6 places into Class A any injectable preparation of Class B drugs (e.g. amphetamine).

One of the effects of paragraph 5, in the light of *Goodchild (No. 2)* is that although a naturally occurring substance containing a controlled drug is not a product or preparation within paragraph 5, any active step or process of preparation may bring it within the paragraph. The drug in relation to which this question most often arises is psilocin contained in the 'magic' mushroom (psilocybin semilanceata). These mushrooms, which have hallucinogenic properties, grow naturally in Britain and are widely eaten as a drug. It is generally accepted that although the act of picking the mushrooms is not sufficient to constitute a preparation, any further process to make them more easily consumable (for example drying them) probably is, and will render the person concerned liable for possession of a Class A drug. In the case of

---

19 A salt normally results from the treatment of a chemical with an acid (e.g. amphetamine sulphate and cocaine hydrochloride). The salts are often more stable than the original substances but the properties (so far as the effect of the drug) remain. A substance exists in different isomeric forms if its molecular structure can be arranged in various different ways.
20 *Goodchild (No. 2)* [1978] 1 All ER 649, 65 Cr App Rep 165, CA.

Stevens[1] it was said that preparation had no technical meaning, but for mushrooms to be prepared they had to cease to be in a natural growing state, and to be in some way altered by hand of man to put them in a condition in which they are usable for human consumption.

Two recent cases have clarified the law as to the degree of forensic precision required in order to prove possession of a particular controlled drug. In *Greensmith*,[2] D was charged with the possession of cocaine with intent to supply. The defence was that the prosecution had failed to show that the substance in question was cocaine as opposed to one of its salts or isomers, etc. as listed in paragraphs 2 to 4 of Part I of the Schedule. In rejecting this argument the court said that the language of paragraph 6 (which refers to separate preceding paragraphs) was no guide to the construction of paragraphs 1 to 5. The drug as specified in paragraph 1 was the generic form, and did not signify the 'pure' drug as opposed to one of its other forms (such as salts or isomers) but rather included all these forms. Thus it was unnecessary for the prosecution to show that the drug was in any particular form. This approach was followed in the case of *Watts*.[3]

Miscellaneous cases on definition
In the case of *Thomas*[4] there was evidence that D possessed a morphous brown substance produced by compacting shakings or scrapings of a cannabis plant. On examination under the microscope it could be seen that the substance contained intact oil-bearing trichomes from which the cannabis had not been removed. D argued that there had been insufficient separation for the substance to constitute resin. He was convicted of possessing resin and the court held that the fact that the substance contained some trichomes did not prevent it from being resin.

The issue of duplicity arose in *Best*[5] where D was charged with 'possession of a controlled drug being either cannabis or cannabis resin'. It was held that this count was not bad for duplicity since cannabis and cannabis resin were linked in Schedule 2 and could therefore be included together in one count in this manner.

Evidence and possession
The following cases are really applications of the general law of criminal evidence but because of their context of drug offences their inclusion may be helpful.

1 [1981] Crim LR 568, CA.
2 [1983] 3 All ER 444, 77 Cr App Rep 202, CA.
3 [1984] 2 All ER 380, [1984] 1 WLR 757, CA.
4 [1981] Crim LR 496, CA.
5 (1979) 70 Cr App Rep 21, [1979] Crim LR 787, CA.

Questions may arise concerning the evidential effect of an admission by D to the police that is later retracted at trial. In *Storey*[6] D was convicted of possessing controlled drugs found on a bed in her flat. When asked to account for them D had pointed to the lavatory from which had emerged a man (A), who told police that he had brought the drugs to the flat without D's consent. At the trial after an unsuccessful submission of no case, D gave no evidence. On appeal it was held that she was rightly convicted as although a statement can be evidence against D if it contains an admission, it is not evidence of the truth of other matters in it but only of the reaction to the charge and the general picture. The statement must be left to the jury.

This rule was applied in a slightly different situation in *Chatwood*.[7] D admitted injecting himself with heroin and was charged with the possession (pre-injection) of it. The prosecution offered no other evidence as to the identity of the drug. After an unsuccessful submission of no case D gave evidence that he had injected himself with flour. In dismissing his appeal against conviction, the court said that the statements were enough to provide *prima facie* evidence against D. The jury had clearly disbelieved D's story and were entitled to convict.[8] A similar case is *Wells*.[9] Here D admitted consuming cannabis and amphetamine and pleaded guilty to possessing them. The prosecution had no evidence other than the admission. D was not permitted to withdraw her plea of guilty. It was held that in the last analysis all evidence as to the nature of a substance was opinion evidence. There was no suggestion that D was mistaken in her belief as to the nature of the substance and there was no need for an analyst to give evidence (contrast *Lang and Evans*[10] which suggests that there should be no conviction without an analyst's report). In some areas it is common practice where there is an admission in cases involving cannabis to proceed without ever sending the substance for analysis.

It is worth noting that where D is charged with possessing cannabis resin the prosecution must prove that the substance possessed was resin as opposed to cannabis.[11] Proving that traces are resin as opposed to cannabis or vice versa can be difficult where the quantities involved are small.[12] A way round this which has been held legitimate[13] is to charge the count in the alternative.

6 (1968) 52 Cr App Rep 334, [1968] Crim LR 387, CA.
7 [1980] 1 All ER 467, 70 Cr App Rep 39, CA.
8 Cf. *Bird v Adams* [1972] Crim LR 174, DC.
9 [1976] Crim LR 518, CA.
10 [1977] Crim LR 286.
11 *Muir v Smith* [1978] Crim LR 293, DC.
12 *Hierowski* [1978] Crim LR 563
13 *Best* (1979) 70 Cr App Rep 21, [1979] Crim LR 787, CA.

MDA, section 5(4)

This section reads as follows:

> In any proceeding for an offence under subsection (2) above in which it is proved that the accused had a controlled drug in his possession, it shall be a defence for him to prove:
>
> (a) that, knowing or suspecting it to be a controlled drug he took possession of it for the purpose of preventing another from committing or continuing to commit an offence in connection with that drug and as soon as possible after taking possession he took all such steps as were reasonably open to him to destroy the drug or to deliver it into the custody of a person lawfully entitled to take custody of it; or
>
> (b) that knowing or suspecting it to be a controlled drug, he took possession of it for the purpose of delivering it into the custody of a person lawfully entitled to take custody of it and that as soon as possible after taking possession of it he took all steps as were reasonably open to him to deliver it into the custody of such a person.

These two separate but related defences, though drafted in a somewhat lengthy manner, are largely self-explanatory. They are intended to cover the type of situation where, for example, a parent discovers an offspring in possession of a controlled drug and takes possession of it in order to stop the offspring using it. The defence in (a) may only operate where the offence is being committed in relation to the controlled drug or D believes that it is. Situations covered by (a) may overlap with those covered by (b) if a person takes possession of a controlled drug with the dual intentions of preventing the commission of an offence and delivering it into lawful custody. If no offences are being committed in relation to the drugs (e.g. they have been dumped by the roadside) only defence (b) is open to D. If D is in possession of a substance which he suddenly discovers is a controlled drug and therefore decides to take it to the police, although he is covered by section 28 before the discovery, it is submitted that he is not covered by section 5(4) after he discovers its true nature. This is because he did not take possession of it with any of the motives listed in the section.

MDA, section 7

Section 7 provides a general defence of lawful authority to charges under various sections of the MDA and will be covered more fully at a later stage. However, the 'prescription' defence is often raised to a charge of possessing controlled drugs and some of the cases are worth mentioning here. If the defence of prescription is raised, the onus of proving a valid prescription falls on D.[14] The prosecution do not have to prove that no such prescription exists.

14 *Ewens* [1967] 1 QB 322, 50 Cr App Rep 171, CCA.

In the case of *Jagger*[15] D was convicted of possessing amphetamine tablets which he had obtained abroad. His defence was that he had mentioned the tablets to his doctor who had said that he could use them in an emergency, and that this amounted to a prescription. The court left open the question of whether there could be an oral prescription (cf. Misuse of Drugs Regulations, regulation 14), but held that the instant facts could not amount to one.

In *Buswell*[16] D was prescribed 70 amphetamine tablets. He used 30 and then his mother washed the trousers which he thought contained the tablets. He obtained a replacement prescription but then, much later, found, used and was charged with the possession of the missing tablets. The prosecution argued that the possession was unlawful:

    (a) because of the existence of the second prescription;
    (b) because the tablets were used for a purpose other than that for which they were prescribed;
    (c) because possession ceased once D believed the tablets to be lost.

D was convicted but his appeal was allowed. In answer to the above three points the court held:

    (a) a prescription set no time limit;
    (b) D was not required to return excess tablets at the end of the course;
    (c) there was no cessation of possession when D believed the tablets to be lost.

A recent case is that of *Dunbar*.[17] D was a doctor but without any patients. He obtained some heroin (in his capacity as a doctor) in order to commit suicide. After taking some of the heroin he felt better and flushed the rest away. He was charged with possession of the heroin and claimed by way of defence that he was within section 7(3)(b) and was therefore acting at all times within his capacity as a doctor. It was held in allowing D's appeal against conviction that even if he had no patients a doctor could often act *qua* doctor. It was a question of fact for the jury to decide whether he was in fact acting in such a capacity.

MDA, section 5(3)

This section, set out above, created the new (in 1971) offence of possession with intent to supply. It is submitted that there is a logical difficulty inherent in the wording of the section in that if D has a controlled drug in his possession with intent to supply it contrary to section 4(1) he cannot be lawfully in possession of it.

15 (1967) 51 Cr App Rep 473, [1967] Crim LR 587, CA.
16 [1972] 1 All ER 75, [1972] 1 WLR 64, CA.
17 [1982] 1 All ER 188, 74 Cr App Rep 88, CA.

Clearly the intention of the draftsman is to catch the person who is entitled to possess a controlled drug but not to supply it. Little need be said here about the offence because its ingredients are possession (explained above) coupled with an intent to supply (the definition of supply being covered in Chapter 8). D need not acquire possession with the intention of supplying; if he later decides to supply he falls within the scope of the section (a rare example of crime by thought). One case worthy of mention here is *King*.[18] (This case has already been referred to and its facts set out in Chapter 8.) It was said by the court that there must be a real and not merely a constructive intent to supply and secondly that the word supply must be given its ordinary everyday meaning. Passing a joint did not amount to supplying.[19] The scope of the expression 'constructive intent' is not entirely clear but would seem to include a conditional intent (i.e. D would be willing to supply only on the occurrence of a particular event such as a friend X arriving or D becoming bankrupt).[20] The word conditional applies to the intent and not to the actual supplying so if D acquired a controlled drug with the intention of selling it if anybody came to buy it he would be within section 5(3).

The *actus reus* of the offence of possession is identical with that of the more serious offence of possession with intent to supply. The only difference between the two is D's state of mind, which cannot, of course, be proved directly. When deciding whether a section 5(3) charge is justified, two principal factors are taken into account:

(a) The quantity involved. If D possesses a quantity of drugs which is unlikely to be used solely for personal consumption, then an inference of intention to supply may be drawn. It is important to take into account all the circumstances, and it is quite possible that a user may buy in bulk for his own use over a long period of time. This is more likely where non-addictive drugs such as cannabis are concerned than with heroin, and where D is not an addict. As a very general guideline it is unusual for a person to possess more than 1 ounce of cannabis or 1 gram of heroin for his own use.

(b) Direct evidence of intention to supply. A common indicator of an intention to supply is that a quantity of drugs is split into several separate lots for distribution. Cannabis is often packaged in plastic bags or silver foil, and heroin in twists of paper. Items such as scales, to be used for weighing quantities of drugs, are also evidence of supplying, especially if they have on them traces of the drug.

18 [1978] Crim LR 228.
19 See Ch. 8 for a more detailed treatment of the meaning of supply as explained by this case.
20 Cf. *Dallaway* 7 October 1983, CA (unreported).

10   Cultivation of Cannabis

Although cannabis is not considered to be the most dangerous of the controlled drugs which occur naturally, there is inserted into the MDA a provision which specifically prohibits the cultivation of cannabis. Drugs such as LSD or amphetamine are synthetic and cannot therefore be cultivated but both cocaine and opium and its derivatives are preepared from plants (the coca plant and the opium poppy). However, it is only the cultivation of cannabis which is in itself an offence. Although the plant *cannabis sativa* has as its natural habitat warmer and drier climates than the British weather, cannabis can be grown effectively in this country, both inside and outside, and indeed it seems that this practice is on the increase as the price of imported cannabis has risen in recent years.

Section 6 of the MDA reads as follows:

(1) Subject to any regulations under section 7 of this Act for the time being in force, it shall not be lawful for a person to cultivate any plant of the genus cannabis.

(2) Subject to section 28 of this Act, it is an offence to cultivate any plant of the genus cannabis.

In keeping with the style of other parts of the Act, the cultivation is prohibited in subsection (1) and contravention of this prohibition is expressly made an offence in subsection (2).

As in sections 3, 4 and 5 the prohibition is subject to section 7, so cultivation is lawful if done under regulations made by the Secretary of State. Section 28 is also expressly applied to section 6, providing the general defence of ignorance of the nature of the drug. (Section 28(2) applies to any fact which the prosecution has to prove, so if in the rather unlikely event that D by emptying his bathwater unknowningly watered some cannabis plants he had noticed growing outside, he would have a defence under this subsection.)

The section is largely self-explanatory and the only difficulty which arises is the precise scope of the word 'cultivate'. Cultivation is defined in the *Oxford English Dictionary*[1] as:

To bestow labour and attention on (a plant) so as to promote its growth; to produce or raise by tillage.

1 1970 edition.

The implication is that cultivation is an active process.

In *Tudhope v Robertson*[2] cannabis plants were found growing in D's window box. The defence was that D did not cultivate the plants but that they were growing by natural process, being watered by the rain and lighted by the sun. D was convicted of cultivating the plants on the basis that the position of the plants to secure light and rain, the condition of the plants and the presence of seeds in D's flat all pointed to the conclusion of cultivation. The court said that although cultivate is an active verb it should not be given too narrow an interpretation.

The degree of activity by D necessary to constitute cultivation will be a question of fact. It is submitted that if D throws some cannabis seeds out of his car window into the verges as he drives along, and they grow into mature plants, he is not guilty of cultivation. However, any interference such as weeding, watering, placing in the light and so on will lead to the inference of cultivation. It will be difficult for D to avoid this inference if the plants are indoors or in a greenhouse. It is suggested that cultivation begins as soon as the seeds are sown and is a continuing process. An initial period of attention to the plants followed by neglect once they are mature enough to survive will be one continuous period of cultivation, otherwise the offence could be avoided unless D was actually caught watering or weeding the plants. Cultivation will only cease once the plant ceases to exist, either by reason of death or harvest.

Much of the argument about the exact meaning of the word cultivation may be avoided if the offence is treated as one of production. In *Taylor v Chief Constable of Kent*[3] a cannabis plant was found in a room which D did not himself occupy, although he knew it was there. He was charged with permitting the production of a controlled drug contrary to section 8(a) of the MDA, and his defence was that he was permitting not production but cultivation. In upholding his conviction, the court said that sections 4 and 6 of the MDA were not mutually exclusive and that production could include production by cultivation. Indeed, MDA, section 37(1) specifically includes cultivation within the scope of production. Since 1977 the term cannabis has not been restricted only to the flowering and fruiting tops, so the offence of production will be complete as soon as the object can be said to be a plant rather than merely a seed. It seems that many offences which are cases of cultivation are now charged under section 4.

The case of *Champ*[4] concerned the application of section 28 to the offence of cultivating cannabis. D was a herbalist who grew

2 1980 SLT 60.
3 [1981] 1 WLR 606, 72 Cr App Rep 318, DC.
4 (1981) 73 Cr App Rep 367, [1982] Crim LR 108, CA.

cannabis in her window box. She claimed that she thought it was hemp and that this was good for certain ailments. The court held that it was first necessary for the prosecution to prove that the plant was cannabis, and then an evidential burden was placed on D to show that she was unaware of the nature of the drug, in order to benefit from the section 28 defence. In this case D had failed to do this. (It is submitted that D would have not been rightly acquitted even if she had shown that she thought the plant was hemp, as hemp is simply another name for cannabis: see Chapter 16.)

11 MDA 1971, section 8

Section 8 of the MDA covers a multitude of sins, although in some respects what is omitted is of more interest than what is included. The section is designed to catch not those persons who use or who are otherwise directly involved in or concerned with controlled drugs, but those who facilitate their production, supply or use by allowing their premises to be abused for such purposes.

Section 8 reads as follows:

8. A person commits an offence, if being the occupier or concerned in the management of any premises, he knowingly permits or suffers any of the following activities to take place on those premises, that is to say—

(a) producing or attempting to produce a controlled drug in contravention of section 4(1) of this Act;

(b) supplying or attempting to supply a controlled drug to another in contravention of section 4(1) of this Act, or offering to supply a controlled drug to another in contravention of section 4(1);

(c) preparing opium for smoking;

(d) smoking cannabis, cannabis resin or prepared opium.

It would appear that the section creates four separate offences (see Chapter 6), and therefore any charge must specify which of the four specified in paragraphs (a) to (d) is involved, otherwise the count will be bad for duplicity.[1] The activities listed in (a) and (b) are offences in their own right. So is smoking prepared opium (in paragraph (d)). Preparing opium is not in itself an offence, athough anybody doing it would fall within the scope of any one of several other offences. Smoking cannabis is not in itself an offence, although it will often involve the possession of cannabis. It is interesting to note that permitting consumption of other controlled drugs whether by smoking, injection or oral means is not prohibited. Neither is eating cannabis or injecting or eating opium. There appears to be no clear rationale behind the structure of this section although the smoking of cannabis is a serious problem in the sense that it is very widespread, even if it is not a

1 See [1972] Crim LR 756 and *Fox v Dingley, Ware v Fox* [1967] 1 All ER 100, [1967] 1 WLR 379, DC.

particularly hazardous misuse of a drug, and for this reason the section is of assistance in discouraging the smoking of cannabis. The cases on section 8 and its predecessors in the earlier drugs legislation are concerned principally with the interpretation of three expressions, namely 'occupier', 'concerned in the management' and 'knowingly permits or suffers'.

Occupier

It is perhaps stating the obvious to say that whether or not a person is an occupier of premises is a question of fact to be decided with regard to all the relevant circumstances. The case law provides some guidelines, however. In *Mogford*[2] the co-defendants were two sisters aged fifteen and twenty who lived in their parents' house. While their parents were on holiday they permitted the smoking of cannabis at the house. They were held not to be occupiers within the meaning of the Dangerous Drugs Act 1965. They were not in legal possession while their parents were away, and their power to invite guests did not imply sufficient control to amount to being occupier. On similar facts in *Campbell and Campbell*[3] D was also acquitted. The court stated that not every transient use of premises would amount to occupation.

However, in *Tao*[4] it was held that an undergraduate living as a licensee in a college room had sufficient exclusivity of possession to be an occupier. It is not, however, necessary to have any legal right to occupation in order to be concerned in the management of premises. In *Josephs*,[5] D ran a card school in the basement of a building belonging to the local authority. Although they were clearly either squatters or trespassers, it was nevertheless held that they were concerned in the management of the building within the meaning of section 8.

The word premises is normally confined to something which may be the subject of a lease.[6] However, land without buildings is not normally considered as premises,[7] even if it is development land[8] and in any event the courts will not be fettered in drugs cases by the technicalities of property law. A houseboat with permanent moorings may be premises,[9] although a mobile boat or caravan probably cannot be.[10]

2 [1970] 1 WLR 988, [1970] Crim LR 401. The reasoning although not the result in this case was disapproved in *Tao*.
3 [1982] Crim LR 595.
4 [1977] QB 141, 63 Cr App Rep 163, CA.
5 (1977) 65 Cr App Rep 253, CA.
6 *Bracey v Read* [1963] Ch 88, [1962] 3 All ER 472.
7 *Bracey v Read*, above.
8 *Metropolitan Water Board v Paine* [1907] 1 KB 285, 76 LJKB 151, DC.
9 *West Mersea UDC v Fraser* [1950] 2 KB 119, [1950] 1 All ER 990, DC.
10 *Cowlairs Co-operative Society Ltd v Glasgow Corpn.* 1957 SLT 288.

Knowingly permits or suffers

This phrase can be given its ordinary commonsense meaning. It was held in *Thomas*[11] that the word 'knowingly' is superfluous, adding nothing to the expression, because both permitting and suffering imply knowledge. However the court also stated that mere suspicion amounted to neither knowledge nor permission, although a deliberate shutting of one's eyes in suspicious circumstances could bring D within the section. On the facts of the case D was convicted under section 8 because although he had told X to stop smoking cannabis on the premises he (D) knew that he (X) continued to do so. In *Ashdown*[12] it was held that a tenant who permits a co-tenant to indulge in any of the activities prohibited by section 8 falls within that section.

Concerned in the management

The juxtaposition of two words which are themselves not easy to define makes this phrase one of the more difficult in the Act to interpret precisely. There can be no management unless there is some business or other enterprise capable of being managed – this expression is indeed the equivalent for commercial-type premises of the occupier for domestic premises, and a colloquial definition might be 'a person responsible for what goes on there'. Residential premises are covered if some business is conducted there (e.g. the letting of flats) and in fact most of the cases on the meaning of the phrase were decided in the context of the management of brothels. 'Being concerned in' is wider than assistance.[13] What is required is evidence indicating the taking of an active part in the running of the business,[14] or an important part of it.[15] Mere participation in an activity does not imply a concern in its management.[16] A leading case on the phrase is the celebrated one of *Sweet v Parsley*.[17] Although the most important aspect of this case is its decision concerning the application of *mens rea*, their Lordships also made some observations on the meaning of the phrase 'concerned in the management'. The charge in question was made under section 5 of the 1965 Dangerous Drugs Act which is similar

---

11 (1976) 63 Cr App Rep 65, [1976] Crim LR 517, CA.
12 (1974) 59 Cr App Rep 193, CA.
13 *A-G v Robson* (1850) 5 Exch 790.
14 *Abbott v Smith* [1965] 2 QB 662n, [1964] 3 All ER 762.
15 *Glanvill Enthoven & Co. v IRC* (1925) 41 TLR 258, HL.
16 *Gorman v Standen* [1964] 1 QB 294, 48 Cr App Rep 30, DC.
17 [1970] AC 132, 53 Cr App Rep 221, HL.

but not identical to the present section 8.[18] The facts of the case were that D had a farmhouse of which she sublet all the rooms but one, which she kept for herself. She rarely visited the premises, except on occasions to collect mail, and only on a few occasions did she stay overnight. The House of Lords upheld her appeal against conviction on the grounds that the offence was one requiring *mens rea*, and said that in order to be concerned in the management of something there must at least be knowledge of what it is being managed. According to Lord Wilberforce, 'one does not manage premises...but rather some human activity on the premises...'

The activities described in section 8(a) and 8(b) are covered in Chapter 8 on production and supply. The activity of smoking cannabis is self-explanatory and would include any process by which D inhales anything which is or contains the smoke of the burning substance in question.

18 Section 5 of the Dangerous Drugs Act 1965 reads: 'If a person—(a) being the occupier of any premises, permits those premises to be used for the purpose of smoking cannabis or cannabis resin...or (b) is concerned in the management of any premises used for any such purpose aforesaid; he shall be guilty of an offence against this Act.' The different wording of section 8 of the MDA avoids the difficulties in the expression 'used for the purpose of' which was considered in *Sweet v Parsley*.

12   MDA 1971, section 9

Section 9 is anomalous in a number of ways. Its form has not changed since the Dangerous Drugs Act of 1920, when the problems of drug abuse were very different from those today. It is submitted that the section could be repealed without in any way impairing the legal control of drugs and without putting the United Kingdom in breach of international obligations to prohibit various activities relating to drugs. The reason for its inclusion appears to be that it was not thought necessary to remove a measure which had been in all the legislation since 1920, when opium smoking was one of the principal activities aimed at by the legislature. The provisions of section 9 are out of keeping with the general structure of the rest of the Act, which classifies offences into possession, supply and so on, but does not make consumption of drugs *per se* an offence. The penalties, too, are anomalous. Although opium is a Class A drug (maximum penalty for possession seven years) the penalty for smoking opium under section 9 is fourteen years. The three separate offences created by the section cannot be legitimised by regulations made pursuant to sections 7 or 10 of the Act.

It is an offence:

(a) To smoke or otherwise use prepared opium.

Presumably the word 'use' must be construed *eiusdem generis* with smoke and be confined to use by way of consumption. By extending the definition of prepared opium to include residue remaining after its use[1] the draftsman has by rather devious means avoided the evidential difficulties of charging possessors of residue with past possession. Normally a drug which has been used is no longer considered to be a drug[2] and where the substance has been smoked the residue will be an entirely different chemical from the original drug.

(b) To frequent a place used for the purposes of opium smoking.

The word 'frequent' has never been interpreted in the context of this section. Most of the cases are concerned with frequenting a

1 Section 37(1).
2 See *Hambleton v Callinan* [1968] 2 QB 427, [1968] 2 All ER 943.

public place. There are two principal lines of thought on the word frequent. Firstly, the case of *Re Cross*[3] suggests that D frequents a place if he is merely physically present there. On this approach the milkman who delivers milk to an opium den would fall within the scope of section 9. The second and, it is submitted, the preferable view is that D frequents a place if he is there long enough for the purpose aimed at.[4] It is, however, possible to frequent a place without having any purpose at all. If D on a single occasion walked into an opium den with no particular purpose in mind, would he be frequenting it? In *Clark v R*[5] it was said that frequent suggests paying repeated visits to the same locality or at the very least to linger in a locality for a period of time. The more modern case of *Nakhla v R*[6] suggests that frequenting connotes more than mere physical presence. The exact meaning will depend on the circumstances, but it involves notions of something continuous or repeated. It is clear from remarks made in *Sweet v Parsley*[7] that the prohibited purpose should be the purpose of the management and not merely of any person who happens to be there. If a person books a room in a hotel for the purposes of smoking opium it does not cause the hotel to become a place used for that purpose. However, the word place is wider than the expression 'premises' used in section 8, and is probable that in the above example, although the hotel might not be such a place, the individual room might be, so that D's friends who visited him in that room would fall within the section. This subsection is one of the few for which section 28(2) can clearly have an application. If D does not know that the place is used for the purpose of smoking opium he will have a defence to any section 9 charge.

  (c) To have in his possession
    (i) any pipes or utensils made or adapted for use in connection with the smoking of opium, being pipes or utensils which have been used by him or with his knowledge and permission in that connection or which he intends to use or permit others to use in that connection; or
    (ii) any utensils which have been used by him or with his knowledge and permission in connection with the preparation of opium for smoking.

These provisions are self explanatory. Sub-paragraph (i) deals with articles 'made or adapted' for the purpose. The mere fact that an article is used for a purpose does not imply adaptation for that purpose so an ordinary tobacco pipe used to smoke opium does

3 (1857) 1 H & N 651, 26 LJMC 28.
4 *Airton v Scott* (1909) 100 LT 393, 73 JP 148.
5 (1884) 14 QBD 92, 52 LT 136.
6 [1976] AC 1, [1975] 2 All ER 138.
7 [1970] AC 132, 53 Cr App Rep 221, HL.

not fall within the section. The requirement of use or intention to use means that the possession of ornamental hookahs and the like is not of itself illegal.

Sub-paragraph (ii) is concerned with articles which have been used for the preparation of opium. They need not be made or adapted for the purpose, so a kitchen knife could fall within the section. Only actual use and not intended use is covered (the latter would present grave problems of proof).

In neither sub-paragraph does the word 'knowledge' add anything, as the term 'permission' implies knowledge.

It should again be emphasised that this chapter is of little practical significance as the days of opium dens in the United Kingdom are past.

13   MDA 1971, section 20

Section 20 is another section which is designed to allow the international control of drugs to transcend national boundaries. It provides that any person who in the UK assists in or induces the commission in any place outside the UK of an offence punishable under the provisions of a corresponding law in force in that place, is guilty of an offence.

The expression 'corresponding law' is defined in section 36(1) and broadly covers any law for the control of drugs in accordance with the provisions of the Single Convention on Narcotic Drugs signed at New York on 30 March 1961, or a similar law made pursuant to a treaty between Her Majesty's Government and the government of the relevant country. As is normal where proof of a foreign law is required, a certificate purporting to be issued by the appropriate government is evidence of the matters stated therein (section 36(2)).

The word 'assist' in section 20 was construed broadly in the case of *Vickers*.[1] Here D and others were charged with conspiracy to contravene section 20. D agreed to hire a vehicle in the UK and take some cabinets to Italy knowing that they would be used to smuggle cannabis into the USA. He was convicted and on appeal the Court of Appeal held that 'assist' was to be given its commonsense meaning, and not the narrow meaning of only acts directly concerned in the prohibited importation.

1 [1975] 2 All ER 945, [1975] 1 WLR 811.

14　Miscellaneous Offences

Offences by corporation

Section 21 of the MDA confirms by implication that offences under the MDA may be committed by corporations,[1] and also expressly states that if an offence is committed by a body corporate, then officers of the corporation may also be liable for the offence in certain circumstances.

The liability of a corporation itself depends on the actions and intentions of its officers. A corporation in itself has no mind or body and acts through human agency. The principles governing when a corporation will become liable for offences through the actions of its officers or employees are laid down in the leading case of *Tesco Supermarkets v Nattrass*,[2] where the earlier cases are also discussed. In essence a corporation can only be liable for the actions of those who 'represent the directing mind and will of a company and control what it does'.

In view of this, the provisions of section 21 are to some extent circular in their effect, and frequently will not attribute criminal liability to any person where it does not already exist. The section provides that if an offence committed by a corporation 'is proved to have been committed with the consent or connivance of, or to be attributable to the neglect on the part of any director, manager, secretary or other similar officer of the body corporate...he shall be guilty of that offence.'

The term 'similar officer' must be construed *eiusdem generis* with the other officers in the list, who are all senior officers of a company, indeed those whose actions are likely to give rise to the corporation's liability initially. So a junior employee is not within the scope of the section. The situation which will be covered by the section is where one senior officer of the corporation by his conduct renders the corporation liable, and other officers consent to or connive in this without their conduct actually amounting to commission of the offence itself. From an evidential point of view, it is clearly easier in general to prove connivance, consent and so on than actual commission of an offence.

1 The Interpretation Act 1978, s. 5 and Sch. 1, define 'person' to include a body of persons corporate or unincorporate.
2 [1972] AC 153, [1971] 2 All ER 127.

The expression 'corporation' is not defined by the Act, but will include any incorporated body.

Offences against the Person Act 1861

Sections 22, 23 and 24 of this Act are concerned with the administration of stupefying drugs or noxious things, and the administration of a controlled drug could fall within one of these sections. These sections are set out in full in Appendix 2.

Section 22 deals with the administration of 'chloroform, laudanum, or other stupefying or overpowering drug, matter or thing' in order to facilitate or enable the commission of an indictable offence. The drug must have a stupefying or overpowering effect, so not every controlled drug would fall into this category. Amphetamine, for example, would have the reverse effect.

Section 23 makes it an offence to 'unlawfully and maliciously administer...any poison or other destructive or noxious thing, so as thereby to endanger the life of such person, or...inflict...grievous bodily harm'. Whether a substance is noxious depends on the effect it has in the actual quantities administered.[3] In Cato,[4] D injected X with heroin. It was held that for the purposes of section 23 a substance was also noxious if liable to cause injury in ordinary use. The court also said that the consent of the victim was irrelevant and that the word 'maliciously' simply meant deliberately.

Section 24 is in similar terms to section 23 except that the relevant intention is 'to injure, aggrieve or annoy'. This includes administration of cantharides in order to excite sexual passion.[5] If the intent is merely to annoy, but grievous bodily harm or death results, this amounts to an offence under section 23.[6]

These Offences against the Person Act offences have a rather archaic flavour, and Cato is a rare example of their use in modern times.

Other offences

In addition to offences under the CEMA 1979 or MDA 1971, a person using drugs may incidentally commit other offences, liability for which is not affected by whether the drug is controlled or not. For example, section 5 of the Road Traffic Act 1972 creates the offence of driving or being in charge of a motor vehicle when

---

3 *Hennah* (1877) 13 Cox CC 547, *Cramp* (1880) 5 QBD 307, 39 LJMC 44, and
   Marcus [1981] 2 All ER 833, [1981] 1 WLR 774.
4 [1976] 1 All ER 260, 62 Cr App Rep 41.
5 *Wilkins* (1861) Le & Ca 89 31 LJMC 72.
6 *Ibid.*

unfit through drink or drugs. For the purposes of this section any drug used as a medicine will suffice, e.g. insulin,[7] as will any controlled drug. It is submitted that any substance which constitutes a drug in the wider sense of producing a state of intoxication, whether or not it is controlled and/or a medicine, will fall within the section. Recently it was held by a crown court judge[8] that driving under the influence of solvent vapours would give rise to liability under the section, on the grounds that glue contained a drug called toluene. Toluene is neither controlled nor used medicinally.

There has been uncertainty as to whether the term 'drunk' can include intoxication by drugs other than alcohol. The logical conclusion is that it cannot, and this is supported by the case of *Neale v RMJE (a minor)*.[9] Here it was held by the Divisional Court that the offence of being guilty of disorderly behaviour in a highway while drunk (contrary to section 91 of the Criminal Justice Act 1967) could not be committed where the intoxication was induced by a substance other than alcohol. This decision will prevent the extension of the scope of the numerous 'drunken' offences to those under the influence of other drugs.

The criminal law has frequently shown considerable ingenuity in adapting ancient laws or laws passed for a totally different purpose in order to combat behaviour which is considered undesirable although *prima facie* legal. In the field of drugs law, this most often occurs in the context of glue sniffing which is not of itself illegal, although the principles could apply to any drugs. The case of *Neale*[10] is one example. The other main type of approach is the use of public order law. There have been several instances[11] of glue sniffers being bound over or fined for offences involving a breach of the peace. In this way the public use of drugs has to some extent been outlawed, although the offence requires that some reaction is provoked, or is likely to be provoked in onlookers. Glue sniffing is an activity which often involves objectively offensive behaviour, it is submitted that a person who ate a barbiturate tablet (or even sipped laudanum) in public could not be rightly convicted of such offences.

In a similar vein there have been convictions under local byelaws which, for example, make it an offence to 'cause annoyance or commit a nuisance to public decency or propriety'.[12]

7 *Armstrong v Clark* [1957] 2 QB 391, [1957] 1 All ER 433.
8 *The Times*, 26 November 1982.
9 (1984) Times, 5 March and see *Lanham v Rickwood* (1984) Times, 10 May, DC.
10 Above.
11 *Sheffield Star*, 9 September 1981, *West Lancs Evening Gazette*, 20 October 1982, *Western Mail*, 12 March 1982. Clearly these reports are illustrative rather than authoritative.
12 *South West Evening Post*, 4 October 1982.

15 Conspiracy and Attempt

Conspiracy

The crime of conspiracy is an ancient common law offence and is in effect an agreement to do something unlawful. At common law the unlawful act need not actually be an offence. However, section 1 of the Criminal Law Act 1977 has abolished all common law conspiracy except the offence of conspiracy to defraud, and replaced it with the statutory offence of conspiracy. This section[1] limits statutory conspiracy to an agreement to a course of conduct the pursuit of which would amount to the commission of any offence by one or more of the parties to the agreement.

Thus an agreement to commit any of the MDA offences (except that under section 19) would be a statutory conspiracy and triable as such. In practice the conspiracy charge is most frequently used in cases involving the importation or exportation of controlled drugs. This is for two reasons.

Firstly, due to the degree of planning by several people which is often necessary to effect an importation of any sizeable quantity of controlled drugs, there is often a conspiracy in existence before any actual importation takes place. The police or Customs are often able to proceed on a conspiracy charge where there would be insufficient evidence to prove the commission of the substantive offence.

Secondly, the MDA does not specifically create offences of importing or exporting controlled drugs, although section 3 does prohibit such activities and thus render them unlawful. Offences involving importation or exportation are often dealt with by a charge of conspiring to evade the prohibition contained in section 3(1)(a). The importation or exportation of controlled drugs is itself an offence under sections 50 or 68 of the Customs and Excise Management Acts 1979.

In the case of *Whitehead*,[2] D was charged with conspiracy to evade the prohibition contained in section 3(1)(a) of the MDA. It was argued on behalf of the defence that as the section did not create an offence there could be no statutory conspiracy. In

1 See Appendix 2.
2 [1982] QB 1272, 75 Cr App Rep 289, CA.

applying *Menocal*[3] and distinguishing *Williams*[4] the court held that the offence of evading the prohibition in section 3(1)(a) was created by the combination of that section and section 304 of the Customs and Excise Act 1952 (the predecessor of section 170 of the 1979 Act) and that the offence of conspiracy was chargeable as it arose under either act.

In *Ardalan*[5] D was charged with conspiring to acquire possession of controlled drugs with intent to evade the prohibition on importation. Two cases of cannabis were sent from Beirut to a Middlesex address. They were delayed for a long period by a postal strike and eventually collected by D. In dismissing his appeal against conviction the Court of Appeal said that the fact that D's act of collecting the cases took place a long way in both time and distance from the actual agreement was no bar to a conviction for conspiracy, which was an offence of a continuing nature. The case of *DPP v Doot*[6] also illustrates the continuing nature of a conspiracy. An offence of importing drugs will almost invariably involve activity and planning abroad, but this will not prevent the participants from being tried in the UK for conspiracy (cf. *Neal*[7]). In *DPP v Doot*, D and various others, all US citizens, planned to ship cannabis to the USA via the UK. They were charged with conspiracy to import the cannabis. The defendants argued that there was no jurisdiction as the conspiracy was made abroad. The House of Lords held in dismissing their appeals that although a conspiracy was complete as soon as the agreement was made, it continued in existence as long as there were two or more persons intending to carry it out, which the defendants were intending when they were arrested in England. The fact that D might not know the identity of his fellow conspirators was no defence to the charge of conspiracy.

There has been much case law on the subject of conspiracy to do something which is inherently impossible. At common law the doctrine enshrined in the case of *Haughton v Smith*[8] on the law of attempt was applied to conspiracy, meaning that an agreement to do something unlawful by means which were inherently impossible was not a criminal conspiracy.[9] If the agreement was not inherently impossible but would only fail because the participants made a minor mistake which rendered it impossible (e.g. one wrong ingredient in a chemical process) then the conspiracy was

3 [1980] AC 598, 69 Cr App Rep 157.
4 [1971] Crim LR 356.
5 56 Cr App Rep 320, [1972] 2 All ER 257, CA.
6 [1973] AC 807, 57 Cr App Rep 600, HL.
7 (1983) 77 Cr App Rep 283, CA.
8 [1975] AC 476, 58 Cr App Rep 198.
9 *DPP v Nock and Alsford* [1978] AC 979, 67 Cr App Rep 116.

not negated.[10] The law is now on a statutory basis, and the Criminal Law Act, section 1(1), as amended by the Criminal Attempts Act 1981, section 5, reads as follows:

> Subject to the following provisions of this part of this Act, if a person agrees with any other person or persons that a course of conduct shall be pursued which, if the agreement is carried out in accordance with their intentions, either—
> (a) will necessarily amount to or involve the commission of any offence or offences by one or more of the parties to the agreement, or
> (b) would do so but for the existence of facts which render the commission of the offence or any of the offences impossible
> he is guilty of conspiracy to commit the offence in question.

This section widens the scope of the offence of conspiracy considerably. For example, the conspirators in *DPP v Nock and Alsford* would now be caught by this provision. The only difficulty lies in the exact meaning of the phrase 'would necessarily amount to the commission of an offence...but for the existence of facts which render [it]...impossible'. Clearly if X and Y agree in the following terms – 'Let us make cocaine by mixing flour and sugar' then they are committing a statutory conspiracy. However, if they say 'Let us mix together chemical B and chemical C. If cocaine is the result we will consume it. If novocaine (not a controlled drug) is the result we will sell it,' then they are not within the section because the intention is conditional. If they say 'Let us make novocaine by mixing chemicals E and F' and indeed they do produce novocaine, but some cocaine is produced as well as a by-product, then are they guilty of conspiracy to produce cocaine? The course of conduct necessarily involves its production. Has the agreement been carried out 'in accordance with their intentions'? If charged with the substantive offence they would, of course, have a defence under section 28. An error of law will not place the conspirators within the section. So if X and Y agree to produce novocaine, believing it to be a controlled drug, they are not guilty of conspiracy as the course of conduct will not involve the commission of an offence.

Attempts and Incitement

Section 19 of the MDA makes it an offence to attempt to commit an offence under any other provision of the Act, or to incite or attempt to incite another to commit such an offence.

The meaning of attempt must now be as defined by section 1 of the Criminal Attempts Act 1981. This abolishes the *Haughton v*

---

10 *Harris* [1979] Cr App Rep 122.

Smith doctrine and brings within the provisions of the criminal law a number of activities which previously did not amount to offences. The important changes are firstly that 'impossible attempts' are now offences and secondly that the common law 'proximate test' for acts amounting to attempt is replaced by the statutory definition of 'acts more than merely preparatory to the commission of the offence'. (It is doubtful whether this second change has much practical significance.) So in either of the following cases D will be guilty of attempt.

(a) D attempts to make LSD using ingredients or a process which are incapable of producing it.

(b) D attempts to supply cannabis, although unknown to him the substance he offers for sale is, as happened in one case, camel dung. (This alters the common law position as expounded in *Mieras v Rees*.[10])

The Criminal Attempts Act abolishes the common law offence of attempt, so the case of *R v Chelmsford Justices, ex p Amos*[11] is no longer good law. In that case D was convicted of attempting to incite supply, contrary to section 18 of the Dangerous Drugs Act 1965. It was held that although no such offence arose under the section, it did at common law.

In *Kyprianou v Reynolds*[12] D was charged with attempting to procure cannabis. He approached a dealer and said, 'What have you got tonight boys, hash or heroin? I've got money upstairs.' He was acquitted on the grounds that the facts amounted only to an invitation to treat, and that further action would be required to constitute attempt. It is submitted that the result would be the same today, as the action would be merely preparatory. It is interesting to note the procedure of some drug squads when raiding suspected drugs dealers. This is to wait inside the house and arrest any suspicious persons who arrive at the house with money and charge them with attempting to possess. It is certainly arguable that going to a house with money is only a preparatory act, unless by previous communication with the supplier a transaction has been arranged. There appears to be no authority on this point, and it must be a question of fact in each case whether D has fulfilled the requirements of section 1(1).

11 [1973] Crim LR 437, DC.
12 [1969] Crim LR 656, DC.

16   MDA 1971, section 28

Section 28 of the MDA was introduced in order to relieve some of the hardships caused by the more technical aspects of the doctrine of possession. The concept of strict possession and the rules developed for container cases had imputed possession and therefore criminal liability in certain situations where it was generally felt that no such liability should arise. The intention of the legislature was to provide a general defence of lack of knowledge (such as ignorance or mistake of fact) in proceedings for certain offences.

The exact scope of section 28 and its relationship with the law of possession is uncertain and has been the subject of much academic debate.[1] The lack of case law has left many questions unresolved. Two particular areas of difficulty are:

(a) the relationship between section 28(2) and section 28(3), and

(b) whether the section alters the concept of possession or merely its consequences.

The answer to the latter question has important practical consequences in that it will alter the burden of proof in certain aspects of possession cases.

Section 28 is by subsection (1) stated to apply only to certain offences under the MDA, which in practice are offences under sections 4(2), 4(3), 5(2), 5(3), 6(2) and section 9. The section provides three specific types of defence which can broadly be described as:

(a) Ignorance that the substance was a controlled drug (section 28(3)(b)(i));

(b) Belief that the substance was a controlled drug which D was entitled to possess, produce, etc. when it was in fact a different controlled drug (section 28(3)(b)(ii));

(c) Ignorance of some other material fact (section 28(2)).

Ignorance that the substance was a controlled drug

In order to establish this defence D must show on balance of probabilities[1] two things. Firstly, D must show that he neither knew nor suspected that the substance was a controlled drug. This test is subjective and merely requires D's honest belief. Secondly, D must then show that he had no reason to suspect that the substance was a controlled drug. This test is objective, taking into account all relevant circumstances. So, for example, if D is given a tablet which he is told is aspirin when in fact it is heroin, in order to invoke section 28(3)(b)(i) successfully he must show that he really did not believe or suspect that it was heroin and that in the circumstances there was no reason to suspect that it was. If D believed the tablet to be amphetamine and had no reason to believe or suspect that it was heroin, he would still be convicted in accordance with section 28(3)(a).

Section 28(3)(b)(ii)
This section will only apply to the tiny percentage of the population who are entitled to possess, produce, etc. controlled drugs in some capacity. If D believes that he possesses controlled drug X (which he is entitled to possess) whereas in fact he possesses controlled drug Y (which he is not entitled to possess) he will have a defence under this subsection. Here there is no objective test of reasonableness – D's honest belief is sufficient.

Section 28(2)
This section is the most widely worded and the most difficult to interpret. It provides for a defence where D is ignorant of any fact which it is necessary for the prosecution to prove. As in section 28(3)(b)(i) there is a twofold test. D must prove (again on balance of probabilities):[1]
  (a) that he neither knew or suspected the existence of the fact (subjective), and
  (b) that he had no reason to suspect it (objective).
The difficulty with section 28 is in deciding what type of 'facts' are referred to in the section. At first sight it would appear to include the fact that the subject was a controlled drug and hence overlap with section 28(3)(b)(i), but section 28(2) is expressed to be subject to subsection (3), and it is submitted that in view of this such a situation does not fall within the scope of subsection (2). (It should be noted that section 28 has the effect of providing a defence to a prosecution and does not legitimise the activities referred to.)

Another possible interpretation of section 28(2) is that it could refer to the issue of knowledge which is a fact which the prosecution have to prove in order to establish possession. This would have the effect of reversing the onus of proof in certain cases where there was an issue whether D was in possession of something. However, in the leading case on section 28, *Ashton*

1 *Carr Briant* [1943] KB 607, 29 Cr App Rep 76, CCA.

Rickhardt,[2] the Court of Appeal held that section 28(2) does not alter the ingredients of possession nor the burden of proof in proving possession. Section 28 will only come into play when the prosecution have already proved the knowledge necessary for possession. Defendants in cases similar to those of *Searle v Randolph*[3] and *Lockyer v Gibb*[4] will now have a defence to a charge of possession, but it will be under subsection (3)(b)(i) and not under subsection (2). On this interpretation it is hard to envisage a practical situation where subsection (2) will apply, apart from ignorance of the fact that premises were used for the purposes of smoking opium as a defence to a section 9 charge.

In the recent case of *Young*[5] D claimed that he was so drunk that he did not know that what he possessed was LSD. The Court of Appeal considered whether on these facts section 28(3)(b)(i) could afford D a defence. D argued that although self-induced intoxication was no defence where 'reasonable grounds for belief' was the criterion, the approach should be different where the words were 'no reason to suspect'. The court agreed with this proposition, supported by the case of *Jaggard v Dickinson*,[6] and stated that the test of the reasonable sober man was irrelevant. However, it went on to say that a reason was not something entirely personal and individual, but involved a wider concept of objective rationality, and for this reason D could not avail himself of the defence under section 28.

For the law on the effect of self-induced intoxication by drink or drugs on *mens rea* and intent generally, see the cases of *DPP v Majewski*[7] and *Lipman*[8].

It very frequently occurs that D is in possession of a controlled drug without knowing the exact chemical name of the drug. D may be in possession of a substance he knows as 'acid' without knowing that he is in possession of lysergide. He may even be unaware that the substance is in fact a controlled drug. This ignorance will not give him any defence under section 28. However, in the following situation D would have a defence under section 28: D is in possession of a substance which he knows of as 'blues'. He thinks that the term 'blues' is common parlance for barbiturate (not a controlled drug). In fact the term 'blues' is common parlance for amphetamine. The substance is in fact amphetamine. To borrow the terminology of a series of contract cases, D must be mistaken as to the identity of a substance and not merely its attribute (such as its name) in order to have a defence under section 28.

2 [1978] 1 All ER 173, 65 Cr App Rep 67, CA.
3 [1972] Crim LR 779, DC.
4 [1967] 2 QB 243, [1966] 2 All ER 653.
5 [1984] 2 All ER 164, [1984] 1 WLR 654.
6 [1981] QB 527, 72 Cr App Rep 33.
7 [1977] AC 443, [1977] Crim LR 532.
8 [1970] 1 QB 15, 53 Cr App Rep 600, CA.

Part IV
Sentencing

17   Sentencing

General policy

The sentencing of persons convicted of any crime involves the consideration of numerous factors, all of which may point in different directions. This is especially true in relation to drug cases. Perhaps more than in any other branch of the criminal law there is a great variety in the nature of the crimes and the circumstances and motives of their perpetrators which can arise for any particular offence. In determining the correct sentence the requirements of deterrence and the needs of the offender frequently conflict.

The basic principles of sentencing are apparent from the maximum penalties set out in the MDA and similar legislation. These depend on

(a) the drug involved, and

(b) the precise offence involved.

The purpose of the division of the list of controlled drugs into Classes A, B and C is in order to indicate the relative harm associated with the misuse of that drug. Class A contains the most dangerous drugs and Class C the least dangerous.

The range of offences specified by the MDA can be graded by severity of maximum punishment. At the bottom end of the scale is the simple possessor. He is least likely to present a danger to society in general and is least likely to have financial gain as a motive for his crime. Next up the scale is the supplier. Suppliers of controlled drugs can be subdivided into two basic categories – the social supplier and the commercial supplier. Although the maximum penalties are the same in either case the courts tend to take into account the wide scope of the offence of supplying. A 'supplier' who collects money from his friends, contributes some himself and then purchases some drugs for their communal use is treated more leniently than a wholesale dealer in drugs who may not use them at all himself and whose sole motive is financial gain. The offence of possession with intent to supply carries the same maximum penalty as supply itself. This is, on indictment, for Class A, B and C drugs respectively fourteen years, fourteen years and five years. Also with this maximum sentence is the offence of production of a controlled drug contrary to section 4(2). This offence is likely to attract the severest sentence per amount of drug involved.

The actual sentence will normally depend on the quantity of drugs involved. An importer of very small amounts which are clearly intended for personal use should be treated in the same way as the simple possessor of an equivalent quantity, whereas a person who imports a large quantity will be treated at least as severely as a supplier of that quantity.

For each offence there is a maximum sentence prescribed by statute and in addition a tarifff developed by the courts which indicates the range of sentences which may be received by the 'average offender'. The trends in drug sentencing have varied considerably over the years since the mid 1960s when drug abuse became a serious problem. Despite the courts' frequent proclamations on the evils of drug trafficking and the need to eliminate it, sentences have in general become less severe in recent years. Many of the earlier cases cannot be regarded as giving valid guidelines on sentencing policy. Indeed all cases previous to *Aramah*[1] should be looked at in the light of this recent case in which the Court of Appeal laid down the principles to be applied and the tariffs which were appropriate when sentencing drug offenders.

Aramah lays down the following guidelines:

Class A drugs: For importers at least seven years is generally appropriate. The sentence should seldom be less than four years unless the offender has co-operated fully with the authorities. Suppliers should seldom receive less than three years. It is not practical to give general guidelines for cases of possession, but prison is often appropriate.

Class B drugs: For importers of up to 20 kilograms, eighteen months to three years, except where small quantities for personal use are involved, where the case should be treated on the same basis as possession. For medium quantities, three to six years. For large quantities, sentences in the region of ten years should be given. For suppliers, persons playing a major role in the supply of large quantities must expect ten years' imprisonment. In lesser cases, one to four years would normally be appropriate. For possession a fine is often sufficient, although persistent flouting of the law is likely to merit imprisonment.

The above guidelines are the basis of the table in Appendix 5. When considering sentence, as well as the tariffs the following points should always be taken into account:

    (a) whether the offender has been convicted summarily or on indictment;

1 (1983) 76 Cr App Rep 190, [1983] Crim LR 271, CA. Further cases on sentencing are cited in Appendix 5.

(b) whether there is a plea of guilty and whether there has been co-operation with the authorities;
(c) the offender's criminal record (or lack of it);
(d) the gain to D involved, if any;
(e) D's personal circumstances.

Other factors which may or may not affect sentence

Quantities of drugs involved
It has already been mentioned in passing that the quantity of drugs involved is of great significance where sentencing is involved. In one sense this is obvious, as importing 200 kilograms of cannabis is clearly more important than importing 20 kilograms, just as the theft of £10,000 is more serious than the theft of £10. In addition to this gradation by quantity there is a clear distinction to be drawn between cases where the amount involved implies the drug is for personal use by the offender, and amounts where it is not. As a matter of policy the law treats a user much less severely than somebody who by trafficking enables or encourages others to use drugs. On this basis a producer or importer of a small quantity of drugs for personal use will be treated more leniently than the possessor of a large quantity which is clearly to be distributed to others.

Age of offender
The majority of drug users are under twenty-five and the drug culture in general is very much associated with youth. In addition to the general statutory restrictions placed on the sentencing of young persons, the courts may take a less stern view of young offenders than those who being of greater age and maturity should be more responsible.

Age of person to whom drugs are supplied
The courts have made it clear that they take a very strong line against anyone supplying drugs to young persons.[2]

Foreign offenders
In two cases[3] it has been stated that the fact that the defendant is foreign is immaterial for sentencing purposes.

Penalty under foreign law
In the case of *Faulkner and Thomas*,[4] D and his fiancée smuggled cannabis from Pakistan to Denmark. The operation was planned

---

2 *Williams* [1969] Crim LR 497, CA, *Macauley* (1967) 52 Cr App Rep 230, [1967] Crim LR 716, CA
3 *Winter* [1973] Crim LR 63, CA, *Palmer* [1974] Crim LR 375, CA.
4 [1977] Crim LR 47 and 679.

in the UK and they were convicted under section 20 of the MDA. It was held that the penalty for the corresponding offence (of importation) under Danish law was irrelevant for the purposes of sentencing.

Co-operation with the police
In keeping with general principles of sentencing, a person who after his arrest co-operates with the authorities may have this fact taken into account when sentenced.[5]

Motive of offender
It has already been mentioned that the personal user is dealt with less severely than the supplier. The category of supplier can be further divided into social and commercial suppliers. The social supplier who distributes small amounts of drugs to friends is less likely to have financial gain as a motive and is less likely to introduce non-users to the use of drugs than a commercial supplier whose aim is to make as much profit as possible. The social supplier is also less likely to dilute or adulterate supplies (a dangerous practice). For this reason social suppliers are usually treated less severely,[6] although they cannot expect to escape prison where it is otherwise appropriate simply on account of this factor.[7] In the recent case of *Davies and Marshall-Price*[8] the Court of Appeal has reiterated that suppliers of hard drugs, regardless of motives, must expect to go to prison, normally for years rather than months. (The term 'hard drugs' is not a term of art, but is loosely used to describe Class A drugs.)

Degree of participation of offender
The courts have, in accordance with general sentencing practice, recognised the different degrees of participation by various members of a gang of people all engaged in a venture to contravene the controlled drugs legislation. Sentences less than the normal tariff may be given for those involved peripherally.[9]

Personal circumstances of offenders
In sentencing drug offenders the need to deter other potential offenders is paramount, and the mitigating personal circumstances

---

5 *Aramah*, (above), *Taonis* (1974) 59 Cr App Rep 160, [1974] Crim LR 322, *Ng and Dhalai* [1978] Crim LR 174, CA.
6 *Lawless* [1981] Crim LR 845, DC.
7 *Powrie* [1973] Crim LR 708, CA; *Jolley* [1971] 56 Cr App Rep 217, [1972] Crim LR 193, CA; *Aramah* (supra).
8 (1982) 4 Cr App Rep (S) 302, [1983] Crim LR 46, CA.
9 *Jusoh* [1979] Crim LR 191, CA; *Hancock and Holdgate* [1978] Crim LR 174, CA; *Bibi* [1980] Crim LR 732

of individual offenders will not always involve a reduction in sentence. In *Fraser*[10] the defendant had no previous convictions and was well-educated and of good background. It was said by the court that this was not a reason for leniency, but rather the contrary. A person with such a background had even less reason than normal to get involved in drugs. There have also been several cases[11] involving the recruitment by traffickers of persons with financial or emotional difficulties to use as couriers. The courts have said that the need to deter this practice prevents them from taking a softer line with such offenders, who are often in themselves people to be pitied.

The sentencing of addicts presents a particularly difficult problem. On the one hand addicts present the greatest danger of all drug offenders to society. Theft, burglary and crimes of violence are often associated with addiction and addicts are also likely to sell drugs, frequently diluted with dangerous additives. On the other hand, an addict is usually a pathetic spectacle and an inadequate personality, for whom prison is not the solution to his problems. The case of *Fraser* makes the point that an addict is sentenced not for being an addict, but for becoming involved in drugs initially and thus exposing himself to the risk of addiction. In general, addiction is not a valid mitigating factor, and again the needs of deterrence take precedence over the individual needs of the offender.[12] Indeed, in some cases, the fact that the offender is an addict may warrant a more severe sentence than usual on the grounds that a period in prison is the offender's only hope for survival (as, for example, in the case of *Roote*[13].

Rehabilitation of offenders

In one sense any offender is in need of rehabilitation on the basis that a person who breaks the criminal law has deviated from the norm of society. However, this extreme view is untenable in practical terms (most people convicted of speeding do not consider themselves deviant) and in the context of drug offences those convicted may be conveniently divided into two broad categories.

Firstly, there are those whose use of drugs is not a problem for themselves (except for the criminal liability involved).

Secondly, there are those who have 'a drug problem' quite separate from any legal issues. The first category need not be considered any further, except to emphasise that a sentencer

10 [1967] Crim LR 597.
11 For example, *Anderson* [1981] Crim LR 270, CA; *Mehagian and Fenwick* (1972) 57 Cr App Rep 488, [1973] Crim LR 250.
12 *Owen* [1973] Crim LR 455, CA.
13 [1981] Crim LR 189, CA.

should not assume that a drug offender is automatically socially maladjusted, disturbed or deviant simply on account of his use of drugs. The type of drugs involved and the personal circumstances of the offender will obviously be relevant in assessing whether this is so or not.

When dealing with those in the second category, a sentencer has a duty to pass a sentence which will be in the best interests of the offender, although this duty may be overridden by the needs of deterrence and the interests of society in general. Many of the ways in which a drug abuser may be helped cannot be implemented by the sentence of a criminal court. The main options available are normally:

(a) a fine (this should take into account the offender's ability to pay);
(b) imprisonment;
(c) probation;
(d) (in certain circumstances) Community Service Order.

A fine is unlikely to have any rehabilitative effect at all, except in that it may in the short term render a user of drugs less able to afford them. Imprisonment, which is the sentence which must be given for serious offences will, however, have some effect. A person who is imprisoned is compulsorily withdrawn from drugs (unless they are necessary for organic disease or injury). A prisoner will normally be given the opportunity to withdraw under medical supervision in the medical unit, if the prison medical officer considers that he is dependent on a drug. However, although a term of imprisonment will ensure that a person stops using drugs for its duration, this is not usually an effective cure for addiction, as it merely treats the symptoms rather than the underlying causes. The hardest part of conquering addiction is generally considered to be not giving up drugs initially, but staying off them. Many addicts return to drug abuse after release from prison. Some prisons (such as Holloway and Wormwood Scrubs) have special drug units where counselling and other help is available to assist withdrawal from drugs. These are likely to be more effect as a long-term solution.[14] It has already been mentioned that a prison sentence may be justified simply for the reason that it is the only way to save the offender's life.

Probation is in theory one of the best methods to encourage an offender to solve his drug problems. Probation officers are trained to deal with such matters, and they should be able to give support and guidance. In addition conditions may be attached to a probation order, and in the context of drugs offences they might include residence at a rehabilitation hostel, or attendance for

14 See Advisory Council's Report on treatment within the prison service.

treatment at a drug clinic. The main difficulty is the practical one of enforcing such conditions. Problem drug users are notoriously disorganised and unmotivated, and all too often such a person will, despite a probation order, continue to lead the same life style as before. In particular, maintaining contact with friends who are users makes it very difficult to keep clear of drugs.

A Community Service Order may only be made as an alternative to imprisonment, but this limitation is of little practical consequence in the context of drug offences. Such an order will give no direct incentive for a user to give up drugs, but the doing of community-type work may well cause a more positive attitude to work or life in general and thus be of assistance.

Other treatment and rehabilitation
Although the following section is not directly concerned with the law, it is sufficiently closely related to the general problem of drug abuse and the law to merit inclusion. In it is listed the general range of services for treatment and rehabilitation for problem drug users. A fuller discussion of this topic can be found in the report of the Advisory Council on Treatment and Rehabilitation.[15]

Hospitals
It has for some years been part of government policy that there should be available special drug units attached to hospitals in order to provide treatment for addicts and other problem drug users. There are about 100 NHS hospitals in the United Kingdom which provide a service of this kind. These units are the responsibility of local area health authorities and so they vary considerably from area to area. Each unit will normally be headed by a consultant psychiatrist. The precise approach to the treatment policy will be decided by the consultant and his assistants. In addition to special drug units, general medical beds will, of course, be available to those who suffer some acute organic crisis as a result of drug abuse (overdose, hepatitis, etc.).

General practitioners
An addict's first step towards treatment may be to consult his GP, or indeed the drug problems may come to light as a result of a visit to the doctor on an unrelated matter. Although a GP may wish to refer a patient to a specialist drug unit, he may also treat the problem himself, and the only limitation on this will be his inability

15 HMSO 1982.

to prescribe heroin, cocaine or dipipanone. It appears that the treatment of drug problems by GPs is on the increase.

Probation service
This has already been mentioned. Probation officers are specifically trained to help problem drug users and are likely to be experienced in this field. The service is only available for those who have been convicted of an offence.

Non-statutory and voluntary groups
This category covers a whole range of organisations, from expensive and well-equipped private clinics to informal parental groups in a number of towns and cities. Some organisations are crisis centres for street users (the best known being City Road in London), others provide residential drug-free hostels where residents are helped to adjust to living and working in society. They embrace a wide variety of aims and methods used to achieve them.[16]

16 A list of some drug-oriented help and information organisations is given in Appendix 8.

18   Forfeiture

Section 27 of the MDA reads as follows:

(1) Subject to subsection (2) below, the court by or before which a person is convicted of an offence under this Act may order anything shown to the satisfaction of the court to relate to the offence to be forfeited and either destroyed or dealt with in such other manner as the court may order.

(2) The court shall not order anything to be forfeited under this section, where a person claiming to be owner of or otherwise interested in it applies to be heard by the court, unless an opportunity has been given to him to show cause why the order should not be made.

This section is designed to ensure that not only are those committing drug offences punished but also that they shall not profit from these offences. The profits to be made in drug dealing are potentially very large and a person may well be prepared to risk a period of imprisonment if he knows that a large sum of money is safely salted away for when he is released.

Any forfeiture order made under section 27 is to be counted as part of the sentence in the case. In *Menocal*,[1] three months after sentence had been passed on D for importing drugs, the court purported to make a forfeiture order concerning money which was the proceeds from the drugs offences. It was held that the definition of sentence in section 57 of the Courts Act 1971 included a section 27 order and that therefore any such order could only be made and/or varied within twenty-eight days of sentencing.

The main problem in interpreting section 27 is to know how directly property or other objects contemplated by section 27 must be connected with an offence under the Act before it may be subject to an order under the section. The case of *Beard*[2] suggests that any money which represents the proceeds of a drug dealing offence is subject to such an order, but a house which is used to harbour drugs is not.[3] It is submitted that any vehicle or other vessel (e.g. a ship) which is directly involved in the commission of an offence under the Act is subject to a forfeiture order. However,

1 [1980] AC 598, 69 Cr App Rep 157.
2 [1974] 1 WLR 1549, [1975] Crim LR 92.
3 The case of *Khan* [1982] 3 All ER 969, 4 Cr App Rep (S) 298, holds that a house cannot be forfeited pursuant to the more general power contained in section 43 of the Powers of Criminal Courts Act 1973.

if a crewman aboard a supertanker hides a few grams of cocaine aboard in order to import it, it is unlikely that the ship would be subject to forfeiture as the smuggling is not the main purpose of the voyage (cf the detailed statutory forfeiture provisions under the Customs and Excise Management Act 1979).

In *Morgan*,[4] D arranged to meet X and Y in order to sell cocaine to them. He was arrested and an amount of cash was found on him. It was held that this cash could not be forfeited because it appeared that although the cash represented part of D's 'stock in trade' as a drug dealer, the money could not be said to be connected with that particular transaction.

In the case of *Cuthbertson*[5] the construction of section 27 was considered by the House of Lords in relation to the famous 'operation Julie' case, where the defendants had manufactured large amounts of LSD and were charged with conspiring to contravene various provisions of the MDA. The House of Lords held (with some reluctance[6] that the list of offences contained in Schedule 4 (and referred to in section 25) of the MDA was an exhaustive list of the offences 'under the Act' for the purposes of section 27 and therefore a conspiracy to contravene a provision of the Act did not fall within the scope of section 27. As a result no forfeiture order could be made in relation to such a conspiracy. Furthermore their Lordships held (Lord Scarman dissenting) that for section 27 to operate the offence had to be one to which something tangible could relate, which was not possible in the case of conspiracy (where the *actus reus* of the offence is an agreement). It also appears from the case that only tangible objects and not choses in action may be the subject of a forfeiture order.

The section does not require that the object forfeited belonged to a person convicted of an offence. So it would seem that if D steals a car from X and uses it to import drugs, then the car may be forfeited (although of course in practice the court would normally order the car to be returned to its owner).

Forfeiture under the Customs and Excise Management Acts
In addition to the provisions of section 27 which apply only to offences under the MDA, there are a series of sections in the Customs and Excise Management Act 1979 dealing with forfeiture. The CEMA was drafted with a wide range of goods in

4 [1977] Crim LR 488, CA.
5 [1980] 2 All ER 401, 71 Cr App Rep 148.
6 Following the result of *Cuthbertson* there has been much criticism of this area of the law and a committee set up by the Howard League for Penal Reform under the chairmanship of Hodgson J is examining the law relating to forfeiture orders by criminal courts.

mind, including both prohibited ones such as controlled drugs and dutiable ones. The relevant sections are 139 to 144 and Schedule 3. Any controlled drugs, the importation of which is prohibited are liable to forfeiture under the CEMA, section 49(1)(b).

By section 139, anything liable to forfeiture may be seized by either a Customs officer or a constable or a member of the armed forces. It appears that if goods are seized in the mistaken belief that they are prohibited, the seizor is not liable in trespass.[7] If the seizure is not by a Customs officer, the person seizing it must, subject to certain exceptions, deliver it to the nearest convenient customs office. Pending forfeiture proceedings the thing may be dealt with in any way the commissioners see fit.

In order to deter smuggling as effectively as possible, it is desirable to have forfeited not only the prohibited goods themselves but anything which has facilitated the smuggling. Section 141 provides in very wide terms for the forfeiture of

> any ship, aircraft, vehicle, animal, container (including any article of passenger's baggage) or any other thing whatsoever which has been used for the carriage, handling, deposit or concealment of the thing so liable for forfeiture...or any other thing mixed, packed or found with the thing so liable...

By subsection (2) 'all tackle, apparel, or furniture' of any ship, aircraft, vehicle or animal liable to forfeiture is also so liable. The term 'used for the carriage of' is widely construed.[8] A vessel is used for the purposes of importation even if the handling was done outside territorial waters,[9] so if a ship carrying cannabis from Colombia unloads her cargo to smaller vessels in mid Atlantic she is still liable to forfeiture. Forfeiture proceedings are actions *in rem*.[10]

Although forfeiture is discretionary, there is a danger of an unfair operation of section 141 in some cases. As the section stands, if a crewman on a supertanker hid a few grams of cannabis in his cabin, the entire ship would be liable to forfeiture. For this reason section 142 makes provisions for forfeiture of larger ships. By section 142(1) a ship of 250 or more tons may only be forfeited under the Act if the offence in respect of which forfeiture is claimed:

> (a) was substantially the object of the voyage during which the offence was committed, or
> (b) was committed while the ship was under chase by a vessel in the service of Her Majesty...

7 *Jacobsohn v Blake* (1844) 6 Man & G 919, 13 LJCP 89.
8 *Customs and Excise Comrs v Jack Bradley (Accrington) Ltd* [1959] 1 QB 219, [1958] Crim LR 786.
9 *A-G v Hunter* [1949] 2 KB 111, [1949] 1 All ER 1006.
10 *Denton v John Lister Ltd* [1971] 3 All ER 669, [1971] 1 WLR 1426.

Procedure

The procedure for forfeiture under the Act is laid down in Schedule 3. This will not be detailed here, but the Schedule provides for giving notice of seizure, giving notice of claims, the jurisdiction of courts and methods of proof of certain matters. Forfeiture proceedings are civil, and may be commenced in a magistrates' court or the High Court.

Part V
Lawful Use

19 Lawful Use

Sections 3, 4, 5 and 6 of the MDA, which prohibit certain activities relating to controlled drugs, are all expressly subject to section 7. This section allows, and in the case of subsection (3) requires, the Secretary of State to make regulations in connection with the lawful use of controlled drugs.

Many controlled drugs have no legitimate medical use, and many drugs used medically are neither controlled nor abused. However there is a certain amount of overlap between the medical and the non-medical use of drugs, and it is essential that doctors, dentists and other medical practitioners should be able to treat their patients appropriately without being hindered by the fact that a particular drug is controlled. Many controlled drugs, especially the synthetic ones, were initially produced for medical use, and even naturally occurring ones such as the opiates are used in this way (the opiates are powerful analgesics). In addition it may be desirable to conduct scientific research into the effects of controlled drugs which have no medical use, and bona fide research establishments need to able to possess and use such drugs lawfully.

Sections 7 and 10 establish the basis for a set of regulations which allow doctors, pharmacists and so on to produce, supply and otherwise deal with certain controlled drugs in the course of their business. These sections, in conjunction with sections 11 to 17 can be broadly classified together as regulating the lawful use of controlled drugs.

This book is principally concerned with misuse of controlled drugs in the popular sense of the word (i.e. by persons who do not have and do not purport to have authority to possess or otherwise deal with controlled drugs). For this reason a comprehensive analysis of the somewhat lengthy regulations concerning the storage, prescription etc. of controlled drugs is inappropriate here. However in this chapter the basic scheme and some of the more important aspects of the regulations will be explained. The various regulations are set out in Appendix 3.

There are three principal sets of regulations made pursuant to the MDA. These are:

a Misuse of Drugs Regulations (SI 1973/797, as amended by SI 1974/402, 1975/499, 1975/1623, 1977/1380, 1979/326). These control the possession, supply and production of controlled drugs by practitioners and research establishments.

b Misuse of Drugs (Safe Custody) Regulations (SI 1973/798). These lay down extremely detailed provisions regarding the manner in which controlled drugs shall be kept by lawful possessors.

c Misuse of Drugs (Notification of and Supply to Addicts) Regulations (SI 1973/799). These continue the 1968 scheme laid down under the 1967 Act whereby a doctor must notify the Home Office of addicts, and whereby only licensed doctors (in practice those who work in special drug units attached to hospitals) may prescribe specific drugs to such addicts.

Misuse of Drugs Regulations 1973 (SI 1973/797)
There are four schedules to these regulations. They each list a number of controlled drugs of various types. In practice the schedules represent the following categories:

Schedule 1   The least dangerous. This contains a list of substances which any person may administer to any other person. They are all dilute preparations of a controlled drug.

Schedule 2   These are controlled drugs which may be administered by a practitioner or produced by a pharmacist. They include the opiates and major stimulants.

Schedule 3   These are a few controlled drugs which may be administered by a practitioner or produced by a pharmacist, or by any person registered for the purpose with the Home Office. They include minor stimulants.

Schedule 4   These are drugs with no accepted medical use, such as LSD and cannabis. They may only be possessed or produced by special licence of the Secretary of State. Such licences will only be given for research purposes.

General provisions
Regulation 1 states the title of the regulations and specifies that 1 July 1974 shall be the date upon which the regulations come into

operation. Regulation 2 is concerned with the definition and interpretation of various terms and expressions used in the regulations, such as 'registered pharmacy', 'matron' etc.

Possession of controlled drugs

Regulation 6 lists six classes of persons who, although unconnected with the medical profession, may legitimately be required to be in possession of controlled drugs in the course of their business. These six classes are permitted to have controlled drugs in their possession and they are: the police, customs officers, forensic laboratory workers, carriers, persons engaged on Post Office business and lastly anybody conveying the drug to one of the first five. The 'scope of duty' doctrine, developed in the law of tort, will apply here. A postman who opens a packet of cannabis and smokes it will no longer be in the course of Post Office business, and will therefore lose the protection afforded by the regulation. It is less clear whether a postman or carrier who delivers a controlled drug to someone whom he knows is not entitled to possess it will be outside the scope of his duty.

Regulation 10 entitles all those listed in regulations 8(2) and 9(2) as entitled to supply controlled drugs in Schedules 2 and 3 respectively to possess those drugs when acting in the capacity stated. Regulations 8 and 9 will be covered below but broadly regulation 10 allows medical practitioners, matrons etc. to possess drugs which they are entitled to supply or manufacture (a necessary prerequisite of that supply or manufacture). Regulation 11, which is concerned with the Class A drug pethidine (a powerful painkiller often used in childbirth), allows a midwife to possess the drug.

Persons to whom drugs are lawfully supplied by practitioners under regulations 8 and 9 are entitled to possess those drugs for the purpose of self-administration by regulation 10(2). This right is subject to two qualifications:
  (a) by regulation 10(2)(a) a person is not so entitled to possess a drug if he is also at that time being prescribed controlled drugs by another doctor and has failed to disclose that fact.
  (b) by regulation 10(2)(b) he is not entitled to possess such a drug if he has made any false declaration or statement in order to obtain the prescription (for example a person who obtains a prescription for methadone by wrongly stating that he is addicted to it loses the protection of this regulation).

Once the drug has been obtained, the fact that D does not use it in accordance with the directions will not vitiate the legality of its possession.[1] There is, however, no authority to possess a drug which was illegally prescribed by a doctor, even if this was done in good faith.

Regulation 4(1) permits the possession, importation and exportation of Schedule 1 drugs and poppy straw (which has been exempted from section 3 of the MDA).

Production and supply of controlled drugs

Regulations 8 and 9 deal with the production and supply of the controlled drugs in Schedules 2 and 3 respectively. The provisions of the two regulations are extremely similar. By regulations 8(1) and 9(1) either a practitioner or a pharmacist or a person lawfully conducting a retail pharmacy business may manufacture or compound any of the drugs listed in Schedules 2 and 3 respectively.

Regulations 8(2) and 9(2) give a long list of persons who are entitled to supply controlled drugs listed in Schedules 2 and 3 respectively. Among those included are practitioners, pharmacists, sisters in hospitals, public analysts and ships' masters. Regulation 9(1)(c), which has no corresponding provision in regulation 8, entitles any person whose name is entered in a register kept for this purpose by the Secretary of State to produce any drug in Schedule 3.

Regulation 11 deals with the supply of pethidine by midwives, and regulation 4(2) permits the production and supply of poppy straw.

Administration (as opposed to supply) of controlled drugs is covered by regulation 7. By regulation 7(1) any person may administer to any other a drug listed in Schedule 1. These are certain specified dilute preparations of controlled drugs. So a mother may give her child kaolin and morphine with no special authorisation. In addition a doctor or dentist may administer to a patient any drug specified in Schedule 2 or 3 (regulation 7(2)), as may any person acting in accordance with the directions of a doctor or dentist (regulation 7(3)).

---

1 Even an apparently subjective decision of the Secretary of State is open to review in accordance with the principles laid down in *Secretary of State for Education and Science v Tameside Metropolitan Borough Council* [1977] AC 1014, if no person acting reasonably could have come to that decision. By virtue of the Tribunals and Inquiries (Misuse of Drugs) Order 1973 (SI 1973/1600), the tribunals, advisory bodies and professional panels referred to in MDA, Sch. 3 are subject to the supervision of the Council on Tribunals. This order is made pursuant to the Tribunals and Inquiries Act 1971.

Licences

Possession, manufacture and supply of certain controlled drugs with no medical uses is only legitimate when done in accordance with the terms of a licence issued by the Secretary of State. Section 30 of the MDA and regulation 5 allow the Secretary of State very wide discretion as to the terms and conditions (including the payment of a fee) which may permit the production, supply and possession of any controlled drug. Licences to use Schedule 4 drugs are normally restricted to special research institutions. For example, there are currently only 5 possession and supply licences and 78 possession only licences for cannabis. For lysergide the figures are 1 and 91, and for other Schedule 4 drugs 1 and 104. For a specimen licence to produce, supply and possess, see Appendix 4.

Ancillary to the power to issue licences are regulations 12 and 13. Regulation 12 confirms that if a person authorised to do so by licence may cultivate cannabis (the MDA, section 6 is expressly made subject to regulations under section 7). Regulation 13 states that section 8 shall not have effect where an occupier of premises is permitted by licence to allow the smoking of cannabis (although section 8 is not expressed to be subject to any regulations).

It is worthy of note that the term 'practitioner' is limited to a British doctor, dentist or veterinary surgeon, so drugs prescribed by a foreign doctor may well be the subject of a possession or importation charge if brought back into this country.[2]

Documentation

Part III of the regulation deals with the documentation and record keeping necessary when supplying controlled drugs. These are somewhat detailed and will be described in outline only. A practitioner will normally supply drugs in one of three ways. Firstly, he may administer it directly, as for example when giving an injection. Secondly, he may supply it directly to the recipient or his representative. Thirdly, he may write a prescription which entitles the recipient to obtain it from a pharmacist.

Regulation 14 deals principally with the second situation and provides safeguards against a controlled drug being supplied to the wrong person or getting into the wrong hands. The practitioner may not deliver the drug to the recipient's representative unless the latter produces a statement in writing signed by the recipient to the effect that the representative is authorised to receive the drug. The practitioner must be satisfied that the signature is genuine. By regulation 14(2) to (6), where a person supplies a controlled drug

---

2 Special group export and import licences are issued if, for example, a party of sick persons wishes to visit Lourdes under the supervision of a doctor.

to others who will themselves resupply the drug, he must obtain a requisition in writing specifying certain particulars from that person.

Regulations 15 and 16 deal with drugs supplied by way of prescription. By regulation 15 certain formalities for prescriptions are laid down. A prescription must be in ink and signed and dated by the practitioner. It must specify the name and address of the recipient and details of the dosage. Regulation 16 states various prerequisites which must be met before a person supplies a controlled drug on prescription. The prescription must comply with regulation 15 and must be issued by someone whose address is in the United Kingdom, and the supplier must be satisfied that the prescription is genuine. When dispensed a prescription must have the date of dispensation marked on it. By regulation 17 certain prescriptions are exempted from the provisions of regulations 15 and 16 if they are issued pursuant to a scheme for testing the quality and amount of drugs supplied under the National Health Service Acts.

Regulation 18 provides for the marking of bottles and containers in which controlled drugs are dispensed, and regulations 19 to 23 specify what records, registers and other documentation must be kept by those engaged in the supply of controlled drugs.

Regulations 24 and 25, classified in Part IV of the regulations as miscellaneous provisions, specify *inter alia*, conditions for the destruction of a controlled drug. Where a drug is kept in circumstances where records are required, that drug shall not be destroyed except in the presence of an authorised person, and records shall be kept specifying details of the destruction. An authorised person is defined (not particularly helpfully) as a person authorised by the Secretary of State for this person. The reason for this provision is to prevent drugs from being diverted to illegitimate channels under the pretence that they have been destroyed.

Misuse of Drugs (Safe Custody) Regulations 1973 (SI 1973/798)
These regulations, as their name suggests, lay down provisions for the manner in which controlled drugs are actually kept, in order that unauthorised persons should not have access to them. These regulations are very important, as people will go to considerable lengths to break into premises where such drugs are kept, either in order to satisfy their own need for the drug, or to make large profits by selling them on the black market. The regulations apply to retail pharmacists, nursing homes and mental nursing homes, but not to hospitals. By regulation 3, controlled drugs kept on premises to which the regulations apply shall, with certain

exceptions, be kept in a locked safe, cabinet or room constructed and maintained to prevent unauthorised access. The cabinet or safe etc. must comply with rigorous standards laid down in Schedule 2, unless it has been inspected by a police officer and granted a certificate of exemption under regulation 4.

By regulation 5, where a controlled drug is kept otherwise than as specified in regulation 3, it should be kept, as far as circumstances permit, in a locked receptacle which can only be opened by authorised persons.[3]

Misuse of Drugs (Notification of and Supply to Addicts) Regulations 1973 (SI 1973/797)

These regulations, which preserve the scheme set up in 1968, are of considerable importance in implementing the policy adopted in the United Kingdom for the treatment of drug addicts. An addict is defined for the purpose of the regulations by regulation 2(2) as follows:

> A person shall be regarded as addicted to a drug if, and only if, he has as a result of repeated administration become so dependent upon the drug that he has an overpowering desire for the administration of it to be continued.

The two key points of the regulations are:
(a) the notification of addicts to the Home Office,
(b) the limitation of supply of certain drugs to specially licensed doctors.

Notification

By regulation 3, a doctor who attends a person who he considers or has reasonable grounds to suspect is addicted to any drug (which is listed in the Schedule) must within seven days notify the Home Office of the name, address, sex, date of birth and national health number of that person, together with the date of attendance and the name of the drug or drugs concerned. The drugs listed in the schedule are heroin, cocaine, dipipanone (Diconal), methadone, opium, morphine and pethidine. A doctor need not give such notification if either it has already been given by an appropriate person or if the doctor is of the opinion that continued administration is necessary for the treatment of organic disease or injury. The word 'attends' implies that a doctor need not notify the Home Office of any addicts he meets socially.

By regulation 4, a doctor may only prescribe heroin or cocaine or their salts (or as from 1 April 1984, dipipanone)[4] if he is specially licensed to do so, unless the supply of the drug is for the purpose of treating an organic disease or injury.

3 *Dhulipala Kameswara Rao v Wyles* [1949] 2 All ER 685, 113 JP 516.
4 SI 1983/1909.

The three above sets of regulations are made under the MDA, sections 7 and 10 and cover the matters listed in those sections. In addition there are the Misuse of Drugs Tribunal (England and Wales) Rules 1974, brought into effect by SI 1974/85, which regulate the procedure for the tribunals constituted under Part I of Schedule 3 of the MDA.

Sections 11–17 of the MDA contain provisions which are in effect ancillary to these regulations. The sections can conveniently be dealt with in numerical order. As well as further regulating the lawful use of controlled drugs and those who supply them, they create various offences in connection with the regulations.

Section 11 provides for stricter measures for safe keeping of controlled drugs on any premises which the Secretary of State may consider necessary, over and above the requirements of the safe custody regulations. By section 11(1) the Secretary of State may by notice in writing require the occupier of any premises to take such precautions for the safe keeping of controlled drugs as may be specified in the notice. Section 11(2) makes it an offence to contravene the terms of such a notice.

Sections 12 and 13 are of considerable practical importance. One of the grave weaknesses of early schemes for the control of drug addiction was the inability of the Home Office to control effectively doctors who overprescribed. Such doctors were often acting from the best of motives but were exploited by addicts, and they created a huge surplus of controlled drugs, many of which were sold on the black market. This problem was tackled in two ways. Firstly, the prescription of heroin, cocaine and more recently dipipanone to addicts was restricted to specially licensed doctors. Secondly what are now sections 12 and 13 of the MDA were inserted into the drugs legislation to deal with overprescribing doctors. Section 12 gives powers in respect of practitioners or pharmacists who have been convicted of offences against the drugs legislation. In this case the Secretary of State may give a direction prohibiting the practitioner or pharmacist from dealing with any of the controlled drugs specified in the notice. A copy of such a notice shall be published in the appropriate gazettes (section 11(4)) and any such notice is revocable. The contravention of such a notice is made an offence by subsection (6).

Section 12 deals with convicted practitioners and pharmacists, but greater problems were caused by doctors who remained within the limits of the law. For many years the medical profession resisted any attempts to control their absolute right to prescribe drugs as they saw fit and until 1968 they were successful. Now, however, section 13 gives the Secretary of State power to prohibit practitioners from prescribing, administering or supplying specified controlled drugs or from authorising the doing of these things.

He may exercise this power if:
- (a) A doctor is in contravention of the regulations made under section 10(2)(h) or (i), which are the Misuse of Drugs (Notification of and Supply to Addicts) Regulations 1973, or in contravention of the terms of a licence, or
- (b) if the Secretary of State is of the opinion that a doctor has been prescribing or administering or supplying controlled drugs in an irresponsible manner.

Section 13(3) states that the contravention of such a prohibition is an offence although contravention of the Misuse of Drugs (Notification of and Supply to Addicts) Regulations 1973 is not an offence. These regulations are the only ones made under the MDA, contravention of which is not an offence.[5]

Although section 13(2) is couched subjectively, the Secretary of State may only issue a direction under the section if he follows the detailed procedures laid down in sections 14 to 16. Section 14 in effect provides that where the Secretary of State wishes to make such a direction he must refer the matter to a tribunal constituted for that purpose. The tribunal considers the matter and if it thinks fit, may recommend that a direction should be made specifying all or any controlled drugs. If this happens, the Secretary of State must notify the doctor as to whether or not he proposes to issue a notice, and if he does propose to, he must inform him that consideration will be given to any relevant written representations received within twenty-eight days. If representations are received within the specified period, the case is then referred to an advisory body constituted for the purpose. This body will consider the case and after receiving their advice, the Secretary of State may either:
- (a) give a direction under section 13(1) or 13(2), or
- (b) order that the case be referred back to the same or another tribunal, or
- (c) take no further proceedings.

It will be seen that the procedure to be followed under section 14 can be rather long and cumbersome. In certain cases action may be required urgently and section 15 provides that in those circumstances temporary directions may be given under section 13(2). If the Secretary of State considers that there are grounds for a direction under section 13(2) and that it is vital to avoid delay, he may refer the matter to a professional panel constituted for the purpose. This panel must afford the doctor an opportunity of appearing before it and then report to the Secretary of State as to whether there appear to be reasonable grounds for the making of a direction. If they report that there are such grounds, the Secretary of State may give a temporary direction lasting for six weeks.

5 MDA, s. 18(1).

Section 16 deals with matters supplementary to sections 14 and 15. By subsection (2) a copy of any direction given under section 14 or 15 must be published in the appropriate gazette. Subsection (3) gives the power to the Secretary of State to cancel or suspend or cancel the suspension of any section 14 notice and to cancel any section 15 direction.

It may happen that a particular geographical area in Great Britain develops drug problems disproportionate to those in the country in general, and in view of this phenomenon section 17 gives powers to the Secretary of State to elicit certain information in order to combat the problem. The existence of a problem area will normally be drawn to the attention of the Secretary of State by the Advisory Council. The section begins:

17.(1) If it appears...that there exists a social problem caused by the extensive misuse of dangerous or otherwise harmful drugs...

The expression 'social problem' is vague but presumably implies that there must be some consequence of the drugtaking other than persons being convicted of offences. The drugs specified are not merely controlled ones, but any dangerous or otherwise harmful ones. The argument as to whether a drug can be harmful without being dangerous is of academic interest only. If this situation arises, the Secretary of State may require from doctors, pharmacists or retail pharmacies such particulars as may be specified relating to quantity of and frequency of supply, prescription and administration of specified drugs. It is an offence to fail to comply with a valid notice under the section[6] or to give false information.[7]

Section 18 lists various offences relating to licences and regulations. By section 18(1), it is an offence to contravene any regulations made under this Act other than those made in pursuance of section 10(2)(h) or (i), which relate to notification of and supply to addicts. This blanket offence would appear to attach criminal liability to any members of a tribunal who failed to comply with the procedure set out in the Misuse of Drugs Tribunal rules, although it is unlikely that this result was intended.

The constitution and procedure of the tribunals, advisory bodies and professional panels referred to in the MDA are laid down in Schedule 3 of the Act, with more detailed provisions for the tribunal set out in the rules mentioned in the previous paragraph, made in pursuance of paragraph 4 of the schedule.

The decisions and procedures of the Secretary of State and the various quasi-judicial bodies referred to will be subject to judicial review in accordance with the normal principles.[8]

6 MDA, s. 17(3).
7 MDA, s. 17(4).
8 See fn. 2, above.

Appendices

1   Misuse of Drugs Act 1971

Arrangement of sections

The Advisory Council on the Misuse of Drugs

Section
1. The Advisory Council on the Misuse of Drugs . .　　. .　　. .　　. .

Controlled drugs and their classification
2. Controlled drugs and their classification for purposes of this Act　　. .

Restrictions relating to controlled drugs etc.
3. Restriction of importation and exportation of controlled drugs　　. .
4. Restriction of production and supply of controlled drugs　　. .　　. .
5. Restriction of possession of controlled drugs　　. .　　. .　　. .　　. .
6. Restriction of cultivation of cannabis plant　　. .　　. .　　. .　　. .
7. Authorisation of activities otherwise unlawful under foregoing provisions　　. .　　. .　　. .　　. .　　. .　　. .　　. .　　. .

Miscellaneous offences involving controlled drugs etc.
8. Occupiers etc. of premises to be punishable for permitting certain activities to take place there　　. .　　. .　　. .　　. .　　. .　　. .
9. Prohibition of certain activities etc. relating to opium　　. .　　. .　　. .

Powers of Secretary of State for preventing misuse of controlled drugs
10. Power to make regulations for preventing misuse of controlled drugs
11. Power to direct special precautions for safe custody of controlled drugs to be taken at certain premises　　. .　　. .　　. .　　. .
12. Directions prohibiting prescribing, supply etc. of controlled drugs by practitioners etc. convicted of certain offences　　. .　　. .
13. Directions prohibiting prescribing, supply etc. of controlled drugs by practitioners in other cases　　. .　　. .　　. .　　. .　　. .
14. Investigation where grounds for a direction under s. 13 are considered to exist　　. .　　. .　　. .　　. .　　. .　　. .　　. .
15. Temporary directions under s. 13 (2)　　. .　　. .　　. .　　. .
16. Provisions supplementary to ss. 14 and 15　　. .　　. .　　. .
17. Power to obtain information from doctors, pharmacists etc. in certain circumstances　　. .　　. .　　. .　　. .　　. .　　. .

Miscellaneous offences and powers
18. Miscellaneous offences　　. .　　. .　　. .　　. .　　. .　　. .
19. Attempts etc. to commit offences　　. .　　. .　　. .　　. .
20. Assisting in or inducing commission outside United Kingdom of offence punishable under a corresponding law　　. .　　. .　　. .

21. Offences by corporations ..   ..
22. Further powers to make regulations   ..   ..

Law enforcement and punishment of offences
23. Powers to search and obtain evidence ..   ..
24. Power of arrest   ..   ..
25. Prosecution and punishment of offences   ..   ..
26. Increase of penalties for certain offences under Customs and Excise
    Act 1952 ..   ..
27. Forfeiture ..   ..

Miscellaneous and supplementary provisions
28. Proof of lack of knowledge etc. to be a defence in proceedings for
    certain offences ..   ..
29. Service of documents   ..   ..
30. Licences and authorities ..   ..
31. General provisions as to regulations   ..   ..
32. Research   ..   ..
33. Amendment of Extradition Act 1870 ..   ..
34. Amendment of Matrimonial Proceedings (Magistrates' Courts) Act
    1960   ..   ..
35. Financial provisions   ..   ..
36. Meaning of 'corresponding law', and evidence of certain matters by
    certificate   ..   ..
37. Interpretation   ..   ..
38. Special provisions as to Northern Ireland   ..   ..
39. Savings and transitional provisions, repeals, and power to amend
    local enactments   ..   ..
40. Short title, extent and commencement ..   ..

SCHEDULES:
    Schedule 1—Constitution etc. of Advisory Council on the Misuse
      of Drugs   ..   ..
    Schedule 2—Controlled drugs   ..   ..
    Schedule 3—Tribunals, advisory bodies and professional panels ..
    Schedule 4—Prosecution and punishment of offences   ..   ..
    Schedule 5—Savings and transitional provisions   ..   ..   ..
    Schedule 6—Repeals ..   ..

An Act to make new provision with respect to dangerous or otherwise harmful drugs and related matters, and for purposes connected therewith   [27 May 1971]

The Advisory Council on the Misuse of Drugs
1. The Advisory Council on the Misuse of Drugs
(1) There shall be constituted in accordance with Schedule 1 to this Act an Advisory Council on the Misuse of Drugs (in this Act referred to as 'the Advisory Cour.cil'); and the supplementary provisions contained in that Schedule shall have effect in relation to the Council.

(2) It shall be the duty of the Advisory Council to keep under review the situation in the United Kingdom with respect to drugs which are being or

appear to them likely to be misused and of which the misuse is having or appears to them capable of having harmful effects sufficient to constitute a social problem, and to give to any one or more of the Ministers, where either the Council consider it expedient to do so or they are consulted by the Minister or Ministers in question, advice on measures (whether or not involving alteration of the law) which in the opinion of the Council ought to be taken for preventing the misuse of such drugs or dealing with social problems connected with their misuse, and in particular on measures which in the opinion of the Council, ought to be taken—

- (a) for restricting the availability of such drugs or supervising the arrangements for their supply;
- (b) for enabling persons affected by the misuse of such drugs to obtain proper advice, and for securing the provision of proper facilities and services for the treatment, rehabilitation and after-care of such persons;
- (c) for promoting co-operation between the various professional and community services which in the opinion of the Council have a part to play in dealing with social problems connected with the misuse of such drugs;
- (d) for educating the public (and in particular the young) in the dangers of misusing such drugs, and for giving publicity to those dangers; and
- (e) for promoting research into, or otherwise obtaining information about, any matter which in the opinion of the Council is of relevance for the purpose of preventing the misuse of such drugs or dealing with any social problem connected with their misuse.

(3) It shall also be the duty of the Advisory Council to consider any matter relating to drug dependence or the misuse of drugs which may be referred to them by any one or more of the Ministers and to advise the Minister or Ministers in question thereon, and in particular to consider and advise the Secretary of State with respect to any communication referred by him to the Council, being a communication relating to the control of any dangerous or otherwise harmful drug made to Her Majesty's Government in the United Kingdom by any organisation or authority established by or under any treaty, convention or other agreement or arrangement to which that Government is for the time being a party.

(4) In this section 'the Ministers' means the Secretary of State for the Home Department, the Secretaries of State respectively concerned with health in England, Wales and Scotland, the Secretaries of State respectively concerned with education in England, Wales and Scotland, the Minister of Home Affairs for Northern Ireland, the Minister of Health and Social Services for Northern Ireland and the Minister of Education for Northern Ireland.

Controlled drugs and their classification
2. Controlled drugs and their classification for purposes of this Act
(1) In this Act—
- (a) the expression 'controlled drug' means any substance or product for the time being specified in Part I, II or III of Schedule 2 to this Act; and

(b) the expressions 'Class A drug', 'Class B drug' and 'Class C drug' mean any of the substances and products for the time being specified respectively in Part I, Part II and Part III of that Schedule; and the provisions of Part IV of that Schedule shall have effect with respect to the meanings of expressions used in that Schedule.

(2) Her Majesty may by Order in Council make such amendments in Schedule 2 to this Act as may be requisite for the purpose of adding any substance or product to, or removing any substance or product from, any of Parts I to III of that Schedule, including amendments for securing that no substance or product is for the time being specified in a particular one of those Parts or for inserting any substance or product into any of those Parts in which no substance or product is for the time being specified.

(3) An Order in Council under this section may amend Part IV of Schedule 2 to this Act, and may do so whether or not it amends any other Part of that Schedule.

(4) An Order in Council under this section may be varied or revoked by a subsequent Order in Council thereunder.

(5) No recommendation shall be made to Her Majesty in Council to make an Order under this section unless a draft of the Order has been laid before Parliament and approved by a resolution of each House of Parliament; and the Secretary of State shall not lay a draft of such an Order before Parliament except after consultation with or on the recommendation of the Advisory Council.

Restrictions relating to controlled drugs etc.

3. Restriction of importation and exportation of controlled drugs
(1) Subject to subsection (2) below—
    (a) the importation of a controlled drug; and
    (b) the exportation of a controlled drug,
are hereby prohibited.

(2) Subsection (1) above does not apply—
    (a) to the importation or exportation of a controlled drug which is for the time being excepted from paragraph (a) or, as the case may be, paragraph (b) of subsection (1) above by regulations under section 7 of this Act; or
    (b) to the importation or exportation of a controlled drug under and in accordance with the terms of a licence issued by the Secretary of State and in compliance with any conditions attached thereto.

4. Restriction of production and supply of controlled drugs
(1) Subject to any regulations under section 7 of this Act for the time being in force, it shall not be lawful for a person—
    (a) to produce a controlled drug; or
    (b) to supply or offer to supply a controlled drug to another.

(2) Subject to section 8 of this Act, it is an offence for a person—
    (a) to produce a controlled drug in contravention of subsection (1) above; or

(b) to be concerned in the production of such a drug in contravention of that subsection by another.

(3) Subject to section 28 of this Act, it is an offence for a person—

(a) to supply or offer to supply a controlled drug to another in contravention of subsection (1) above; or

(b) to be concerned in the supplying of such a drug to another in contravention of that subsection; or

(c) to be concerned in the making to another in contravention of that subsection of an offer to supply such a drug.

5. Restriction of possession of controlled drugs

(1) Subject to any regulations under section 7 of this Act for the time being in force, it shall not be lawful for a person to have a controlled drug in his possession.

(2) Subject to section 28 of this Act and to subsection (4) below, it is an offence for a person to have a controlled drug in his possession in contravention of subsection (1) above.

(3) Subject to section 28 of this Act, it is an offence for a person to have a controlled drug in his possession, whether lawfully or not, with intent to supply it to another in contravention of section 4 (1) of this Act.

(4) In any proceedings for an offence under subsection (2) above in which it is proved that the accused had a controlled drug in his possession, it shall be a defence for him to prove—

(a) that, knowing or suspecting it to be a controlled drug, he took possession of it for the purpose of preventing another from committing or continuing to commit an offence in connection with that drug and that as soon as possible after taking possession of it he took all such steps as were reasonably open to him to destroy the drug or to deliver it into the custody of a person lawfully entitled to take custody of it; or

(b) that, knowing or suspecting it to be a controlled drug, he took possession of it for the purpose of delivering it into the custody of a person lawfully entitled to take custody of it and that as soon as possible after taking possession of it he took all such steps as were reasonably open to him to deliver it into the custody of such a person.

(5) Subsection (4) above shall apply in the case of proceedings for an offence under section 19 (1) of this Act consisting of an attempt to commit an offence under subsection (2) above as it applies in the case of proceedings for an offence under subsection (2), subject to the following modifications, that is to say—

(a) for the references to the accused having in his possession, and to his taking possession of, a controlled drug there shall be substituted respectively references to his attempting to get, and to his attempting to take, possession of such a drug; and

(b) in paragraphs (a) and (b) the words from 'and that as soon as possible' onwards shall be omitted.

(6) Nothing in subsection (4) or (5) above shall prejudice any defence which it is open to a person charged with an offence under this section to raise apart from that subsection.

6. Restriction of cultivation of cannabis plant

(1) Subject to any regulations under section 7 of this Act for the time being in force, it shall not be lawful for a person to cultivate any plant of the genus *Cannabis*.

(2) Subject to section 28 of this Act, it is an offence to cultivate any such plant in contravention of subsection (1) above.

7. Authorisation of activities otherwise unlawful under foregoing provisions

(1) The Secretary of State may by regulations—

    (a) except from section 3 (1) (a) or (b), 4 (1) (a) or (b) or 5 (1) of this Act such controlled drugs as may be specified in the regulations; and

    (b) make such other provision as he thinks fit for the purpose of making it lawful for persons to do things which under any of the following provisions of this Act, that is to say sections 4 (1), 5 (1) and 6 (1), it would otherwise be unlawful for them to do.

(2) Without prejudice to the generality of paragraph (b) of subsection (1) above, regulations under that subsection authorising the doing of any such thing as is mentioned in that paragraph may in particular provide for the doing of that thing to be lawful—

    (a) if it is done under and in accordance with the terms of a licence or other authority issued by the Secretary of State and in compliance with any conditions attached thereto; or

    (b) if it is done in compliance with such conditions as may be prescribed.

(3) Subject to subsection (4) below, the Secretary of State shall so exercise his power to make regulations under subsection (1) above as to secure—

    (a) that it is not unlawful under section 4 (1) of this Act for a doctor, dentist, veterinary practitioner or veterinary surgeon, acting in his capacity as such, to prescribe, administer, manufacture, compound or supply a controlled drug, or for a pharmacist or a person lawfully conducting a retail pharmacy business, acting in either case in his capacity as such, to manufacture, compound or supply a controlled drug; and

    (b) that it is not unlawful under section 5 (1) of this Act for a doctor, dentist, veterinary practitioner, veterinary surgeons, pharmacist or person lawfully conducting a retail pharmacy business to have a controlled drug in his possession for the purpose of acting in his capacity as such.

(4) If in the case of any controlled drug the Secretary of State is of the opinion that it is in the public interest—

    (a) for production, supply and possession of that drug to be either wholly unlawful or unlawful except for purposes of research or other special purposes; or

    (b) for it to be unlawful for practitioners, pharmacists and persons lawfully conducting retail pharmacy businesses to do in relation to that drug any of the things mentioned in subsection (3) above except under a licence or other authority issued by the Secretary of State, he may by order designate that drug as a drug to which this subsection applies; and while there is in force an order under this subsection designating a controlled drug as one to which this subsection applies, subsection (3) above shall not apply as regards that drug.

(5) Any order under subsection (4) above may be varied or revoked by a subsequent order thereunder.

(6) The power to make orders under subsection (4) above shall be exercisable by statutory instrument, which shall be subject to annulment in pursuance of a resolution of either House of Parliament.

(7) The Secretary of State shall not make any order under subsection (4) above except after consultation with or on the recommendation of the Advisory Council.

(8) References in this section to a person's 'doing' things include references to his having things in his possession.

(9) In its application to Northern Ireland this section shall have effect as if for references to the Secretary of State there were substituted references to the Ministry of Home Affairs for Northern Ireland and as if for subsection (6) there were substituted—

'(6) Any order made under subsection (4) above by the Ministry of Home Affairs for Northern Ireland shall be subject to negative resolution within the meaning of section 41 (6) of the Interpretation Act (Northern Ireland) 1954 as if it were a statutory instrument within the meaning of that Act.'

Miscellaneous offences involving controlled drugs etc.

8. Occupiers etc. of premises to be punishable for permitting certain activities to take place there

A person commits an offence if, being the occupier or concerned in the management of any premises, he knowingly permits or suffers any of the following activities to take place on those premises, that is to say—

(a) producing or attempting to produce a controlled drug in contravention of section 4 (1) of this Act;

(b) supplying or attempting to supply a controlled drug to another in contravention of section 4 (1) of this Act, or offering to supply a controlled drug to another in contravention of section 4 (1);

(c) preparing opium for smoking;

(d) smoking cannabis, cannabis resin or prepared opium.

9. Prohibition of certain activities etc. relating to opium

Subject to section 28 of this Act, it is an offence for a person—

(a) to smoke or otherwise use prepared opium; or

(b) to frequent a place used for the purpose of opium smoking; or

(c) to have in his possession

(i) any pipes or other utensils made or adapted for use in connection with the smoking of opium, being pipes or utensils which have been used by him or with his knowledge and permission in that connection or which he intends to use or permit others to use in that connection; or

(ii) any utensils which have been used by him or with his knowledge and permission in connection with the preparation of opium for smoking.

Powers of Secretary of State for preventing misuse of controlled drugs

10. Power to make regulations for preventing misuse of controlled drugs
(1) Subject to the provisions of this Act, the Secretary of State may by regulations make such provision as appears to him necessary or expedient for preventing the misuse of controlled drugs.

(2) Without prejudice to the generality of subsection (1) above, regulations under this section may in particular make provision—

(a) for requiring precautions to be taken for the safe custody of controlled drugs;

(b) for imposing requirements as to the documentation of transactions involving controlled drugs, and for requiring copies of documents relating to such transactions to be furnished to the prescribed authority;

(c) for requiring the keeping of records and the furnishing of information with respect to controlled drugs in such circumstances and in such manner as may be prescribed;

(d) for the inspection of any precautions taken or records kept in pursuance of regulations under this section;

(e) as to the packaging and labelling of controlled drugs;

(f) for regulating the transport of controlled drugs and the methods used for destroying or otherwise disposing of such drugs when no longer required;

(g) for regulating the issue of prescriptions containing controlled drugs and the supply of controlled drugs on prescriptions, and for requiring persons issuing or dispensing prescriptions containing such drugs to furnish to the prescribed authority such information relating to those prescriptions as may be prescribed;

(h) for requiring any doctor who attends a person who he considers, or has reasonable grounds to suspect, is addicted (within the meaning of the regulations) to controlled drugs of any description to furnish to the prescribed authority such particulars with respect to that person as may be prescribed;

(i) for prohibiting any doctor from administering, supplying and authorising the administration and supply to persons so addicted, and from prescribing for such persons, such controlled drugs as may be prescribed, except under and in accordance with the terms of a licence issued by the Secretary of State in pursuance of the regulations.

11. Power to direct special precautions for safe custody of controlled drugs to be taken at certain premises
(1) Without prejudice to any requirement imposed by regulations made in pursuance of section 10 (2) (a) of this Act, the Secretary of State may by notice in writing served on the occupier of any premises on which controlled drugs are or are proposed to be kept give directions as to the taking of precautions or further precautions for the safe custody of any controlled drugs of a drescription specified in the notice which are kept on those premises.

(2) It is an offence to contravene any directions given under subsection (1) above.

12. Directions prohibiting prescribing, supply etc. of controlled drugs by practitioners etc. convicted of certain offences

(1) Where a person who is a practitioner or pharmacist has after the coming into operation of this subsection been convicted—

(a) of an offence under this Act or under the Dangerous Drugs Act 1965 or any enactment repealed by that Act; or

(b) of an offence under section 45, 56 or 304 of the Customs and Excise Act 1952 in connection with a prohibition of or restriction on importation or exportation of a controlled drug having effect by virtue of section 3 of this Act or which had effect by virtue of any provision contained in or repealed by the Dangerous Drugs Act 1965,

the Secretary of State may give a direction under subsection (2) below in respect of that person.

(2) A direction under this subsection in respect of a person shall—

(a) if that person is a practitioner, be a direction prohibiting him from having in his possession, prescribing, administering, manufacturing, compounding and supplying and from authorising the administration and supply of such controlled drugs as may be specified in the direction;

(b) if that person is a pharmacist, be a direction prohibiting him from having in his possession, manufacturing, compounding and supplying and from supervising and controlling the manufacture, compounding and supply of such controlled drugs as may be specified in the direction.

(3) The Secretary of State may at any time give a direction cancelling or suspending any direction given by him under subsection (2) above, or cancelling any direction of this under his subsection by which a direction so given is suspended.

(4) The Secretary of State shall cause a copy of any direction given by him under this section to be served on the person to whom it applies, and shall cause notice of any such direction to be published in the London, Edinburgh and Belfast Gazettes.

(5) A direction under this section shall take effect when a copy of it is served on the person to whom it applies.

(6) It is an offence to contravene a direction given under subsection (2) above.

(7) In section 80 of the Medicines Act 1968 (under which a body corporate carrying on a retail pharmacy business may be disqualified for the purposes of Part IV of that Act and have its premises removed from the register kept under section 75 of that Act, where that body or any member of the board of that body or any officer or any employee of that body is convicted of an offence under any of the relevant Acts as defined in subsection (5)), for the words 'and this Act' in subsection (5) there shall be substituted the words 'this Act and the Misuse of Drugs Act 1971'.

13. Directions prohibiting prescribing, supply etc. of controlled drugs by practitioners in other cases

(1) In the event of a contravention by a doctor of regulations made in pursuance of paragraph (h) or (i) of section 10 (2) of this Act, or of the

terms of a licence issued under regulations made in pursuance of the said paragraph (i), the Secretary of State may, subject to and in accordance with section 14 of this Act, give a direction in respect of the doctor concerned prohibiting him from prescribing, administering and supplying and from authorising the administration and supply, of such controlled drugs as may be specified in the direction.

(2) If the Secretary of State is of the opinion that a practitioner is or has after the coming into operation of this subsection been prescribing, administering or supplying or authorising the administration or supply of any controlled drugs in an irresponsible manner, the Secretary of State may, subject to and in accordance with section 14 or 15 of this Act, give a direction in respect of the practitioner concerned prohibiting him from prescribing, administering and supplying and from authorising the administration and supply of such controlled drugs as may be specified in the direction.

(3) A contravention such as is mentioned in subsection (1) above does not as such constitute an offence, but it is an offence to contravene a direction given under subsection (1) or (2) above.

14. Investigation where grounds for a direction under s. 13 are considered to exist

(1) If the Secretary of State considers that there are grounds for giving a direction under subsection (1) of section 13 of this Act on account of such a contravention by a doctor as is there mentioned, or for giving a direction under subsection (2) of that section on account of such conduct by a practitioner as is mentioned in the said subsection (2), he may refer the case to a tribunal constituted for the purpose in accordance with the following provisions of this Act; and it shall be the duty of the tribunal to consider the case and report on it to the Secretary of State.

(2) In this Act 'the respondent', in relation to a reference under this section, means the doctor or other practitioner in respect of whom the reference is made.

(3) Where—
(a) in the case of a reference relating to the giving of a direction under the said subsection (1), the tribunal finds that there has been no such contravention as aforesaid by the respondent or finds that there has been such a contravention but does not recommend the giving of a direction under that subsection in respect of the respondent; or
(b) in the case of a reference relating to the giving of a direction under the said subsection (2), the tribunal finds that there has been no such conduct as aforesaid by the respondent or finds that there has been such conduct by the respondent but does not recommend the giving of a direction under the said subsection (2) in respect of him, the Secretary of State shall cause notice to that effect to be served on the respondent.

(4) Where the tribunal finds—
(a) in the case of a reference relating to the giving of a direction under the said subsection (1), that there has been such a contravention as aforesaid by the respondent; or

    (b) in the case of a reference relating to the giving of a direction under the said subsection (2), that there has been such conduct as aforesaid by the respondent,

and considers that a direction under the subsection in question should be given in respect of him, the tribunal shall include in its report a recommendation to that effect indicating the controlled drugs which it considers should be specified in the direction or indicating that the direction should specify all controlled drugs.

    (5) Where the tribunal makes such a recommendation as aforesaid, the Secretary of State shall cause a notice to be served on the respondent stating whether or not he proposes to give a direction pursuant thereto, and where he does so propose the notice shall—

    (a) set out the terms of the proposed direction; and

    (b) inform the respondent that consideration will be given to any representations relating to the case which are made by him in writing to the Secretary of State within the period of twenty-eight days beginning with the date of service of the notice.

    (6) If any such representations are received by the Secretary of State within the period aforesaid, he shall refer the case to an advisory body constituted for the purpose in accordance with the following provisions of this Act; and it shall be the duty of the advisory body to consider the case and to advise the Secretary of State as to the exercise of his powers under subsection (7) below.

    (7) After the expiration of the said period of twenty-eight days and, in the case of a reference to an advisory body under subsection (6) above, after considering the advice of that body, the Secretary of State may either—

    (a) give in respect of the respondent a direction under subsection (1) or, as the case may be, subsection (2) of section 13 of this Act specifying all or any of the controlled drugs indicated in the recommendation of the tribunal; or

    (b) order that the case be referred back to the tribunal, or referred to another tribunal constituted as aforesaid; or

    (c) order that no further proceedings under this section shall be taken in the case.

    (8) Where a case is referred or referred back to a tribunal in pursuance of subsection (7) above, the provisions of subsections (2) to (7) above shall apply as if the case had been referred to the tribunal in pursuance of subsection (1) above, and any finding, recommendation or advice previously made or given in respect of the case in pursuance of those provisions shall be disregarded.

15. Temporary directions under s. 13 (2)

(1) If the Secretary of State considers that there are grounds for giving a direction under subsection (2) of section 13 of this Act in respect of a practitioner on account of such conduct by him as is mentioned in that subsection and that the circumstances of the case require such a direction to be given with the minimum of delay, he may, subject to the following provisions of this section, give such a direction in respect of him by virtue of this section; and a direction under section 13 (2) given by virtue of this

section may specify such controlled drugs as the Secretary of State thinks fit.

(2) Where the Secretary of State proposes to give such a direction as aforesaid by virtue of this section, he shall refer the case to a professional panel constituted for the purpose in accordance with the following provisions of this Act; and

(a) it shall be the duty of the panel, after affording the respondent an opportunity of appearing before and being heard by the panel, to consider the circumstances of the case, so far as known to it, and to report to the Secretary of State whether the information before the panel appears to it to afford reasonable grounds for thinking that there has been such conduct by the respondent as is mentioned in section 13 (2) of this Act; and

(b) the Secretary of State shall not by virtue of this section give such a direction as aforesaid in respect of the respondent unless the panel reports that the information before it appears to it to afford reasonable grounds for so thinking.

(3) In this Act 'the respondent', in relation to a reference under subsection (2) above, means the practitioner in respect of whom the reference is made.

(4) Where the Secretary of State gives such a direction as aforesaid by virtue of this section he shall, if he has not already done so, forthwith refer the case to a tribunal in accordance with section 14 (1) of this Act.

(5) Subject to subsection (6) below, the period of operation of a direction under section 13 (2) of this Act given by virtue of this section shall be a period of six weeks beginning with the date on which the direction takes effect.

(6) Where a direction under section 13 (2) of this Act has been given in respect of a person by virtue of this section and the case has been referred to a tribunal in accordance with section 14 (1), the Secretary of State may from time to time, by notice in writing served on the person to whom the direction applies, extend or further extend the period of operation of the direction for a further twenty-eight days from the time when that period would otherwise expire, but shall not so extend or further extend that period without the consent of that tribunal, or, if the case has been referred to another tribunal in pursuance of section 14 (7) of this Act, of that other tribunal.

(7) A direction under section 13 (2) of this Act given in respect of a person by virtue of this section shall (unless previously cancelled under section 16 (3) of this Act) cease to have effect on the occurrence of any of the following events, that is to say—

(a) the service on that person of a notice under section 14 (3) of this Act relating to his case;

(b) the service on that person of a notice under section 14 (5) of this Act relating to his case stating that the Secretary of State does not propose to give a direction under section 13 (2) of this Act pursuant to a recommendation of the tribunal that such a direction should be given;

(c) the service on that person of a copy of such a direction given in respect of him in pursuance of section 14 (7) of this Act;

(d) the making of an order by the Secretary of State in pursuance of section 14 (7) that no further proceedings under section 14 shall be taken in the case;

(e) the expiration of the period of operation of the direction under section 13 (2) given by virtue of this section.

16. Provisions supplementary to ss. 14 and 15

(1) The provisions of Schedule 3 to this Act shall have effect with respect to the constitution and procedure of any tribunal, advisory body or professional panel appointed for the purposes of section 14 or 15 of this Act, and with respect to the other matters there mentioned.

(2) The Secretary of State shall cause a copy of any order or direction made or given by him in pursuance of section 14 (7) of this Act or any direction given by him by virtue of the said section 15 to be served on the person to whom it applies and shall cause notice of any such direction, and a copy of any notice served under section 15 (6) of this Act, to be published in the London, Edinburgh and Belfast Gazettes.

(3) The Secretary of State may at any time give a direction—

(a) cancelling or suspending any direction given by him in pursuance of section 14 (7) of this Act or cancelling any direction of his under this subsection by which a direction so given is suspended; or

(b) cancelling any direction given by him by virtue of section 15 of this Act.

and shall cause a copy of any direction of his under this subsection to be served on the person to whom it applies and notice of it to be published as aforesaid.

(4) A direction given under section 13 (1) or (2) of this Act or under subsection (3) above shall take effect when a copy of it is served on the person to whom it applies.

17. Power to obtain information from doctors, pharmacists etc. in certain circumstances

(1) If it appears to the Secretary of State that there exists in any area in Great Britain a social problem cause by the extensive misuse of dangerous or otherwise harmful drugs in that area, he may by notice in writing served on any doctor or pharmacist practising in or in the vicinity of that area, or on any person carrying on a retail pharmacy business within the meaning of the Medicines Act 1968 at any premises situated in or in the vicinity of that area, require him to furnish to the Secretary of State, with respect to any such drugs specified in the notice and as regards any period so specified, such particulars as may be so specified relating to the quantities in which and the number and frequency of the occasions on which those drugs—

(a) in the case of a doctor, were prescribed, administered or supplied by him:

(b) in the case of a pharmacist, were supplied by him; or

(c) in the case of a person carrying on a retail pharmacy business, were supplied in the course of that business at any premises so situated which may be specified in the notice.

(2) A notice under this section may require any such particulars to be furnished in such manner and within such time as may be specified in the notice and, if served on a pharmacist or person carrying on a retail pharmacy business, may require him to furnish the names and addresses of doctors on whose prescriptions any dangerous or otherwise harmful drugs to which the notice relates were supplied, but shall not require any person to furnish any particulars relating to the identity of any person for or to whom any such drug has been prescribed, administered or supplied.

(3) A person commits an offence if without reasonable excuse (proof of which shall lie on him) he fails to comply with any requirement to which he is subject by virtue of subsection (1) above.

(4) A person commits an offence if in purported compliance with a requirement imposed under this section he gives any information which he knows to be false in a material particular or recklessly gives any information which is so false.

(5) In its application to Northern Ireland this section shall have effect as if for the references to Great Britain and the Secretary of State there were substituted respectively references to Northern Ireland and the Ministry of Home Affairs for Northern Ireland.

Miscellaneous offences and powers

18. Miscellaneous offences

(1) It is an offence for a person to contravene any regulations made under this Act other than regulations made in pursuance of section 10 (2) (h) or (i).

(2) It is an offence for a person to contravene a condition or other term of a licence issued under section 3 of this Act or of a licence or other authority issued under regulations made under this Act, not being a licence issued under regulations made in pursuance of section 10 (2) (i).

(3) A person commits an offence if, in purported compliance with any obligation to given information to which he is subject under or by virtue of regulations made under this Act, he gives any information which he knows to be false in a material particular or recklessly gives any information which is so false.

(4) A person commits an offence if, for the purpose of obtaining, whether for himself or another, the issue or renewal of a licence or other authority under this Act or under any regulations made under this Act, he—

(a) makes any statement or gives any information which he knows to be false in a material particular or recklessly gives any information which is so false; or

(b) produces or otherwise makes use of any book, record or other document which to his knowledge contains any statement or information which he knows to be false in a material particular.

19. Attempts etc. to commit offences

It is an offence for a person to attempt to commit an offence under any other provision of this Act or to incite or attempt to incite another to commit such an offence.

20. Assisting in or inducing commission outside United Kingdom of offence punishable under a corresponding law

A person commits an offence if in the United Kingdom he assists in or induces the commission in any place outside the United Kingdom of an offence punishable under the provisions of a corresponding law in force in that place.

21. Offences by corporations

Where any offence under this Act committed by a body corporate is proved to have been committed with the consent or connivance of, or to be attributable to any neglect on the part of, any director, manager, secretary or other similar officer of the body corporate, or any person purporting to act in any such capacity, he as well as the body corporate shall be guilty of that offence and shall be liable to be proceeded against accordingly.

22. Further powers to make regulations

The Secretary of State may by regulations make provision—
  (a) for excluding such cases as may be prescribed—
    (i)   the application of any provision of this Act which creates an offence; or
    (ii) the application of any of the following provisions of the Customs and Excise Act 1952, that is to say sections 45 (1), 56 (2) and 304, in so far as they apply in relation to a prohibition or restriction on importation or exportation having effect by virtue of section 3 of this Act;
  (b) for applying any of the provisions of sections 14 to 16 of this Act and Schedule 3 thereto, with such modifications (if any) as may be prescribed—
    (i)   in relation to any proposal by the Secretary of State to give a direction under section 12 (2) of this Act; or
    (ii) for such purposes of regulations under this Act as may be prescribed;
  (c) for the application of any of the provisions of this Act or regulations or orders thereunder to servants or agents of the Crown, subject to such exceptions, adaptations and modifications as may be prescribed.

Law enforcement and punishment of offences

23. Power to search and obtain evidence

(1) A constable or other person authorised in that behalf by a general or special order of the Secretary of State (or in Northern Ireland either of the Secretary of State or the Ministry of Home Affairs for Northern Ireland) shall, for the purposes of the execution of this Act, have power to enter the premises of a person carrying on business as a producer or supplier of any controlled drugs and to demand the production of, and to inspect, any books or documents relating to dealings in any such drugs and to inspect any stocks of any such drugs.

(2) If a constable has reasonable grounds to suspect that any person is in possession of a controlled drug in contravention of this Act or of any regulations made thereunder, the constable may—

    (a) search that person, and detain him for the purpose of searching him;

    (b) search any vehicle or vessel in which the constable suspects that the drug may be found, and for that purpose require the person in control of the vehicle or vessel to stop it;

    (c) seize and detain, for the purposes of proceedings under this Act, anything found in the course of the search which appears to the constable to be evidence of an offence under this Act.

In this subsection 'vessel' includes a hovercraft within the meaning of the Hovercraft Act 1968; and nothing in this subsection shall prejudice any power of search or any power to seize or detain property which is exercisable by a constable apart from this subsection.

(3) If a justice of the peace (or in Scotland a justice of the peace, a magistrate or a sheriff) is satisfied by information on oath that there is reasonable ground for suspecting—

    (a) that any controlled drugs are, in contravention of this Act or of any regulations made thereunder, in the possession of a person on any premises; or

    (b) that a document directly or indirectly relating to, or connected with, a transaction or dealing which was, or an intended transaction or dealing which would if carried out be, an offence under this Act, or in the case of a transaction or dealing carried out or intended to be carried out in a place outside the United Kingdom, an offence against the provisions of a corresponding law in force in that place, is in the possession of a person on any premises,

he may grant a warrant authorising any constable acting for the police area in which the premises are situated at any time or times within one month from the date of the warrant, to enter, if need be by force, the premises named in the warrant, and to search the premises and any persons found therein and, if there is reasonable ground for suspecting that an offence under this Act has been committed in relation to any controlled drugs found on the premises or in the possession of any such persons, or that a document so found is such a document as is mentioned in paragraph (b) above, to seize and detain those drugs or that document, as the case may be.

(4) A person commits an offence if he—

    (a) intentionally obstructs a person in the exercise of his powers under this section; or

    (b) conceals from a person acting in the exercise of his power under subsection (1) above any such books, documents, stocks or drugs as are mentioned in that subsection; or

    (c) without reasonable excuse (proof of which shall lie on him) fails to produce any such books or documents as are so mentioned where their production is demanded by a person in the exercise of his powers under that subsection.

(5) In its application to Northern Ireland subsection (3) above shall have effect as if the words 'acting for the police area in which the premises are situated' were omitted.

24. Power of arrest
(1) A constable may arrest without warrant a person who has committed, or whom the constable, with reasonable cause, suspects to have committed, an offence under this Act, if—
- (a) he, with reasonable cause, believes that that person will abscond unless arrested; or
- (b) the name and address of that person are unknown to, and cannot be ascertained by, him; or
- (c) he is not satisfied that a name and address furnished by that person as his name and address are true.

(2) This section shall not prejudice any power of arrest conferred by law apart from this section.

25. Prosecution and punishment of offences
(1) Schedule 4 to this Act shall have effect, in accordance with subsection (2) below, with respect to the way in which offences under this Act are punishable on conviction.

(2) In relation to an offence under a provision of this Act specified in the first column of the Schedule (the general nature of the offence being described in the second column)—
- (a) the third column shows whether the offence is punishable on summary conviction or on indictment or in either way;
- (b) the fourth, fifth and sixth columns show respectively the punishments which may be imposed on a person convicted of the offence in the way specified in relation thereto in the third column (that is to say, summarily or on indictment) according to whether the controlled drug in relation to which the offence was committed was a Class A drug, a Class B drug or a Class C drug; and
- (c) the seventh column shows the punishments which may be imposed on a person convicted of the offence in the way specified in relation thereto in the third column (that is to say, summarily or on indictment), whether or not the offence was committed in relation to a controlled drug and, if it was so committed, irrespective of whether the drug was a Class A drug, a Class B drug or a Class C drug;

and in the fourth, fifth, sixth and seventh columns a reference to a period gives the maximum term of imprisonment and a reference to a sum of money the maximum fine.

(3) An offence under section 19 of this Act shall be punishable on summary conviction, on indictment or in either way according to whether, under Schedule 4 to this Act, the substantive offence is punishable on summary conviction, on indictment or in either way; and the punishments which may be imposed on a person convicted of an offence under that section are the same as those which, under that Schedule, may be imposed on a person convicted of the substantive offence.

In this subsection 'the substantive offence' means the offence under this Act to which the attempt or, as the case may be, the incitement or attempted incitement mentioned in section 19 was directed.

26. [*Repealed*]

27. Forfeiture

(1) Subject to subsection (2) below, the court by or before which a person is convicted of an offence under this act may order anything shown to the satisfaction of the court to relate to the offence, to be forfeited and either destroyed or dealt with in such other manner as the court may order.

(2) The court shall not order anything to be forfeited under this section, where a person claiming to be the owner of or otherwise interested in it applies to be heard by the court, unless an opportunity has been given to him to show cause why the order should not be made.

Miscellaneous and supplementary provisions
28. Proof of lack of knowledge etc. to be a defence in proceedings for certain offences

(1) This section applies to offences under any of the following provisions of this Act, that is to say section 4 (2) and (3), section 5 (2) and (3), section 6 (2) and section 9.

(2) Subject to subsection (3) below, in any proceedings for an offence to which this section applies it shall be a defence for the accused to prove that he neither knew of nor suspected nor had reason to suspect the existence of some fact alleged by the prosecution which it is necessaryy for the prosecution to prove if he is to be convicted of the offence charged.

(3) Where in any proceedings for an offence to which this section applies it is necessary, if the accused is to be convicted of the offence charged, for the prosecution to prove that some substance or product involved in the alleged offence was the controlled drug which the prosecution alleges it to have been, and it is proved that the substance or product in question was that controlled drug, the accused—

  (a) shall not be acquitted of the offence charged by reason only of proving that he neither knew nor suspected nor had reason to suspect that the substance or product in question was the particular controlled drug alleged; but

  (b) shall be acquitted thereof—

    (i) if he proves that he neither believed nor suspected nor had reason to suspect that the substance or product in question was a controlled drug; or

    (ii) if he proves that he believed the substance or product in question to be a controlled drug, or a controlled drug of a description, such that, if it had in fact been that controlled drug or a controlled drug of that description, he would not at the material time have been committing any offence to which this section applies.

(4) Nothing in this section shall prejudice any defence which it is open to a person charged with an offence to which this section applies to raise apart from this section.

29. Service of documents

(1) Any notice or other document required or authorised by any provision of this Act to be served on any person may be served on him either by delivering it to him or by leaving it at his proper address or by sending it by post.

(2) Any notice or other document so required or authorised to be served on a body corporate shall be duly served if it is served on the secretary or clerk of that body.

(3) For the purposes of this section, and of section 26 of the Interpretation Act 1889 in its application to this section, the proper address of any person shall, in the case of the secretary or clerk of a body corporate, be that of the registered or principal office of that body, and in any other case shall be the last address of the person to be served which is known to the Secretary of State.

(4) Where any of the following documents, that is to say—

(a) a notice under section 11 (1) or section 15 (6) of this Act; or

(b) a copy of a direction given under section 12 (2), section 13 (1) or (2) or section 16 (3) of this Act,

is served by sending it by registered post or by the recorded delivery service, service thereof shall be deemed to have been effected at the time when the letter containing it would be delivered in the ordinary course of post; and so much of section 26 of the Interpretation Act 1889 as relates to the time when service by post is deemed to have been effected shall not apply to such a document if it is served by so sending it.

30. Licences and authorites

A licence or other authority issued by the Secretary of State for purposes of this Act or of regulations made under this Act may be, to any degree, general or specific, may be issued on such terms and subject to such conditions (including in the case of a licence, the payment of a prescribed fee) as the Secretary of State thinks proper, and may be modified or revoked by him at any time.

31. General provisions as to regulations

(1) Regulations made by the Secretary of State under any provision of this Act—

(a) may make different provision in relation to different controlled drugs, different classes of persons, different provisions of this Act or other different cases or circumstances; and

(b) may make the opinion, consent or approval of a prescribed authority or of any person authorised in a prescribed manner material for purposes of any provision of the regulations; and

(c) may contain such supplementary, incidental and transitional provisions as appear expedient to the Secretary of State.

(2) Any power of the Secretary of State to make regulations under this Act shall be exercisable by statutory instrument, which shall be subject to annulment in pursuance of a resolution of either House of Parliament.

(3) The Secretary of State shall not make any regulations under this Act except after consultation with the Advisory Council.

(4) In its application to Northern Ireland this section shall have effect as if for references to the Secretary of State there were substituted references to the Ministry of Home Affairs for Northern Ireland and as if for subsection (2) there were substituted—

'(2) Any regulations made under this Act by the Ministry of Home Affairs for Northern Ireland shall be subject to negative resolution

within the meaning of section 41 (6) of the Interpretation Act
(Northern Ireland) 1954 as if they were a statutory instrument within
the meaning of that Act.'

32. Research
The Secretary of State may conduct or assist in conducting research into
any matter relating to the misuse of dangerous or otherwise harmful
drugs.

33. Amendement of Extradition Act 1870
The Extradition Act 1870 shall have effect as if conspiring to commit any
offence against any enactment for the time being in force relating to
dangerous drugs were included in the list of crimes in Schedule 1 to that
Act.

34. Amendement of Matrimonial Proceedings (Magistrates' Courts) Act 1960
In the definition of 'drug addict' contained in section 16 (1) of the
Matrimonial Proceedings (Magistrates' Courts) Act 1960, for the words
from 'any drug' to 'applies' there shall be substituted the words 'any
controlled drug within the meaning of the Misuse of Drugs Act 1971'.

35. Financial provisions
There shall be defrayed out of moneys provided by Parliament—
   (a) any expenses incurred by the Secretary of State under or in
       consequence of the provisions of this Act other than section 32; and
   (b) any expenses incurred by the Secretary of State with the consent of
       the Treasury for the purposes of his functions under that section.

36. Meaning of 'corresponding law', and evidence of certain matters by certificate
(1) In this Act the expression 'corresponding law' means a law stated in a
certificate purporting to be issued by or on behalf of the government of a
country outside the United Kingdom to be a law providing for the control
and regulation in that country of the production, supply, use, export and
import of drugs and other substances in accordance with the provisions of
the Single convention on Narcotic Drugs signed at New York on 30th
March 1961 or a law providing for the control and regulation in that
country of the production, supply, use, export and import of dangerous or
otherwise harmful drugs in pursuance of any treaty, convention or other
agreement or arrangement to which the government of that country and
Her Majesty's Government in the United Kingdom are for the time being
parties.

(2) A statement in any such certificate as aforesaid to the effect that any
facts constitute an offence against the law mentioned in the certificate
shall be evidence and in Scotland sufficient evidence of the matters stated.

37. Interpretation
(1) In this Act, except in so far as the context otherwise requires, the
following expressions have the meanings hereby assigned to them
respectively, that is to say:—
   'the Advisory Council' means the Advisory Council on the Misuse of
       Drugs established under this Act;

'cannabis' (except in the expression 'cannabis resin') means any plant of the genus *Cannabis* or any part of any such plant (by whatever name designated) except that it does not include cannabis resin or any of the following products after separation from the rest of the plant, namely—

   (a)   mature stalk of any such plant,
   (b)   fibre produced from mature stalk of any such plant, and
   (c)   seed of any such plant;

'contravention' includes failure to comply, and 'contravene' has a corresponding meaning'

'controlled drug' has the meaning assigned by section 2 of this act;

'corresponding law' has the meaning assigned by section 36 (1) of this Act;

'dentist' means a person registered in the dentists register under the Dentists Act 1957;

'doctor' means a fully registered person within the meaning of the Medical Acts 1956 to 1969;

'enactment' includes an enactment of the Parliament of Northern Ireland;

'person lawfully conducting a retail pharmacy business', subject to subsection (5) below, means a person lawfully conducting such a business in accordance with section 69 of the Medicines Act 1968;

'pharmacist' has the same meaning as in the Medicines Act 1968;

'practitioner' (except in the expression 'veterinary practitioner') means a doctor, dentist, veterinary practitioner or veterinary surgeon;

'prepared opium' means opium prepared ·for smoking and includes dross and any other residues remaining after opium has been smoked;

'prescribed' means prescribed by regulations made by the Secretary of State under this Act;

'produce' where the reference is to producing a controlled drug, means producing it by manufacture, cultivation or any other method and 'production' has a corresponding meaning;

'supplying' includes distributing;

'veterinary practitioner' means a person registered in the supplementary veterinary register kept under section 8 of the Veterinary Surgeons Act 1966;

'veterinary surgeon' means a person registered in the register of veterinary surgeons kept under section 2 of the Veterinary Surgeons Act 1966.

(2) References in this Act to misusing a drug are references to misusing it by taking it; and the reference in the foregoing provision to the taking of a drug is a reference to the taking of it by a human being by way of any form of self-administration, whether or not involving assistance by another.

(3) For the purposes of this Act the things which a person has in his possession shall be taken to include any thing subject to his control which is in the custody of another.

(4) Except in so far as the context otherwise requires, any reference in this Act to an enactment shall be construed as a reference to that enactment as amended, or extended by or under any other enactment.

(5) So long as sections 8 to 10 of the Pharmacy and Poisons Act 1933 remain in force, this Act in its application to Great Britain shall have effect as if for the definition of 'person lawfully conducting a retail pharmacy business' in subsection (1) above there were substituted—

'person lawfully conducting a retail pharmacy business' means an authorised seller of poisons within the meaning of the Pharmacy and Poisons Act 1933;'

and so long as sections 16 to 18 of the Medicines, Pharmacy and Poisons Act (Northern Ireland) 1945 remain in force, this Act in its application to Northern Ireland shall have effect as if for the definition of 'person lawfully conducting a retail pharmacy business' in subsection (1) above there were substituted—

'person lawfully conducting a retail pharmacy business' means an authorised seller of poisons within the meaning of the Medicines, Pharmacy and Poisons Act (Northern Ireland) 1945;'.

38. Special provisions as to Northern Ireland

(1) In the application of this Act to Northern Ireland, for any reference to the Secretary of State (except in sections 1, 2, 7, 17, 23(1), 31, 35, 39(3) and 40(3) and Schedules 1 and 3) there shall be substituted a reference to the Ministry of Home Affairs for Northern Ireland.

(2) Nothing in this Act shall authorise any department of the Government of Northern Ireland to incur any expenses attributable to the provisions of this Act until provision has been made by the Parliament of Northern Ireland for those expenses to be defrayed out of moneys provided by that Parliament; and no expenditure shall be incurred by the Ministry of Home Affairs for Northern Ireland for the purposes of its functions under section 32 of this Act except with the consent of the Ministry of Finance for Northern Ireland.

(3) This Act shall be deemed for the purposes of section 6 of the Government of Ireland Act 1920 to have been passed before the day appointed for the purposes of that section.

(4) Without prejudice to section 37 (4) of this Act, any reference in this Act to an enactment of the Parliament of Northern Ireland includes a reference to any enactment re-enacting it with or without modifications.

39. Savings and transitional provisions, repeals, and power to amend local enactments

(1) The savings and transitional provisions contained in Schedule 5 to this Act shall have effect.

(2) The enactments mentioned in Schedule 6 to this Act are hereby repealed to the extent specified in the third column of that Schedule.

(3) The Secretary of State may by order made by statutory instrument subject to annulment in pursuance of a resolution of either House of Parliament repeal or amend any provision in any local Act, including an Act confirming a provisional order, or in any instrument in the nature of a local enactment under any Act, where it appears to him that that provision is inconsistent with, or has become unnecessary or requires modification in consequence of, any provision of this Act.

40. Short title, extent and commencement

(1) This Act may be cited as the Misuse of Drugs Act 1971.

(2) This Act extends to Northern Ireland.

(3) This Act shall come into operation on such day as the Secretary of State may by order made by statutory instrument appoint, and different dates may be appointed under this subsection for different purposes.

SCHEDULES

SCHEDULE 1

Section 1

CONSTITUTION ETC. OF ADVISORY COUNCIL ON THE MISUSE OF DRUGS

1. (1) The members of the Advisory Council, of whom there shall be not less than twenty, shall be appointed by the Secretary of State after consultation with such organisations as he considers appropriate, and shall include—
   - (a) in relation to each of the activities specified in sub-paragraph (2) below, at least one person appearing to the Secretary of State to have wide and recent experience of that activity; and
   - (b) persons appearing to the Secretary of State to have wide and recent experience of social problems connected with the misuse of drugs.

   (2) The activities referred to in sub-paragraph (1) (a) above are—
   - (a) the practice of medicine (other than veterinary medicine);
   - (b) the practice of dentistry;
   - (c) the practice of veterinary medicine;
   - (d) the practice of pharmacy;
   - (e) the pharmaceutical industry;
   - (f) chemistry other than pharmaceutical chemistry.

   (3) The Secretary of State shall appoint one of the members of the Advisory Council to be chairman of the Council.

2. The advisory Countil may appoint committees, which may consist in part of persons who are not members of the Council, to consider and report to the Council on any matter referred to them by the Council.

3. At meetings of the Advisory Council the quorum shall be seven, and subject to that the Council may determine their own procedure.

4. The Secretary of State may pay to the members of the Advisory Council such remuneration (if any) and such travelling and other allowances as may be determined by him with the consent of the Minister for the Civil Service.

5. Any expenses incurred by the Advisory Council with the approval of the Secretary of State shall be defrayed by the Secretary of State.

SCHEDULE 2

Section 2

PART I: CLASS A DRUGS

(a) The following substances and products, namely—

Acetorphine.	Benerethidine.
Allylprodine.	Benzylmorphine (3-benzylmorphine).
Alphacetylmethadol.	Betacetylmethadol.
Alphameprodine.	Betameprodine.
Alphamethadol.	Betamethadol.
Alphaprodine	Betaprodine.
Anileridine.	Bezitramide.

Bufotenine.

Cannabinol, except where contained in cannabis or cannabis resin.

Cannabinol derivatives [see Pt. IV, *post* for definition].

Clonitazene.

Coca leaf [see Pt. IV, *post* for definition].

Cocaine.

Desomorphine.

Dextromoramide.

Diamorphine.

Diampromide.

Diethylthiambutene.

Difenoxin (1-(3-cyano-3, 3-diphenyl propyl)-4-phenylpiperidine-4-caboxylic acid)

Dihydrocodeinone O-barboxymethyl-oxime.

Dihydromorphine.

Dimenoxadole.

Dimepheptanol.

Dimethylthiambutene.

Dioxaphetyl butyrate.

Diphenoxylate.

Dipipanone.

Drotebanol (3, 4-dimethoxy-17- Methyl-morphinan-6β, 14-diol)

Ecgonine, and any derivative of ecgonine which is convertible to ecgonine or to cocaine.

Ethylmethylthiambutene.

Etonitazene.

Etorphine.

Etoxeridine.

Fentanyl.

Furethidine.

Hydrocodone.

Hydromorphinol.

Hydromorphone.

Hydroxypethidine.

Isomethadone.

Ketobemidone.

Levomethorphan.

Levomoramide.

Levophenacylmorphan.

Levorphanol.

Lysergamide.

Lysergide and other N-alkyl derivatives of lysergamide.

Mescaline.

Metazocine.

Methadone.

Methadyl acetate.

Methyldesorphine.

Methyldihydromorphine (6-methyl-dihydromorphine).

Metopon.

Morpheridine.

Morphine.

Morphine methobromide, morphine N-oxide and other pentavalent nitrogen morphine derivatives.

Myrophine.

Nicomorphine (3,6-dinicotinoylmorphine).

Noracymethadol.

Norlevorphanol.

Normethadone.

Normorphine.

Norpipanone.

Opium, whether raw, prepared or medicinal [see pt. IV, *post* for definition].

Oxycodone.

Oxymorphone.

Pethidine.

Phenadoxone.

Phenampromide.

Phenazocine.

Phencyclidine.

Phenomorphan.

Phenoperidine.

Piminodine.

Piritramide.

Poppy-straw and concentrate of poppy-straw [see Pt. IV, *post* for definition].

Proheptazine.

Properidine (1-methyl-4-phenyl-piperidine-4-carboxylic acid isopropyl ester).

Psilocin.

Racemethorphan.

Racemoramide.

Racemorphan.

Sufentanil.

Thebacon.

Thebaine.

Tilidate.

Trimeperidine.

4-Bromo-2,5-dimethoxy-α-methyl-phenethylamine.

4-Cyano-2-dimethylamino-4, 4-diphenylbutane.

4-Cyano-1-methyl-4-phenyl-piperidine.

N,N-Diethyltryptamine.

N,N-Dimethyltryptamine.

2,5-Dimethyoxy-α,4-dimethylphene-thylamine.

1-Methyl-4-phenylpiperidine-4-carboxylic acid.

2-Methyl-3-morpholino-1, 1 diphenyl-propanecarboxylic acid.

4-Phenylpiperidine-4-carboxylic acid ethyl ester.

(b) any compound (not being a compound for the time being specified in sub-paragraph (a) above) structurally derived from tryptamine or from a ring-hydroxy tryptamine by substitution at the nitrogen atom of the sidechain with one or more alkyl substituents but no other substituent;

(c) any compound (not being methoxyphenamine or a compound for the time being specified in sub-paragraph (a) above) structurally derived from phenethylamine, an *N*-alkylphenethylamine, α-methylphenethylamine, an *N*-alkyl-α-methylphenethylamine, α-ethylphenethylamine, or an *N*-alkyl-α-ethylphenethylamine by substitution in the ring to any extent with alkyl, alkoxy, alkylenedioxy or halide substituents, whether or not further substituted in the ring by one or more other univalent substituents.

2. Any stereoisomeric form of a substance for the time being specified in paragraph 1 above not being dextromethorphan or dextrorphan.

3. Any ester or ether of a substance for the time being specified in paragraph 1 or 2 above not being a substance for the time being specified in Part II of this Schedule.

4. Any salt of a substance for the time being specified in any of paragraphs 1 to 3 above.

5. Any preparation or other product containing a substance or product for the time being specified in any of paragraphs 1 to 4 above.

6. Any preparation designed for administration by injection which includes a substance or product for the time being specified in any of paragraphs 1 to 3 of Part II of this Schedule.

PART II: CLASS B DRUGS

1. The following substances and products, namely—

Acetyldihydrocodeine	Methylphenidate
Amphetamine	Nicocodine
Cannabis and cannabis resin	Nicodilodine (6-nicotinoyldihydro
Codeine	-codeine)
Dexamphetamine	Norcodeine
Dihydrocodeine	Phenmetrazine
Ethylmorphine (3-ethylmorphine)	Pholcodine
Methylamphetamine	Propiram

2. Any stereoisomeric form of a substance for the time being specified in paragraph 1 of this Part of this Schedule.

3. Any salt of a substance for the time being specified in paragraph 1 or 2 of this Part of this Schedule.

4. Any preparation or other product containing a substance or product for the time being specified in any of paragraphs 1 to 3 of this Part of this Schedule, not being a preparation falling within paragraph 6 of Part I of this Schedule.

PART III: CLASS C DRUGS

1. The following substances, namely—

Benzphetamine	Methaqualone
Chlorphentermine	Phendimetrazine
Dextropropoxyphene	Pipradol
Mephentermine	

2. Any stereoisomeric form of a substance for the time being specified in paragraph 1 of this Part of this Schedule.

3. Any salt of a substance for the time being specified in paragraph 1 or 2 of this Part of this Schedule.

4. Any preparation or other product containing a substance for the time being specified in any of paragraphs 1 to 3 of this Part of this Schedule.

PART IV: MEANING OF CERTAIN EXPRESSIONS USED IN THIS SCHEDULE

For the purposes of this Schedule the following expressions (which are not among those defined in section 37 (1) of this Act) have the meanings hereby assigned to them respectively, that is to say—

'Cannabinol derivatives' means the following substances, except where contained in cannabis or cannabis resin, namely tetrahydro derivatives of cannabinol and 3-alkyl homologues of cannabinol or of its tetrahydro derivatives;

'coca leaf' means the leaf of any plant of the genus *Erythroxylon* from whose leaves cocaine can be extracted either directly or by chemical transformation;

'concentrate of poppy-straw' means the material produced when poppy-straw has entered into a process for the concentration of its alkaloids;

'medicinal opium' means raw opium which has undergone the process necessary to adapt it for medicinal use in accordance with the requirements of the British Pharmacopoeia, whether it is in the form of powder or is granulated or is in any other form, and whether it is or is not mixed with neutral substances;

'opium poppy' means the plant of the species *Papaver somniferum* L;

'poppy straw' means all parts, except the seeds, of the opium poppy, after mowing;

'raw opium' includes powdered or granulated opium but does not include medicinal opium.

SCHEDULE 3

Section 16

Tribunals, Advisory Bodies and Professional Panels

PART I: TRIBUNALS

Membership

1. (1) A tribunal shall consist of five persons of whom—
    (a) one shall be a barrister, advocate or solicitor of not less than seven years' standing appointed by the Lord Chancellor to be the chairman of the tribunal; and
    (b) the other four shall be persons appointed by the Secretary of State from among members of the respondent's profession nominated for the purposes of this Schedule by any of the relevant bodies mentioned in sub-paragraph (2) below.
    (2) The relevant bodies aforesaid are—
    (a) where the respondent is a doctor, the General Medical Council, the Royal Colleges of Physicians of London and Edinburgh, the Royal Colleges of Surgeons of England and Edinburgh, the Royal College of Physicians and Surgeons (Glasgow), the Royal College of Obstetricians and Gynaecologists, the Royal College of General Practitioners, the Royal Medico-Psychological Association and the British Medical Association;
    (b) where the respondent is a dentist, the General Dental Council and the British Dental Association;
    (c) where the respondent is a veterinary practitioner or veterinary surgeon, the Royal College of Veterinary Surgeons and the British Veterinary Association.
    (3) (*Applies to Scotland*).

Procedure

2. The quorum of a tribunal shall be the chairman and two other members of the tribunal.

3. Proceedings before a tribunal shall be held in private unless the respondent requests otherwise and the tribunal accedes to the request.

4. (1) Subject to paragraph 5 below, the Lord Chancellor may make rules as to the procedure to be followed, and the rules of evidence to be observed, in proceedings before tribunals, and in particular—

(a) for securing that notice that the proceedings are to be brought shall be given to the respondent at such time and in such manner as may be specified by the rules;

(b) for determining who, in addition to the respondent, shall be a party to the proceedings;

(c) for securing that any party to the proceedings shall, if he so requires, be entitled to be heard by the tribunal;

(d) for enabling any party to the proceedings to be represented by counsel or solicitor.

(2) (*Applies to Scotland.*)

(3) The power to make rules under this paragraph shall be exercisable by statutory instrument, which shall be subject to annulment in pursuance of a resolution of either House of Parliament.

5. (1) For the purpose of any proceedings before a tribunal in England or Wales or Northern Ireland the tribunal may administer oaths and any party to the proceedings may sue out writs of subpoena and testificandum and duces tecum, but no person shall be compelled under any such writ to give any evidence or produce any document which he could not be compelled to give or produce on the trial of an action.

(2) The provisions of section 49 of the Supreme Court of Judicature (Consolidation) Act 1925, or of the Attendance of Witnesses Act 1854 (which provide special procedures for the issue of such writs so as to be in force throughout the United Kingdom) shall apply in relation to any proceedings before a tribunal in England or Wales or, as the case may be, in Northern Ireland as those provisions apply in relation to causes or matters in the High Court or actions or suits pending in the High Court of Justice in Northern Ireland.

(3) (*Applies to Scotland.*)

6. Subject to the foregoing provisions of this Schedule, a tribunal may regulate its own procedure.

7. The validity of the proceedings of a tribunal shall not be affected by any defect in the appointment of a member of the tribunal or by reason of the fact that a person not entitled to do so took part in the proceedings.

Financial provisions

8. The Secretary of State may pay to any member of a tribunal fees and travelling and other allowances in respect of his services in accordance with such scales and subject to such conditions as the Secretary of State may determine with the approval of the Treasury.

9. The Secretary of State may pay to any person who attends as a witness before the tribunal sums by way of compensation for the loss of his time and travelling and other allowances in accordance with such scales and subject to such conditions as may be determined as aforesaid.

10. If a tribunal recommends to the Secretary of State that the whole or part of the expenses properly incurred by the respondent for the purposes of proceedings before the tribunal should be defrayed out of public funds, the Secretary of State may if he thinks fit make to the respondent such payments in respect of those expenses as the Secretary of State considers appropriate.

11. Any expenses incurred by a tribunal with the approval of the Secretary of State shall be defrayed by the Secretary of State.

Supplemental

12. The Secretary of State shall make available to a tribunal such accommodation, the services of such officers and such other facilities as he considers appropriate for the purpose of enabling the tribunal to perform its functions.

Part II: Advisory Bodies

Membership

13. (1) An advisory body shall consist of three persons of whom—

(a) one shall be a person who is of counsel to Her Majesty and is appointed by the Lord Chancellor to be the chairman of the advisory body; and

(b) another shall be a person appointed by the Secretary of State, being a member of the respondent's profession who is an officer of a department of the Government of the United Kingdom; and

(c) the other shall be a person appointed by the Secretary of State from among the members of the respondent's proofession nominated as mentioned in paragraph 1 above.

(2) (*Applies to Scotland.*)

Procedure

14. The respondent shall be entitled to appear before and be heard by the advisory body either in person or by counsel or solicitor.

15. Subject to the provisions of this Part of this Schedule, an advisory body may regulate its own procedure.

Application of provisions of Part I

16. Paragraphs 3, 7, 8 and 10 to 12 of this Schedule shall apply in relation to an advisory body as they apply in relation to a tribunal.

Part III: Professional Panels

Membership

17. A professional panel shall consist of a chairman and two other persons appointed by the Secretary of State from among the members of the respondent's profession after consultation with such one or more of the relevant bodies mentioned in paragraph 1 (2) above as the Secretary of State considers appropriate.

Procedure

18. The respondent shall be entitled to appear before, and be heard by, the professional panel either in person or by counsel or solicitor.

19. Subject to the provisions of this Part of this Schedule, a professional panel may regulate its own procedure.

Application of provisions of Part I

20. Paragraphs 3, 7 and 8 of this Schedule shall apply in relation to a professional panel as they apply in relation to a tribunal.

Part IV: Application of Parts I to III to Northern Ireland

21. In the application of Parts I to III of this Schedule to Northern Ireland the provisions specified in the first column of the following Table shall have effect subject to the modifications specified in relation thereto in the second column of that Table.

TABLE

Provision of this Schedule	*Modification*
Paragraph 1	In sub-paragraph (1), for the references to the Lord Chancellor and the Secretary of State there shall be substituted respectively references to the Lord Chief Justice of Northern Ireland and the Minister of Home Affairs for Northern Ireland.
Paragraph 4	In sub-paragraph (1), for the reference to the Lord Chancellor there shall be substituted a reference to the Ministry of Home Affairs for Northern Ireland. For sub-paragraph (3) there shall be substituted— '(3) Any rules made under this paragraph by the Ministry of Home Affairs for Northern Ireland shall be subject to negative resolution within the meaning of section 41 (6) of the Interpretation Act (Northern Ireland) 1954 as if they were a statutory instrument within the meaning of that Act.'
Paragraphs 8 to 12 ..	For the references to the Secretary of State and the Treasury there shall be substituted respectively references to the Ministry of Home Affairs for Northern Ireland and the Ministry of Finance for Northern Ireland.
Paragraph 13	In sub-paragraph (1)— (a) for the references to the Lord Chancellor and Secretary of State there shall be substituted respectively references to the Lord Chief Justice of Northern Ireland and the Minister of Home Affairs for Northern Ireland; and (b) for the reference to a department of the Government of the United Kingdom there shall be substituted a reference to a department of the Government of Northern Ireland.
Paragraph 16	The references to paragraphs 8 and 10 to 12 shall be construed as references to those paragraphs as modified by this Part of this Schedule.
Paragraph 17	For the reference to the Secretary of State there shall be substituted a reference to the Minister of Home Affairs for Northern Ireland.
Paragraph 20	The reference to paragraph 8 shall be construed as a reference to that paragraph as modified by this Part of this Schedule.

SCHEDULE 4

PROSECUTION AND PUNISHMENT OF OFFENCES

Section Creating Offence	General Nature of Offence	Mode of Prosecution	Punishment			
			Class A drug involved	Class B drug involved	Class C drug involved	General
Section 4 (2)	Production, or being concerned in the production, of a controlled drug.	(a) Summary	12 months or £400, or both.	12 months or £400, or both.	6 months or £200, or both.	
		(b) On indictment	14 years or a fine, or both.	14 years or a fine, or both.	5 years or a fine, or both.	
Section 4 (3)	Supplying or offering to supply a controlled drug or being concerned in the doing of either activity by another.	(a) Summary	12 months or £400, or both.	12 months or £400, or both.	6 months or £200, or both.	
		(b) On indictment	14 years or a fine, or both.	14 years or a fine, or both.	5 years or a fine, or both.	
Section 5 (2)	Having possession of a controlled drug.	(a) Summary	12 months or £400, or both.	6 months or £400, or both.	6 months or £200, or both.	
		(b) On indictment	7 years or a fine, or both.	5 years or a fine, or both.	2 years or a fine, or both.	
Section 5 (3)	Having possession of a controlled drug with intent to supply it to another.	(a) Summary	12 months or £400, or both.	12 months or £400, or both.	6 months or £200, or both.	
		(b) On indictment	14 years or a fine, or both.	14 years or a fine, or both.	5 years or a fine, or both.	
Section 6 (2)	Cultivation of cannabis plant	(a) Summary	—	—	—	12 months or £400, or both.
		(b) On indictment	—	—	—	14 years or a fine, or both.
Section 8	Being the occupier, or concerned in the management, of premises and permitting or suffering certain activities to take place there.	(a) Summary	12 months or £400, or both.	12 months or £400, or both.	6 months or £200, or both.	
		(b) On indictment	14 years or a fine or both.	14 years or a fine or both.	5 years or a fine, or both.	

Section	General nature of offence	Mode of prosecution				
Section 9	Offences relating to opium.	(a) Summary	—	—	—	12 months or £400, or both.
		(b) On indictment	—	—	—	14 years or a fine, or both.
Section 11 (2)	Contravention of directions relating to safe custody of controlled drugs.	(a) Summary	—	—	—	6 months or £400, or both.
		(b) On indictment	—	—	—	2 years or a fine, or both.
Section 12 (6)	Contravention of direction prohibiting practitioner etc. from possessing, supplying etc. controlled drugs.	(a) Summary	12 months or £400, or both.	12 months or £400, or both.	6 months or £200, or both.	
		(b) On indictment	14 years or a fine, or both.	14 years or a fine, or both.	5 years or a fine, or both.	
Section 13 (3)	Contravention of direction prohibiting practitioner etc. from prescribing, supplying etc. controlled drugs.	(a) Summary	12 months or £400, or both.	12 months or £400, or both.	6 months or £200, or both.	
		(b) On indictment	14 years or a fine, or both.	14 years or a fine, or both.	5 years or a fine, or both.	
Section 17 (3)	Failure to comply with notice requiring information relating to prescribing, supply etc. of drugs.	Summary	—	—	—	£100.
Section 17 (4)	Giving false information in purported compliance with notice requiring information relating to prescribing, supply etc. of drugs.	(a) Summary	—	—	—	6 months or £400, or both.
		(b) On indictment	—	—	—	2 years or a fine, or both.
Section 18 (1)	Contravention of regulations (other than regulations relating to addicts).	(a) Summary	—	—	—	6 months or £400, or both.
		(b) On indictment	—	—	—	2 years or a fine, or both.
Section 18 (2)	Contravention of terms of licence or other authority (other than licence issued under regulations relating to addicts).	(a) Summary	—	—	—	6 months or £400, or both.
		(b) On indictment	—	—	—	2 years or a fine, or both.

Section 25

SCHEDULE 4 (*contd.*)

PROSECUTION AND PUNISHMENT OF OFFENCES

Section Creating Offence	General Nature of Offence	Mode of Proosecution	Class A drug involved	Class B drug involved	Class C drug involved	General
Section 18 (3)	Giving false information in purported compliance with obligation to give information imposed under or by virtue of regulations.	(a) Summary	—	—	—	6 months or £400, or both.
		(b) On indictment	—	—	—	2 years or a fine, or both.
Section 18 (4)	Giving false information, or producing document etc. containing false statement etc., for purposes of obtaining issue or renewal of a licence or other authority.	(a) Summary	—	—	—	6 months or £400, or both.
		(b) On indictment	—	—	—	2 years or a fine, or both.
Section 20	Assisting in or inducing commission outside United Kingdom of an offence punishable under a corresponding law.	(a) Summary	—	—	—	12 months or £400, or both.
		(b) On indictment	—	—	—	14 years or a fine, or both.
Section 23 (4)	Obstructing exercise of powers of search etc. or concealing books, drugs etc.	(a) Summary	—	—	—	6 months or £400, or both.
		(b) On indictment	—	—	—	2 years or a fine, or both.

SCHEDULE 5

SAVINGS AND TRANSITIONAL PROVISIONS

1. (1) Any addiction regulations which could have been made under this Act shall not be invalidated by any repeal effected by this Act but shall have effect as if made under the provisions of this Act which correspond to the provisions under which the regulations were made; and the validity of any licence issued under any such adddiction regulations shall not be affected by any such repeal.

(2) Any order, rule or other instrument or document whatsoever made or issued, any direction given, and any other thing done, under or by virtue of any of the following provisions of the Dangerous Drugs Act 1967, that is to say section 1 (2), 2 or 3 or the Schedule, shall be deemed for the purposes of this Act to have been made, issued or done, as the case may be, under the corresponding provision of this Act; and anything begun under any of the said provisions of that Act may be continued under this Act as if begun under this Act.

(3) In this paragraph 'addiction regulations' means any regulations made under section 11 of the Dangerous Drugs Act 1965 which include provision for any of the matters for which regulations may be so made by virtue of section 1 (1) of the Dangerous Drugs Act 1967.

2. As from the coming into operation of section 3 of this Act any licence granted for the purpose of section 5 of the Drugs (Prevention of Misuse) Act 1964 or sections 2, 3 or 10 of the Dangerous Drugs Act 1965 shall have effect as if granted for the purposes of section 3 (2) of this Act.

3. (1) The Secretary of State may at any time before the coming into operation of section 12 of this Act give a direction under subsection (2) of that section in respect of any practitioner or pharmacist whose general authority under the Dangerous Drugs Regulations is for the time being withdrawn; but a direction given by virtue of this sub-paragraph shall not take effect until section 12 comes into operation, and shall not take effect at all if the general authority of the person concerned is restored before that section comes into operation.

(2) No direction under section 12 (2) of this Act shall be given by virtue of sub-paragraph (1) above in respect of a person while the withdrawal of his general authority under the Dangerous Drugs Regulations is suspended; but where, in the case of any practitioner or pharmacist whose general authority has been withdrawn, the withdrawal is suspended at the time when section 12 comes into operation, the Secretary of State may at any time give a direction under section 12 (2) in respect of him by virtue of this sub-paragraph unless the Secretary of State has previously caused to be served on him a notice stating that he is no longer liable to have such a direction given in respect of him by virtue of this sub-paragraph.

(3) In this paragraph 'the Dangerous Drugs Regulations' means, as regards Great Britain, the Dangerous Drugs (No. 2) Regulations 1964 or, as regards Northern Ireland, the Dangerous Drugs Regulations (Northern Ireland) 1965.

4. Subject to paragraphs 1 to 3 above, and without prejudice to the generality of section 31 (1) (c) of this Act, regulations made by the Secretary of State under any provision of this Act may include such provision as the Secretary of State thinks fit for effecting the transition from any provision made by or by virtue of any of the enactments repealed by this Act to any provision made by or by virtue of this Act, and in particular may provide for the continuation in force, with or without modifications, of any licence or other authority issued or having effect as if issued under or by virtue of any of those enactments.

5. For purposes of the enforcement of the enactments repealed by this Act as regards anything done or omitted before their repeal, any powers of search, entry, inspection, seizure of detention conferred by those enactments shall continue to be exercisable as if those enactments were still in force.

6. The mention of particular matters in this Schedule shall not prejudice the general application of section 38 (2) of the Interpretation Act 1889 with regard to the effect of repeals.

SCHEDULE 6

Section 39

REPEALS

Chapter	Short Title	Extent of Repeal
1964 c. 64	The Drugs (Prevention of Misuse) Act 1964)	The whole Act.
1965 c. 15	The Dangerous Drugs Act 1965	The whole Act.
1967 c. 82	The Dangerous Drugs Act 1967	The whole Act.
1968 c. 59	The Hovercraft Act 1968	Paragraph 6 of the Schedule.
1968 c. 67	The Medicines Act 1968	In Schedule 5, paragraphs 14 and 15.

2 Other Statutory Provisions

Selected sections of the Customs and Excise Management Act 1979

5. Time of importation, exportation, etc.

(1) The provisions of this section shall have effect for the purposes of the customs and excise Acts.

(2) Subject to subsections (3) and (6) below, the time of importation of any goods shall be deemed to be—

    (a) where the goods are brought by sea, the time when the ship carrying them comes within the limits of a port;

    (b) where the goods are brought by air, the time when the aircraft carrying them lands in the United Kingdom or the time when the goods are unloaded in the United Kingdom, whichever is the earlier;

    (c) where the goods are brought by land, the time when the goods are brought across the boundary into Northern Ireland.

(3) In the case of goods brought by sea of which entry is not required under section 37 below, the time of importation shall be deemed to be the time when the ship carrying them came within the limits of the port at which the goods are discharged.

(4) Subject to subsections (5) and (7) below, the time of exportation of any goods from the United Kingdom shall be deemed to be—

    (a) where the goods are exported by sea or air, the time when the goods are shipped for exportation;

    (b) where the goods are exported by land, the time when they are cleared by the proper officer at the last customs and excise station on their way to the boundary.

(5) In the case of goods of a class or description with respect to the exportation of which any prohibition or restriction is for the time being in force under or by virtue of any enactment which are exported by sea or air, the time of exportation shall be deemed to be the time when the exporting ship or aircraft departs from the last port or customs and excise airport at which it is cleared before departing for a destination outside the United Kingdom.

16. Obstructions of officers, etc.

(1) Any person who—

    (a) obstructs, hinders, molests or assaults any person duly engaged in the performance of any duty or the exercise of any power imposed or conferred on him by or under any enactment relating to an assigned matter, or any person acting in his aid; or

(b) does anything which impedes or is calculated to impede the carrying out of any search for any thing liable to forfeiture under any such enactment or the detention, seizure or removal or any such thing; or

(c) rescues, damages or destroys any thing so liable to forfeiture or does anything calculated to prevent the procuring or giving of evidence as to whether or not any thing is so liable to forfeiture; or

(d) prevents the detention of any person by a person duly engaged or acting as aforesaid or rescues any person so detained,

or who attempts to do any of the aforementioned things, shall be guilty of an offence under this section.

(2) A person guilty of an offence under this section shall be liable—

(a) on summary conviction, to a penalty of the prescribed sum, or to imprisonment for a term not exceeding 3 months, or to both; or

(b) on conviction on indictment, to a penalty of any amount, or to imprisonment for a term not exceeding 2 years, or to both.

(3) Any person committing an offence under this section and any person aiding or abetting the commission of such an offence may be detained.

27. Officers' powers of boarding

(1) At any time while a ship is within the limits of a port, or an aircraft is at a customs and excise airport, or a vehicle is on an approved route, any officer and any other person duly engaged in the prevention of smuggling may board the ship, aircraft or vehicle and remain therein and rummage and search any part thereof.

(2) The Commissioners may station officers in any ship at any time while it is within the limits of a port, and if the master of any ship neglects or refuses to provide—

(a) reasonable accommodation below decks for any officer stationed therein; or

(b) means of safe access to and egress from the ship in accordance with the requirements of any such officer,

the master shall be liable on summary conviction to a penalty of £50.

28. Officers' powers of access, etc.

(1) Without prejudice to section 27 above, the proper officer shall have free access to every part of any ship or aircraft at a port or customs and excise airport and of any vehicle brought to a customs and excise station, and may—

(a) cause any goods to be marked before they are unloaded from that ship, aircraft or vehicle;

(b) lock up, seal, mark or otherwise secure any goods carried in the ship, aircraft or vehicle or any place or container in which they are so carried; and

(c) break open any place or container which is locked and of which the keys are withheld.

29. Officers' powers of detention of ships, etc.

(1) Where, in the case of a ship, aircraft or vehicle of which due report has been made under section 35 below, any goods are still on board that ship,

aircraft or vehicle at the expiration of the relevant period, the proper officer may detain that ship, aircraft or vehicle until there have been repaid to the Commissioners—

(a) any expenses properly incurred in watching and guarding the goods beyond the relevant period, except, in the case of a ship or aircraft, in respect of the day of clearance inwards; and

(b) where the goods are removed by virtue of any provisions of the Customs and Excise Acts 1979 from the ship, aircraft or vehicle to a Queen's warehouse, the expenses of that removal.

(2) In subsection (1) above, 'the relevant period' means—

(a) in the case of a ship or vehicle, 21 clear days from the date of making due report of the ship or vehicle under section 35 below or such longer period as the Commissioners may in any case allow;

(b) in the case of an aircraft, 7 clear days from the date of making due report of the aircraft under that section or such longer period as the Commissioners may in any case allow.

(3) Where, in the case of—

(a) any derelict or other ship or aircraft coming, driven or brought into the United Kingdom under legal process, by stress of weather or for safety; or

(b) any vehicle in Northern Ireland which suffers any mishap,

it is necessary for the protection of the revenue to station any officer in charge thereof, whether on board or otherwise, the proper officer may detain that ship, aircraft or vehicle until any expenses thereby incurred by the Commissioners have been repaid.

Forfeiture, offences, etc. in connection with importation
49. Forfeiture of goods improperly imported
(1) Where—

(a) except as provided by or under the Customs and Excise Acts 1979, any imported goods, being goods chargeable on their importation with customs or excise duty, are, without payment of that duty—

(i) unshipped in any port,

(ii) unloaded from any aircraft in the United Kingdom,

(iii) unloaded from any vehicle in, or otherwise brought across the boundary into, Northern Ireland, or

(iv) removed from their place of importation or from any approved wharf, examination station or transit shed; or

(b) any goods are imported, landed or unloaded contrary to any prohibition or restriction for the time being in force with respect thereto under or by virtue of any enactment; or

(c) any goods, being goods chargeable with any duty or goods the importation of which is for the time being prohibited or restricted by or under any enactment, are found, whether before or after the unloading thereof, to have been concealed in any manner on board any ship or aircraft or, while in Northern Ireland, in any vehicle; or

(d) any goods are imported concealed in a container holding goods of a different description; or

(e) any imported goods are found, whether before or after delivery, not to correspond with the entry made thereof; or

(f) any imported goods are concealed or packed in any manner appearing to be intended to deceive an officer,

those goods shall, subject to subsection (2) below, be liable to forfeiture.

50. Penalty for improper importation of goods

(1) Subsection (2) below applies to goods of the following descriptions, that is to say—

(a) goods chargeable with a duty which has not been paid; and

(b) goods the importation, landing or unloading of which is for the time being prohibited or restricted by or under any enactment.

(2) If any person with intent to defraud Her Majesty of any such duty or to evade any such prohibition or restriction as is mentioned in subsection (1) above—

(a) unships or lands in any port or unloads from any aircraft in the United Kingdom or from any vehicle in Northern Ireland any goods to which this subsection applies, or assists or is otherwise concerned in such unshipping, landing or unloading; or

(b) removes from their place of importation or from any approved wharf, examination station, transit shed or customs and excise station any goods to which this subsection applies or assists or is otherwise concerned in such removal,

he shall be guilty of an offence under this subsection and may be detained.

(3) If any person imports or is concerned in importing any goods contrary to any prohibition or restriction for the time being in force under or by virtue of any enactment with respect to those goods, whether or not the goods are unloaded, and does so with intent to evade the prohibition or restriction, he shall be guilty of an offence under this subsection and may be detained.

(4) Subject to subsection (5) below, a person guilty of an offence under subsection (2), or (3) above shall be liable—

(a) on summary conviction, to a penalty of the prescribed sum or of three times the value of the goods, whichever is the greater, or to imprisonment for a term not exceeding 6 months, or to both; or

(b) on conviction on indictment, to a penalty of any amount, or to imprisonment for a term not exceeding 2 years, or to both.

(5) In the case of an offence under subsection (2) or (3) above in connection with a prohibition or restriction on importation having effect by virtue of section 3 of the Misuse of Drugs Act 1971, subsection (4) above shall have effect subject to the modifications specified in Schedule 1 to this Act.

(6) If any person—

(a) imports or causes to be imported any goods concealed in a container holding goods of a different description; or

(b) directly or indirectly imports or causes to be imported or entered any goods found, whether before or after delivery, not to correspond with the entry made thereof,

he shall be liable on summary conviction to a penalty of three times the value of the goods or £100, whichever is the greater.

(7) In any case where a person would, apart from this subsection, be guilty of—

(a) an offence under this section in connection with the importation of goods contrary to a prohibition or restriction; and

(b) a corresponding offence under the enactment or other instrument imposing the prohibition or restriction, being an offence for which a fine or other penalty is expressly provided by that enactment or other instrument,

he shall not be guilty of the offence mentioned in paragraph (a) of this subsection.

68. Offences in relation to exportation of prohibited or restricted goods

(1) If any goods are—

(a) exported or shipped as stores; or

(b) brought to any place in the United Kingdom for the purpose of being exported or shipped as stores,

and the exportation or shipment is or would be contrary to any prohibition or restriction for the time being in force with respect to those goods under or by virtue of any enactment, the goods shall be liable to forfeiture and the exporter or intending exporter of the goods and any agent of his concerned in the exportation or shipment or intended exportation or shipment shall each be liable on summary conviction to a penalty of three times the value of the goods or £100, whichever is the greater.

(2) Any person knowingly concerned in the exportation or shipment as stores, or in the attempted exportation or shipment as stores, of any goods with intent to evade any such prohibition or restriction as is mentioned in subsection (1) above shall be guilty of an offence under this subsection and may be detained.

(3) Subject to subsection (4) below, a person guilty of an offence under subsection (2) above shall be liable—

(a) on summary conviction, to a penalty of the prescribed sum or of three times the value of the goods, whichever is the greater, or to imprisonment for a term not exceeding 6 months, or to both; or

(b) on conviction on indictment, to a penalty of any amount, or to imprisonment for a term not exceeding 2 years, or to both.

(4) In the case of an offence under subsection (2) above in connection with a prohibition or restriction on exportation having effect by virtue of section 3 of the Misuse of Drugs Act 1971, subsection (3) above shall have effect subject to the modifications specified in Schedule 1 to this Act.

(5) If by virtue of any such restriction as is mentioned in subsection (1) above any goods may be exported only when consigned to a particular place or person and any goods so consigned are delivered to some other place or person, the ship, aircraft or vehicle in which they were exported shall be liable to forfeiture unless it is proved to the satisfaction of the Commissioners that both the owner of the ship, aircraft or vehicle and the master of the ship, commander of the aircraft or person in charge of the vehicle—

(a) took all reasonable steps to secure that the goods were delivered to the particular place to which or person to whom they were consigned; and

(b) did not connive at or, except under duress, consent to the delivery of the goods to that other place or person.

(6) In any case where a person would, apart from this subsection, be guilty of—

(a) an offence under subsection (1) or (2) above; and
(b) a corresponding offence under the enactment or instrument imposing the prohibition or restriction in question, being an offence for which a fine or other penalty is expressly provided by that enactment or other instrument,

he shall not be guilty of the offence mentioned in paragraph (a) of this subsection.

Forfeiture of ships, etc. for certain offences

88. Forfeiture of ship, aircraft or vehicle constructed, etc. for concealing goods

Where—

(a) a ship is or has been within the limits of any port or within 3 or, being a British ship, 12 nautical miles of the coast of the United Kingdom, or
(b) an aircraft is or has been at any place, whether on land or on water, in the United Kingdom; or
(c) a vehicle is or has been within the limits of any port or at any aerodrome or, while in Northern Ireland, within the prescribed area,

while constructed, adapted, altered or fitted in any manner for the purpose of concealing goods, that ship, aircraft of vehicle shall be liable to forfeiture.

89. Forfeiture of ship jettisoning cargo, etc.

(1) If any part of the cargo of a ship is thrown overboard or is staved or destroyed to prevent seizure—

(a) while the ship is within 3 nautical miles of the coast of the United Kingdom; or
(b) where the ship, having been properly summoned to bring to by any vessel in the service of Her Majesty, fails so to do and chase is given, at any time during the chase,

the ship shall be liable to forfeiture.

(2) For the purposes of this section a ship shall be deemed to have been properly summoned to bring to—

(a) if the vessel making the summons did so by means of an international signal code or other recognised means and while flying her proper ensign; and
(b) in the case of a ship which is not a British ship, if at the time when the summons was made the ship was within 3 nautical miles of the coast of the United Kingdom.

Detention of persons

138. Provisions as to detention of persons

(1) Any person who has committed, or whom there are reasonable grounds to suspect of having committed, any offence for which he is liable to be detained under the customs and excise Acts may be detained by any

officer or constable or any member of Her Majesty's armed forces or coastguard at any time within 3 years from the date of the commission of the offence.

(2) Where it was not practicable to detain any person so liable at the time of the commission of the offence, or where any such person having been then or subsequently detained for that offence has escaped, he may be detained by any officer or constable or any member of Her Majesty's armed forces or coastguard at any time and may be proceeded against in like manner as if the offence had been committed at the date when he was finally detained.

(3) Where any person who is a member of the crew of any ship in Her Majesty's employment or service is detained by an officer for an offence under the customs and excise Acts, the commanding officer of the ship shall, if so required by the detaining officer, keep that person secured on board that ship until he can be brought before a court and shall then deliver him up to the proper officer.

(4) Where any person has been detained by virtue of this section otherwise than by an officer, the person detained him shall give notice of the detention to an officer at the nearest convenient office of customs and excise.

Forfeiture

139. Provisions as to detention, seizure and condemnation of goods, etc.
(1) Any thing liable to forfeiture under the customs and excise Acts may be seized or detained by any officer or constable or any member of Her Majesty's armed forces or coastguard.

(2) Where any thing is seized or detained as liable to forfeiture under the customs and excise Acts by a person other than an officer, that person shall, subject to subsection (3) below, either—

(a) deliver that thing to the nearest convenient office of customs and excise; or

(b) if such delivery is not practicable, give to the Commissioners at the nearest convenient office of customs and excise notice in writing of the seizure or detention with full particulars of the thing seized or detained.

(3) Where the person seizing or detaining any thing as liable to forfeiture under the customs and excise Acts is a constable and that thing is or may be required for use in connection with any proceedings to be brought otherwise than under those Acts it may, subject to subsection (4) below, be retained in the custody of the police until either those proceedings are completed or it is decided that no such proceedings shall be brought.

(4) The following provisions apply in relation to things retained in the custody of the police by virtue of subsection (3) above, that is to say—

(a) notice in writing of the seizure or detention and of the intention to retain the thing in question in the custody of the police, together with full particulars as to that thing, shall be given to the Commissioners at the nearest convenient office of customs and excise;

(b) any officer shall be permitted to examine that thing and take account thereof at any time while it remains in the custody of the police;

(c) nothing in the Police (Property) Act 1897 shall apply in relation to that thing.

(5) Subject to subsections (3) and (4) above and to Schedule 3 to this Act any thing seized or detained under the customs and excise Acts shall, pending the determination as to its forfeiture or disposal, be dealt with, and, if condemned or deemed to have been condemned or forfeited, shall be disposed of in such manner as the Commissioners may direct.

(6) Schedule 3 to this Act shall have effect for the purpose of forfeiture and of proceedings for the condemnation of any thing as being forfeited under the customs and excise Acts.

(7) If any person, not being an officer, by whom any thing is seized or detained or who has custody thereof after its seizure or detention, fails to comply with any requirement of this section or with any direction of the Commissioners given thereunder, he shall be liable on summary conviction to a penalty of £50.

(8) Subsections (2) to (7) above shall apply in relation to any dutiable goods seized or detained by any person other than an officer notwithstanding that they were not so seized as liable to forfeiture under the customs and excise Acts.

141. Forfeiture of ships, etc. used in connection with goods liable to forfeiture

(1) Without prejudice to any other provision of the Customs and Excise Acts 1979, where any thing has become liable to forfeiture under the customs and excise Acts—

(a) any ship, aircraft, vehicle, animal, container (including any article of passengers' baggage) or other thing whatsoever which has been used for the carriage, handling, deposit or concealment of the thing so liable to forfeiture, either at a time when it was so liable or for the purposes of the commission of the offence for which it later became so liable; and

(b) any other thing mixed, packed or found with the thing so liable, shall also be liable to forfeiture.

(2) Where any ship, aircraft, vehicle or animal has become liable to forfeiture under the customs and excise Acts, whether by virtue of subsection (1) above or otherwise, all tackle, apparel or furniture thereof shall also be liable to forfeiture.

142. Special provision as to forfeiture of larger ships

(1) Notwithstanding any other provision of the Customs and Excise Acts 1979, a ship of 250 or more tons register shall not be liable to forfeiture under or by virtue of any provision of the Customs and Excise Acts 1979, except under section 88 above, unless the offence in respect of or in connection with which the forfeiture is claimed—

(a) was substantially the object of the voyage during which the offence was committed; or

(b) was committed while the ship was under chase by a vessel in the service of Her Majesty after failing to bring to when properly summoned to do so by that vessel.

(2) For the purposes of this section, a ship shall be deemed to have been properly summoned to bring to—

(a) if the vessel making the summons did so by means of an international signal code or other recognised means and while flying her proper ensign; and

(b) in the case of a ship which is not a British ship, if at the time when the summons was made the ship was within 3 nautical miles of the coast of the United Kingdom.

(3) For the purposes of this section, all hovercraft (of whatever size) shall be treated as ships of less than 250 tons register.

(4) The exemption from forfeiture of any ship under this section shall not affect any liability to forfeiture of goods carried therein.

143. Penalty in lieu of forfeiture of larger ship where responsible officer implicated in offence

(1) Where any ship of 250 or more tons register would, but for section 142 above, be liable to forfeiture for or in connection with any offence under the customs and excise Acts and, in the opinion of the Commissioners, a responsible officer of the ship is implicated either by his own act or by neglect in that offence, the Commissioners may fine that ship such sum not exceeding £50 as they see fit.

(2) For the purposes of this section, all hovercraft (of whatever size) shall be treated as ships of less than 250 tons register.

(3) Where any ship is liable to a fine under subsection (1) above but the Commissioners consider that fine an inadequate penalty for the offence, they may take proceedings in accordance with Schedule 3 to this Act, in like manner as they might but for section 142 above have taken proceedings for the condemnation of the ship if notice of claim had been given in respect thereof, for the condemnation of the ship in such sum not exceeding £500 as the court may see fit.

(4) Where any fine is to be imposed or any proceedings are to be taken under this section, the Commissioners may require such sum as they see fit, not exceeding £50 or, as the case may be, £500, to be deposited with them to await their final decision or, as the case may be, the decision of the court, and may detain the ship until that sum has been so deposited.

(5) No claim shall lie against the Commissioners for damages in respect of the payment of any deposit or the detention of any ship under this section.

(6) For the purposes of this section—

(a) 'responsible officer', in relation to any ship, means the master, a mate or an engineer of the ship and, in the case of a ship carrying a passenger certificate, the purser or chief steward and, in the case of a ship manned wholly or partly by Asiatic seamen, the serang or other leading Asiatic officer of the ship;

(b) without prejudice to any other grounds upon which a responsible officer of any ship may be held to be implicated by neglect, he may be so held if goods not owned to by any member of the crew are discovered in a place under that officer's supervision in which they could not reasonably have been put if he had exercised proper care at the time of the loading of the ship or subsequently.

144. Protection of officers, etc. in relation to seizure and detention of goods, etc.

(1) Where, in any proceedings for the condemnation of any thing seized as liable to forfeiture under the customs and excise Acts, judgment is given for the claimant, the court may, if it sees fit, certify that there were reasonable grounds for the seizure.

(2) Where any proceedings, whether civil or criminal, are brought against the Commissioners, a law officer of the Crown or any person authorised by or under the Customs and Excise Acts 1979 to seize or detain any thing liable to forfeiture under the customs and excise Acts on account of the seizure or detention of any thing, and judgment is given for the plantiff or prosecutor, then if either—

(a) a certificate relating to the seizure has been granted under subsection (1) above; or

(b) the court is satisfied that there were reasonable grounds for seizing or detaining that thing under the customs and excise Acts,

the plaintiff or prosecutor shall not be entitled to recover any damages or costs and the defendant shall not be liable to any punishment.

(3) Nothing in subsection (2) above shall affect any right of any person to the return of the thing seized or detained or to compensation in respect of any damage to the thing or in respect of the destruction thereof.

(4) Any certificate under subsection (1) above may be proved by the production of either the original certificate or a certified copy thereof purporting to be signed by an officer of the court by which it was granted.

General provisions as to legal proceedings

145. Institution of proceedings

(1) Subject to the following provisions of this section, no proceedings for an offence under the customs and excise Acts or for condemnation under Schedule 3 to this Act shall be instituted except by order of the Commissioners.

(2) Subject to the following provisions of this section, any proceedings under the customs and excise Acts instituted in a magistrates' court, and any such proceedings instituted in a court of summary jurisdiction in Northern Ireland, shall be commenced in the name of an officer.

(3) (*Applies to Scotland.*)

(4) In the case of the death, removal, discharge or absence of the officer in whose name any proceedings were commenced under subsection (2) above, those proceedings may be continued by any officer authorised in that behalf by the Commissioners.

(5) Nothing in the foregoing provisions of this section shall prevent the institution of proceedings for an offence under the customs and excise Acts by order and in the name of a law officer of the Crown in any case in which he thinks it proper that proceedings should be so instituted.

(6) Notwithstanding anything in the foregoing provisions of this section, where any person has been detained for any offence for which he is liable

to be detained under the customs and excise Acts, any court before which he is brought may proceed to deal with the case although the proceedings have not been instituted by order of the Commissioners or have not been commenced in the name of an officer.

146. Service of process

(1) Any summons or other process issued anywhere in the United Kingdom for the purpose of any proceedings under the customs and excise Acts may be served on the person to whom it is addressed in any part of the United Kingdom without any further endorsement, and shall be deemed to have been duly served—

   (a) if delivered to him personally; or
   (b) if left at his last known place of abode or business or, in the case of a body corporate, at their registered or principal office; or
   (c) if left on board any vessel or aircraft to which he may belong or have lately belonged.

(2) Any summons, notice, order or other document issued for the purposes of any proceedings under the customs and excise Acts, or of any appeal from the decision of the court in any such proceedings, may be served by an officer.

In this subsection 'appeal' includes an appeal by way of case stated

(3) This section shall not apply in relation to proceedings instituted in the High Court or Court of Session.

147. Proceedings for offences

(1) Save as otherwise expressly provided in the customs and excise Acts and notwithstanding anything in any other enactment, any proceedings for an offence under those Acts—

   (a) may be commenced at any time within 3 years from the date of the commission of the offence; and
   (b) shall not be commenced later than 3 years from that date.

(2) Where, in England or Wales, a magistrates' court has begun to inquire into an information charging a person with an offence under the customs and excise Acts as examining justices court shall not proceed under section 25 (3) of the Criminal Law Act 1977 to try the information summarily without the consent of—

   (a) the Attorney General, in a case where the proceedings were instituted by his order and in his name; or
   (b) the Commissioners, in any other case.

(3) In the case of proceedings in England or Wales, without prejudice to any right to require the statement of a case for the opinion of the High Court, the prosecutor may appeal to the Crown Court against any decision of a magistrates' court in proceedings for an offence under the customs and excise Acts.

(4) In the case of proceedings in Northern Ireland, without prejudice to any right to require the statement of a case for the opinion of the High Court, the prosecutor may appeal to the county court against any decision of a court of summary jurisdiction in proceedings for an offence under the customs and excise Acts.

(5) (*Applies to Scotland.*)

148. Place of trial for offences
(1) Proceedings for an offence under the customs and excise Acts may be commenced—
   (a) in any court having jurisdiction in the place where the person charged with the offence resides or is found; or
   (b) if any thing was detained or seized in connection with the offence, in any court having jurisdiction in the place where that thing was so detained or seized or was found or condemned as forfeited; or
   (c) in any court having jurisdiction anywhere in that part of the United Kingdom, namely—
      (i)   England and Wales,
      (ii) Scotland, or
      (iii) Northern Ireland,
   in which the place where the offence was committed is situated.
(2) Where any such offence was committed at some place outside the area of any commission of the peace, the place of the commission of the offence shall, for the purposes of the jurisdiction of any court, be deemed to be any place in the United Kingdom where the offender is found or to which he is first brought after the commission of the offence.
(3) The jurisdiction under subsection (2) above shall be in addition to and not in derogation of any jurisdiction or power of any court under any other enactment.

149. Non-payment of penalties, etc.: maximum terms of imprisonment
(1) Where, in any proceedings for an offence under the customs and excise Acts, a magistrates' court in England or Wales or a court of summary jurisdiction in Scotland, in addition to ordering the person convicted to pay a penalty for the offence—
   (a) orders him to be imprisoned for a term in respect of the same offence; and
   (b) further (whether at the same time or subsequently) orders him to be imprisoned for a term in respect of non-payment of that penalty or default of a sufficient distress to satisfy the amount of that penalty;
the aggregate of the terms for which he is so ordered to be imprisoned shall not exceed 15 months.
(2) (*Applies to Scotland.*)
(3) Where, under any anactment for the time being in force in Northern Ireland, a court of summary jurisdiction has power to order a person to be imprisoned in respect of the non-payment of a penalty, or of the default of a sufficient distress to satisfy the amount of that penalty, for a term in addition and succession to a term of imprisonment imposed for the same offence as the penalty, then in relation to a sentence for an offence under the customs and excise Acts the aggregate of those terms of imprisonment may, notwithstanding anything in any such enactment, be any period not exceeding 15 months.

150. Incidental provisions as to legal proceedings
(1) Where liability for any offence under the customs and excise Acts is incurred by two or more persons jointly, those persons shall each be liable for the full amount of any pecuniary penalty and may be proceeded against jointly or severally as the Commissioners may see fit.

(2) In any proceedings for an offence under the customs and excise Acts instituted in England, Wales or Northern Ireland, any court by whom the matter is considered may mitigate any pecuniary penalty as they see fit.

(3) In any proceedings for an offence or for the condemnation of any thing as being forfeited under the customs and excise Acts, the fact that security has been given by bond or otherwise for the payment of any duty or for compliance with any condition in respect of the non-payment of which or non-compliance with which the proceedings are instituted shall not be a defence.

151. Application of penalties

The balance of any sum paid or recovered on account of any penalty imposed under the customs and excise Acts, after paying any such compensation or costs as are mentioned in section 114 of the Magistrates' Courts Act 1952 to persons other than the Commissioners shall, notwithstanding any local or other special right or privilege of whatever origin, be accounted for and paid to the Commissioners or as they direct.

152. Power of Commissioners to mitigate penalties, etc.

The Commissioners may, as they see fit—

(a) stay, sist or compound any proceedings for an offence or for the condemnation of any thing as being forfeited under the customs and excise Acts; or

(b) restore, subject to such conditions (if any) as they think proper, any thing forfeited or seized under those Acts; or

(c) after judgment, mitigate or remit any pecuniary penalty imposed under those Acts; or

(d) order any person who has been imprisoned to be discharged before the expiration of his term of imprisonment, being a person imprisoned for any offence under those Acts or in respect of the non-payment of a penalty or other sum adjudged to be paid or awarded in relation to such an offence or in respect of the default of a sufficient distress to satisfy such a sum;

(Applies to Scotland)

153. Proof of certain documents

(1) Any document purporting to be signed either by one or more of the Commissioners, or by their order, or by any other person with their authority, shall, until the contrary is proved, be deemed to have been so signed and to be made and issued by the Commissioners, and may be proved by the production of a copy thereof purporting to be so signed.

(2) Without prejudice to subsection (1) above, the Documentary Evidence Act 1868 shall apply in relation to—

(a) any document issued by the Commissioners;

(b) any document issued before 1st April 1909, by the Commissioners of Customs or the Commissioners of Customs and the Commissioners of Inland Revenue jointly;

(c) any document issued before that date in relation to the revenue of excise by the Commissioners of Inland Revenue,

as it applies in relation to the documents mentioned in that Act.

(3) That Act shall, as applied by subsection (2) above, have effect as if the persons mentioned in paragraphs (a) to (c) of that subsection were included in the first column of the Schedule to that Act, and any of the Commissioners or any secretary or assistant secretary to the Commissioners were specified in the second column of that Schedule in connection with those persons.

154. Proof of certain other matters
(1) An averment in any process in proceedings under the customs and excise Acts—
  (a) that those proceedings were instituted by the order of the Commissioners; or
  (b) that any person is or was a Commissioner, officer or constable, or a member of Her Majesty's armed forces or coastguard; or
  (c) that any person is or was appointed or authorised by the Commissioners to discharge, or was engaged by the orders or with the concurrence of the Commissioners in the discharge of, any duty; or
  (d) that the Commissioners have or have not been satisfied as to any matter as to which they are required by any provision of those Acts to be satisfied; or
  (e) that any ship is a British ship; or
  (f) that any goods thrown overboard, staved or destroyed were so dealt with in order to prevent or avoid the seizure of those goods,
shall, until the contrary is proved, be sufficient evidence of the matter in question.
  (2) Where in any proceedings relating to customs or excise any question arises as to the place from which any goods have been brought or as to whether or not—
  (a) any duty has been paid or secured in respect of any goods; or
  (b) any goods or other things whatsoever are of the description or nature alleged in the information, writ or other process; or
  (c) any goods have been lawfully imported or lawfully unloaded from any ship or aircraft; or
  (d) any goods have been lawfully loaded into any ship or aircraft or lawfully exported or were lawfully water-borne; or
  (e) any goods were lawfully brought to any place for the purpose of being loaded into any ship or aircraft or exported; or
  (f) any goods are or were subject to any prohibition of or restriction on their importation or exportation,
then, where those proceedings are brought by or against the Commissioners, a law officer of the Crown or an officer, or against any other person in respect of anything purporting to have been done in pursuance of any power or duty conferred or imposed on him by or under the customs and excise Acts, the burden of proof shall lie upon the other party to the proceedings.

155. Persons who may conduct proceedings
(1) Any officer or any other person authorised in that behalf by the Commissioners may, although he is not a barrister, advocate or solicitor,

conduct any proceedings before any magistrates' court in England or Wales or court of summary jurisdiction in Scotland or Northern Ireland or before any examining justices, being proceedings under any enactment relating to an assigned matter or proceedings arising out of the same circumstances as any proceedings commenced under any such enactment, whether or not the last mentioned proceedings are persisted in.

(2) Any person who has been admitted as a solicitor and is employed by the Commissioners may act as a solicitor in any proceedings in England, Wales or Northern Ireland relating to any assigned matter notwithstanding that he does not hold a current practising certificate.

161. Power to search premises

(1) Without prejudice to any other power conferred by the Customs and Excise Acts 1979 but subject to subsection (2) below, where there are reasonable grounds to suspect that any thing liable to forfeiture under the customs and excise Acts is kept or concealed in any building or place, any officer having a writ of assistance may—

   (a) enter that building or place at any time, whether by day or night, on any day, a search for, seize, and detain or remove any such thing; and

   (b) so far as is reasonably necessary for the purpose of such entry, search, seizure, detention or removal, break open any door window or container and force and remove any other impediment or obstruction.

(2) No officer shall exercise the power of entry conferred on him by subsection (1) above by night unless he is accompanied by a constable.

(3) Without prejudice to subsection (1) above or to any other power conferred by the Customs and Excise Acts 1979, if a justice of the peace is satisfied by information upon oath given by an officer that there are reasonable grounds to suspect that any thing liable to forfeiture under the customs and excise Acts is kept or concealed in any building or place, he may by warrant under his hand given on any day authorise that officer or any other person named in the warrant to enter and search any building or place so named.

(4) An officer or person named in a warrant under subsection (3) above shall thereupon have the like powers in relation to the building or place named in the warrant, subject to the like conditions as to entry by night, as if he were an officer having a writ of assistance and acting upon reasonable grounds of suspicion.

(5) Where there are reasonable grounds to suspect that any still, vessel, utensil, spirits or materials for the manufacture of spirits is or are unlawfully kept or deposited in any building or place, subsections (3) and (4) above shall apply in relation to any constable as they would apply in relation to an officer.

(6) A writ of assistance shall continue in force during the reign in which it is issued and for 6 months thereafter.

163. Power to search vehicles or vessels

Without prejudice to any other power conferred by the Customs and Excise Acts 1979, where there are reasonable grounds to suspect that any vehicle or vessel is or may be carrying any goods which are—

(a) chargeable with any duty which has not been paid or secured; or

(b) in the course of being unlawfully removed from or to any place; or

(c) otherwise liable to forfeiture under the customs and excise Acts,

any officer or constable or member of Her Majesty's armed forces or coastguard may stop and search that vehicle or vessel.

(2) If when so required by any such officer, constable or member the person in charge or any such vehicle or vessel refuses to stop or to permit the vehicle or vessel to be searched, he shall be liable on summary conviction to a penalty of £100.

164. Power to search persons

(1) Where there are reasonable grounds to suspect that any person to whom this section applied is carrying any article—

(a) which is chargeable with any duty which has not been paid or secured; or

(b) with respect to the importation or exportation of which any prohibition or restriction is for the time being in force under or by virtue of any enactment,

any officer or any person acting under the directions of an officer may, subject to subsections (2) and (3) below, search him and any article he has with him.

(2) A person who is to be searched in pursuance of this section may require to be taken before a justice of the peace or a superior of the officer or other person concerned, and the justice or superior shall consider the grounds for suspicion and direct accordingly whether or not the search is to take place.

(3) No woman or girl shall be searched in pursuance of this section except by a woman.

(4) This section applies to the following persons, namely—

(a) Any person who is on board or has landed from any ship or aircraft;

(b) any person entering or about to leave the United Kingdom;

(c) any person within the dock area of a port;

(d) any person at a customs and excise airport;

(e) any person in, entering or leaving any approved wharf or transit shed which is not in a port;

(f) in Northern Ireland, any person travelling from or to any place which is on or beyond the boundary.

170. Penalty for fraudulent evasion of duty, etc.

(1) Without prejudice to any other provision of the Customs and Excise Acts 1979, if any person—

(a) knowingly acquires possession of any of the following goods, that is to say—

(i)   goods which have been unlawfully removed from a warehouse or Queen's warehouse;

(ii) goods which are chargeable with a duty which has not been paid;

(iii) goods with respect to the importation or exportation of which any prohibition or restriction is for the time being in force under or by virtue of any enactment; or

(b) is in any way knowingly concerned in carrying, removing, depositing, harbouring, keeping or concealing or in any manner dealing with any such goods,

and does so with intent to defraud Her Majesty of any duty payable on the goods or to evade any such prohibition or restriction with respect to the goods he shall be guilty of an offence under this section and may be detained.

(2) Without prejudice to any other provision of the Customs and Excise Acts 1979, if any person is, in relation to any goods, in any way knowingly concerned in any fraudulent evasion or attempt at evasion—

(a) of any duty chargeable on the goods;

(b) of any prohibition or restriction for the time being in force with respect to the goods under or by virtue of any enactment; or

(c) of any provision of the Customs and Excise Acts 1979 applicable to the goods,

he shall be guilty of an offence under this section and may be detained.

(3) Subject to subsection (4) below, a person guilty of an offence under this section shall be liable—

(a) on summary conviction, to a penalty of the prescribed sum or of three times the value of the goods, whichever is the greater, or to imprisonment for a term not exceeding 6 months, or to both; or

(b) on conviction on indictment, to a penalty of any amount, or to imprisonment for a term not exceeding 2 years, or to both.

(4) In the case of an offence under this section in connection with a prohibition or restriction on importation or exportation having effect by virtue of section 3 of the Misuse of Drugs Act 1971, subsection (3) above shall have effect subject to the modifications specified in Schedule 1 to this Act.

(5) In any case where a person would, part from this subsection, be guilty of—

(a) an offence under this section in connection with a prohibition or restriction; and

(b) a corresponding offence under the enactment or other instrument imposing the prohibition or restriction, being an offence for which a fine or other penalty is expressly provided by that enactment or other instrument,

he shall not be guilty of the offence mentioned in paragraph (a) of this subsection.

171. General provisions as to offences and penalties

(1) Where—

(a) by any provision of any enactment relating to an assigned matter a punishment is prescribed for any offence thereunder or for any contravention of or failure to comply with any regulation, direction, condition or requirement made, given or imposed thereunder; and

(b) any person is convicted in the same prooceedings of more than one such offence, contravention or failure,

that person shall be liable to that punishment for each such offence, contravention or failure of which he is so convicted.

(2) In this Act the 'prescribed sum', in relation to the penalty provided for an offence, means—

(a) if the offence was committed in England, Wales or Northern Ireland, the prescribed sum within the meaning of section 28 of the Criminal Law Act 1977 (£1,000 or other sum substituted by order under section 61 (1) of that Act);

(b) (*applies to Scotland*);

and in subsection (1) (a) above, the reference to a provision by which a punishment is prescribed includes a reference to a provision which makes a person liable to a penalty of the prescribed sum within the meaning of this subsection.

(3) Where a penalty for an offence under any enactment relating to an assigned matter is required to be fixed by reference to the value of any goods, that value shall be taken as the price which those goods might reasonably be expected to have fetched, after payment of any duty or tax chargeable thereon, if they had been sold in the open market at or about the date of the commission of the offence for which the penalty is imposed.

(4) Where an offence under any enactment relating to an assigned matter which has been committed by a body corporate is proved to have been committed with the conset or connivance of, or to be attributable to any neglect on the part of, any director, manager, secretary or other similar officer of the body corporate or any person purporting to act in any such capacity, he ass well as the body corporate shall be guilty of that offence and shall be liable to be proceeded against and punished accordingly.

In this subsection 'director', in relation to any body corporate established by or under any enactment for the purpose of carrying on under national ownership any industry or part of an industry or undertaking, being a body corporate whose affairs are managed by the members thereof, means a member of that body corporate.

(5) Where in any proceedings for an offence under the customs and excise Acts any question arises as to the duty or the rate thereof chargeable on any imported goods, and it is not possible to ascertain the relevant time specified in section 43 above, that duty or rate shall be determined as if the goods had been imported without entry at the time when the proceedings were commenced.

SCHEDULES

SCHEDULE 1

Sections 50 (5), 68 (4) and 170 (4)

CONTROLLED DRUGS: VARIATION OF PUNISHMENTS FOR CERTAIN OFFENCES UNDER THIS ACT

1. Section 50 (4), 68 (3) and 170 (3) of this Act shall have effect in a case where the goods in respect of which the offence referred to in that subsection was committed were a Class A drug or a Class B drug as if for the words from 'shall be liable' onwards there were substituted the following words, that is to say—

'shall be liable—

(a) on summary conviction, to a penalty of the prescribed sum or of three times the value of the goods, whichever is the greater, or to imprisonment for a term not exceeding 6 months, or to both;

(b) on conviction on indictment, to a penalty of any amount, or to imprisonment for a term not exceeding 14 years, or to both.'.

2. Section 50 (4), 68 (3) and 170 (3) of this Act shall have effect in a case where the goods in respect of which the offence referred to in that subsection was committed were a Class C drug as if for the words from 'shall be liable' onwards there were substituted the following words, that is to say—
'shall be liable—
- (a) on summary conviction in Great Britain, to a penalty of three times the value of goods or £500, whichever is the greater, or to imprisonment for a term not exceeding 3 months, or to both;
- (b) on summary conviction in Northern Ireland, to a penalty of three times the value of the goods or £100, whichever is the greater, or to imprisonment for a term not exceeding 6 months, or to both;
- (c) on conviction on indictment, to a penalty of any amount, or to imprisonment for a term not exceeding 5 years, or to both.'.

3. In this Schedule 'Class A drug', 'Class B drug' and 'Class C drug' have the same meanings as in the Misuse of Drugs Act 1971.

SCHEDULE 3

Sections 139, 143, 145

PROVISIONS RELATING TO FORFEITURE*

Notice of seizure

1. (1) The Commissioners shall, except as provided in sub-paragraph (2) below, give notice of the seizure of any thing as liable to forfeiture and of the grounds therefor to any person who to their knowledge was at the time of the seizure the owner or one of the owners thereof.

(2) Notice need not be given under this paragraph if the seizure was made in the presence of—
- (a) the person whose offence or suspected offence occasioned the seizure; or
- (b) the owner or any of the owners of the thing seized or any servant or agent of his; or
- (c) in the case of any thing seized in any ship or aircraft, the master or commander.

2. Notice under paragraph 1 above shall be given in writing and shall be deemed to have been duly served on the person concerned—
- (a) if delivered to him personally; or
- (b) if addressed to him and left or forwarded by post to him at his usual or last known place of abode or business or, in the case of a body corporate, at their registered or principal office; or
- (c) where he has no address within the United Kingdom [or the Isle of Man], or his address is unknown, by publication of notice of the seizure in the London, Edinburgh or Belfast Gazette.

Notice of claim

3. Any person claiming that any thing seized as liable to forfeiture is not so liable shall, within one month of the date of the notice of seizure or, where no such notice has been served on him, within one month of the date of the seizure, give notice of his claim in writing to the Commissioners at any office of customs and excise.

4. (1) Any notice under paragraph 3 above shall specify the name and address of the claimant and, in the case of a claimant who is outside the United Kingdom [and the Isle of Man], shall specify the name and address of a solicitor in the United Kingdom who is authorised to accept service of process and to act on behalf of the claimant.

(2) Service of process upon a solicitor so specified shall be deemed to be proper service upon the claimant.

* Forfeiture proceedings under this Schedule are proceedings *in rem* and not *in personam*; see *Denton v John Lister Ltd*, [1971] 3 All ER 669 [1971] 1WLR 1426, DC.

Condemnation

5. If on the expiration of the relevant period under paragraph 3 above for the giving of notice of claim in respect of any thing no such notice has been given to the Commissioners, or if, in the case of any such notice given, any requirement of paragraph 4 above is not complied with, the thing in question shall be deemed to have been duly condemned as forfeited.

6. Where notice of claim in respect of any thing is duly given in accordance with paragraphs 3 and 4 above, the Commissioners shall take proceedings for the condemnation of that thing by the court, and if the court finds that the thing was at the time of seizure liable to forfeiture the court shall condemn it as forfeited.

7. Where any thing is in accordance with either of paragraphs 5 or 6 above condemned or deemed to have been condemned as forfeited, the, without prejudice to any delivery up or sale of the thing by the Commissioners under paragraph 16 below, the forfeiture shall have effect as from the date when the liability to forfeiture arose.

Proceedings for condemnation by court

8. Proceedings for condemnation shall be civil proceedings and may be instituted—

  (a) in England or Wales either in the High Court or in a magistrates' court;
  (b) *(applies to Scotland)*;
  (c) in Northern Ireland either in the High Court or in a court of summary jurisdiction.

9. Proceedings for the condemnation of any thing instituted in a magistrates' court in England or Wales, in the sheriff court in Scotland or in a court of summary jurisdiction in Northern Ireland may be so instituted—

  (a) in any such court having jurisdiction in the place where any offence in connection with that thing was committed or where any proceedings for such an offence are instituted; or
  (b) in any such court having jurisdiction in the place where the claimant resides or, if the claimant has specified a solicitor under paragraph 4 above, in the place where that solicitor has his office; or
  (c) in any such court having jurisdiction in the place where that thing was found, detained or seized or to which it is first brought after being found, detained or seized.

10. (1) In any proceedings for condemnation instituted in England, Wales or Northern Ireland, the claimant or his solicitor shall make oath that the thing seized was, or was to the best of his knowledge and belief, the property of the claimant at the time of the seizure.

(2) In any such proceedings instituted in the High Court, the claimant shall give such security for the costs of the proceedings as may be determined by the Court.

(3) If any requirement of this paragraph is not complied with, the court shall give judgment for the Commissioners.

11. (1) In the case of any proceedings for condemnation instituted in a magistrates' court in England or Wales, without prejudice to any right to require the statement of a case for the opinion of the High Court, either party may appeal against the decision of that court to the Crown Court.

(2) In the case of any proceedings for condemnation instituted in a court of summary jurisdiction in Northern Ireland, without prejudice to any right to require the statement of a case for the opinion of the High Court, either party may appeal against the decision of that court to the county court.

12. Where an appeal, including an appeal by way of case stated, has been made against the decision of the court in any proceedings for the condemnation of any thing, that thing shall, pending the final determination of the matter, be left with the Commissioners or at any convenient office of customs and excise.

Provisions as to proof

13. In any proceedings arising out of the seizure of any thing, the fact, form and manner of the seizure shall be taken to have been as set forth in the process without any further evidence thereof, unless the contrary is proved.

14. In any proceedings, the condemnation by a court of any thing as forfeited may be proved by the production either of the order or certificate of condemnation or of a certified copy thereof purporting to be signed by an officer of the court by which the order or certificate was made or granted.

Special provisions as to certain claimants

15. For the purposes of any claim to, or proceedings for the condemnation of, any thing, where that thing is at the time of seizure the property of a body corporate, of two or more partners or of any number of persons exceeding five, the oath required by paragraph 10 above to be taken and any other thing required by this Schedule or by any rules of the court to be done by, or by any person authorised by, the claimant or owner may be taken or done by, or by any other person authorised by, the following persons respectively, that is to say—

    (a) where the owner is a body corporate, the secretary or some duly authorised officer of that body;

    (b) where the owners are in partnership, any one of those owners;

    (c) where the owners are any number of persons exceeding five not being in partnership, any two of those persons on behalf of themselves and their co-owners.

Power to deal with seizures before condemnation, etc.

16. Where any thing has been seized as liable to forfeiture the Commissioners may at any time if they see fit and notwithstanding that the thing has not yet been condemned, or is not yet deemed to have been condemned, as forfeited—

    (a) deliver it up to any claimant upon his paying to the Commissioners such sum as they think proper, being a sum not exceeding that which in their opinion represents the value of the thing, including any duty or tax chargeable thereon which has not been paid;

    (b) if the thing seized is a living creature or is in the opinion of the Commissioners of a perishable nature, sell or destroy it.

17. (1) If, where any thing is delivered up, sold or destroyed under paragraph 16 above, it is held in proceedings taken under this Schedule that the thing was not liable to forfeiture at the time of its seizure, the Commissioners shall, subject to any deduction allowed under sub-paragraph (2) below, on demand by the claimant tender to him—

    (a) an amount equal to any sum paid by him under sub-paragraph (a) of that paragraph; or

    (b) where they have sold the thing, an amount equal to the proceeds of sale; or

    (c) where they have destroyed the thing, an amount equal to the market value of the thing at the time of its seizure.

(2) Where the amount to be tendered under sub-paragraph (1) (a), (b) or (c) above includes any sum on account of any duty or tax chargeable on the thing which had not been paid before its seizure the Commissioners may deduct so much of that amount as represents that duty or tax.

(3) If the claimant accepts any amount tendered to him under sub-paragraph (1) above, he shall not be entitled to maintain any action on account of the seizure, detention, sale or destruction of the thing.

(4) For the purposes of sub-paragraph (1) (c) above, the market value of any thing at the time of its seizure shall be taken to be such amount as the Commissioners and the claimant may agree or, in default of agreement, as may be determined by a referee appointed by the Lord Chancellor (not being an official of any government department), whose decision shall be final and conclusive; and the procedure on any reference to a referee shall be such as may be determined by the referee.

Offences against the Person Act 1861

22. Whosoever shall unlawfully apply or administer to, or cause to be taken by, or attempt to apply or administer to, or attempt to cause to be administered to or taken by, any person, any chloroform, laudanum, or other stupefying or overpowering drug, matter, thing, or with intent in any of such cases thereby to enable himself or any other person to commit, or with intent in any of such cases thereby to assist any other person in committing, any indictable offence, . . . shall be liable . . . to *imprisonment* for life. . . .

23. Whosoever shall unlawfully and maliciously administer to, or cause to be administered to or taken by any other person any poison, or other destructive or noxious thing, so as thereby to endanger the life of such person, or so as thereby to inflict upon such person any grievous bodily harm, shall be guilty of [felony], and being convicted thereof shall be liable . . . to *imprisonment* for any term not exceeding ten years.

24. Whosoever shall unlawfully and maliciously administer to, or cause to be administered to or taken by any other person, any poison or other destructive or noxious thing, with intent to injure, aggrieve, or annoy such person, shall be guilty of a misdemeanor, and being convicted thereof shall be liable . . . to *imprisonment* . . . [for not more than five years (*Penal Servitude Act* 1891, s. 1 (1) and *Criminal Justice Act* 1948, s. 1 (1)).]

Criminal Law Act 1967

2. Arrest without warrant
(1) The powers of summary arrest conferred by the following subsections shall apply to offences for which the sentence is fixed by law or for which a person (not previously convicted) may under or by virtue of any enactment be sentenced to imprisonment for a term of five years, and to attempts to commit any such offence; and in this Act, including any amendment made by this Act in any other enactment, 'arrestable offence' means any such offence or attempt.

(2) Any person may arrest without warrant anyone who is, or whom he, with reasonable causes suspects to be, in the act of committing an arrestable offence.

(3) Where an arrestable offence has been committed, any person may arrest without warrant anyone who is, or whom he, with reasonable cause, suspects to be, guilty of the offence.

(4) Where a constable, with reasonable cause, suspects that an arrestable offence has been committed, he may arrest without warrant anyone whom he, with reasonable cause, suspects to be guilty of the offence.

(5) A constable may arrest without warrant any person who is, or whom he with reasonable cause suspects to be, about to commit an arrestable offence.

(6) For the purpose of arresting a person under any power conferred by this section a constable may enter (if need be, by force) and search any place where that person is or where the constable, with reasonable cause, suspects him to be.

(7) This section shall not affect the operation of any enactment restricting the institution of proceedings for an offence, nor prejudice any power of arrest conferred by law apart from this section.

Criminal Law Act 1977

PART I: CONSPIRACY

1. The offence of conspiracy

(1) Subject to the following provisions of this Part of this Act, if a person agrees with any other person or persons that a course of conduct shall be pursued which, if the agreement is carrried out in accordance with their intentions, either—

(a) will necessarily amount to or involve the commission of any offence or offences by one or more of the parties to the agreement, or

(b) would do so but for the existence of facts which render the commission of the offence or any of the offences impossible.

he is guilty of conspiracy to commit the offence or offences in question.

This section shall not apply where an agreement was entered into before the commencement of this Act unless the conspiracy continued to exist after that date.

(2) Where liability for any offence may be incurred without knowledge on the part of the person committing it of any particular fact or circumstance necessary for the commission of the offence, a person shall nevertheless not be guilty of conspiracy to commit that offence by virtue of subsection (1) above unless he and at least one other party to the agreement intend or know that that fact or circumstance shall or will exist at the time when the conduct constituting the offence is to take place.

(3) Where in pursuance of any agreement the acts in question in relation to any offence are to be done in contemplation or furtherance of a trade dispute (within the meaning of the Trade Union and Labour Relations Act 1974) that offence shall be disregarded for the purposes of subsection (1) above provided that it is a summary offence which is not punishable with imprisonment.

(4) In this Part of this Act 'offence' means an offence triable in England and Wales, except that it includes murder notwithstanding that the murder in question would not be so triable if committed in accordance with the intentions of the parties to the agreement.

3 Regulations

Misuse of Drugs Regulations 1973
SI 1973/797

PART I: GENERAL

1. Citation and commencement   These Regulations may be cited as the Misuse of Drugs Regulations 1973 and shall come into operation on 1st July 1973.

2. Interpretation   (1) In these Regulations, unless the context otherwise requires, the expression—

'the Act' means the Misuse of Drugs Act 1971;

'authorised as a member of a group' means authorised by virtue of being a member of a class as respects which the Secretary of State has granted an authority under and for the purposes of Regulations 8 (3), 9 (3) or 10 (3) which is in force, and 'his group authority', in relation to a person who is a member of such a class, means the authority so granted to that class;

['cannabis' has the same meaning as in the Act as amended by section 52 of the Criminal Law Act 1977;]

'health prescription' means a prescription issued by a doctor or a dentist either under the [National Health Service Acts 1946 to 1973], the [National Health Service (Scotland) Acts 1947 to 1973], the Health Services Act (Northern Ireland) 1971 or the National Health Service (Isle of Man) Act 1948 (an Act of Tynwald) or upon a form issued by a local authority for use in connection with the health service of that authority;

'installation manager' and 'offshore installation' have the same meanings as in the Mineral Workings (Offshore Installations) Act 1971;

'master' has the same meaning as in the Merchant Shipping Act 1894;

'matron or acting matron' includes any male nurse occupying a similar position;

'the Merchant Shipping Acts' means the Merchant Shipping Acts 1894 to 1971;

'officer of customs and excise' means an officer within the meaning of the Customs and Excise Act 1952;

'prescription' means a presciption issued by a doctor for the medical treatment of a single individual, by a dentist for the dental treatment of a single individual or by a veterinary surgeon or veterinary practitioner for the purposes of animal treatment;

'register' means a bound book and does not include any form of loose leaf register or card index;

'registered pharmacy' has the same meaning as in the Medicines Act 1968;

'retail dealer' means a person lawfully conducting a retail pharmacy business or a pharmacist engaged in supplying drugs to the public at a health centre within the meaning of the Medicines Act 1968;

'sister or acting sister' includes any male nurse occupying a similar position;

'wholesale dealer' means a person who carries on the business of selling drugs to persons who buy to sell again

(2) In these Regulations any reference to a Regulation or Schedule shall be construed as a reference to a Regulation contained in these Regulations or, as the case may be, to a Schedule thereto; and any reference in a Regulation or Schedule to a paragraph shall be construed as a reference to a paragraph of that Regulation or Schedule.

(3) In these Regulations any reference to any enactment shall be construed as a reference to that enactment as amended, and as including a reference thereto as extended or applied, by or under any other enactment.

(4) Nothing in these Regulations shall be construed as derogating from any power or immunity of the Crown, its servants or agents.

(5) The Interpretation Act 1889 shall apply for the interpretation of these Regulations as it applies for the interpretation of an Act of Parliament.

3. Metric system and imperial system   (1) For the purposes of these Regulations—

(a) a controlled drug shall not be regarded as supplied otherwise than on a prescription or other order by reason only that the prescription or order specifies a quantity of the controlled drug in terms of the imperial system and the quantity supplied is the equivalent of that amount in the metric system;

(b) where any person may lawfully be in possession of a quantity of a controlled drug determined by or under these Regulations in terms of the imperial system he shall be deemed not to be in possession of a quantity of that controlled drug in excess of the first-mentioned quantity by reason only that he is in possession of a quantity of that drug which is the equivalent of the first-mentioned quantity in the metric system.

(2) For the purposes of this Regulation the quantity of a controlled drug in the metric system which is the equivalent of a particular quantity in the imperial system shall be taken to be the appropriate quantity ascertained in accordance with the provisions of the Weights and Measures (Equivalents for dealing with drugs) Regulations 1970.

4. Exceptions for drugs in Schedule 1 and poppy-straw   (1) Sections 3 (1) and 5 (1) of the Act (which prohibit the importation, exportation and possession of controlled drugs) shall not have effect in relation to the controlled drugs specified in Schedule 1.

(2) Sections 4 (1) (which prohibits the production and supply of controlled drugs) and 5 (1) of the Act shall not have effect in relation to poppy-straw.

5. Licences to produce etc. controlled drugs   Where any person is authorised by a licence of the Secretary of State issued under this Regulation and for the time being in force to produce, supply, offer to supply or have in his possession any controlled drug, it shall not by virtue of section 4 (1) or 5 (1) of the Act be unlawful for that person to produce, supply, offer to supply or have in his possession that drug in accordance with the terms of the licence and in compliance with any conditions attached to the licence.

6. General authority to possess   Any of the following persons may, notwithstanding the provisions of section 5 (1) of the Act, have any controlled drug in his possession, that is to say—
- (a) a constable when acting in the course of his duty as such;
- (b) a person engaged in the business of a carrier when acting in the course of that business;
- (c) a person engaged in the business of the Post Office when acting in the course of that business;
- (d) an officer of customs and excise when acting in the course of his duty as such;
- (e) a person engaged in the work of any laboratory to which the drug has been sent for forensic examination when acting in the course of his duty as a person so engaged;
- (f) a person engaged in conveying the drug to a person authorised by these Regulations to have it in his possession.

7. Administration of drugs in Schedules 1, 2 and 3   (1) Any person may administer to another any drug specified in Schedule 1.

(2) A doctor or dentist may administer to a patient any drug specified in Schedule 2 or 3.

(3) Any person other than a doctor or dentist may administer to a patient, in accordance with the directions of a doctor or dentist, any drug specified in Schedule 2 or 3.

8. Production and supply of drugs in Schedules 1 and 2   (1) Notwithstanding the provisions of section 4 (1) (a) of the Act—
- (a) a practitioner or pharmacist, acting in his capacity as such, may manufacture or compound any drug specified in Schedule 1 or 2;
- (b) a person lawfully conducting a retail pharmacy business and acting in his capacity as such may, at the registered pharmacy at which he carries on that business, manufacture or compound any drug specified in Schedule 1 or 2.

(2) Notwithstanding the provisions of section 4 (1) (b) of the Act any of the following persons, that is say:
- (a) a practitioner;
- (b) a pharmacist;
- (c) a person lawfully conducting a retail pharmacy business;

(d) the matron or acting matron of a hospital or nursing home which is wholly or mainly maintained by a public authority out of public funds or by a charity or by voluntary subscriptions;

(e) the dispensing and supply of medicines at the hospital or nursing home, the sister or acting sister for the time being in charge of a ward, theatre or other department in such a hospital or nursing home as aforesaid;

(f) a person who is in charge of a laboratory the recognised activities of which consist in, or include, the conduct of scientific education or research and which is attached to a university, university college or such a hospital as aforesaid or to any other institution approved for the purpose by the Secretary of State;

(g) a public analyst appointed under section 89 of the Food and Drugs Act 1955 or section 27 of the Food and Drugs (Scotland) Act 1956;

(h) a sampling officer within the meaning of the Food and Drugs Act 1955 or the Food and Drugs (Scotland) Act 1956;

(i) a sampling officer within the meaning of Schedule 3 to the Medicines Act 1968;

(j) a person employed or engaged in connections with a scheme for testing the quality or amount of the drugs, preparations and appliances supplied under the National Health Service Acts 1946 to 1973 or the National Health Service (Scotland) Acts 1947 to 1973 and the Regulations made thereunder;

(k) an inspector appointed by the Pharmaceutical Society of Great Britain under section 25 of the Pharmacy and Poisons Act 1933,

may, when acting in his capacity as such, supply or offer to supply any drug specified in Schedule 1 or 2 to any person who may lawfully have that drug in his possession:

Provided that nothing in this paragraph authorises—

(i) the matron or acting matron of a hospital or nursing home, having a pharmacist responsible for the dispensing and supply of medicines, to supply or offer to supply any drug;

(ii) a sister or acting sister for the time being in charge of a ward, theatre or other department to supply any drug otherwise than for administration to a patient in that ward, theatre or department in accordance with the directions of a doctor or dentist.

(3) Notwithstanding the provisions of section 4 (1) (b) of the Act, a person who is authorised as a member of a group may, under and in accordance with the terms of his group authority and in compliance with any conditions attached thereto, supply or offer to supply any drug specified in Schedule 1 or 2 to any person who may lawfully have that drug in his possession.

(4) Notwithstanding the provisions of section 4 (1) (b) of the Act, a person whose name is for the time being entered in the register kept for the purposes of this paragraph by the Secretary of State may, at the premises in respect of which his name is so entered and in compliance with any conditions subject to which his name is so entered, supply or offer to supply any drug specified in Schedule 1 to any person who may lawfully have that drug in his possession.

(5) Notwithstanding the provisions of section 4 (1) (b) of the Act—

(a) the owner of a ship, or the master of a ship which does not carry a doctor on board as part of her complement, may supply or offer to supply any drug specified in Schedule 1 or 2—
   (i) to any member of the crew;
   (ii) to any person who may lawfully supply that drug; or
   (iii) to any constable for the purpose of destruction;

(b) the installation manager of an offshore installation may supply or offer to supply any drug specified in Schedule 1 or 2—
   (i) to any person on that installation, whether present in the course of his employment or not;
   (ii) to any person who may lawfully supply that drug; or
   (iii) to any constable for the purpose of destruction.

9. Production and supply of drugs in Schedule 3 (1) Notwithstanding the provisions of section 4 (1) (a) of the Act—

(a) a practitioner or pharmacist, acting in his capacity as such, may manufacture or compound any drug specified in Schedule 3;

(b) a person lawfully conducting a retail pharmacy business and acting in his capacity as such may, at the registered pharmacy at which he carries on that business, manufacture or compound any drug specified in Schedule 3;

(c) a person whose name is for the time being entered in the register kept for the purposes of this sub-paragraph by the Secretary of State may produce, at the premises in respect of which his name is so entered and in compliance with any conditions subject to which his name is so entered, any drug specified in Schedule 3.

Notwithstanding the provisions of section 4 (1) (b) of the Act, any of the following persons, that is to say—

(a) a practitioner;

(b) a pharmacist;

(c) a person lawfully conducting a retail pharmacy business;

(d) the matron or acting matron of a hospital or nursing home;

(e) in the case of such a drug supplied to her by a person responsible for the dispensing and supply of medicines at the hospital or nursing home, the sister or acting sister for the time being in charge of a ward, theatre or other department in a hospital or nursing home;

(f) a person in charge of a laboratory the recognised activities of which consist in, or include, the conduct of scientific education or research;

(g) a public analyst appointed under section 89 of the Food and Drugs Act 1955 or section 27 of the Food and Drugs (Scotland) Act 1956;

(h) a sampling officer within the meaning of the Food and Drugs Act 1955 or the Food and Drugs (Scotland) Act 1956;

(i) a sampling officer within the meaning of Schedule 3 to the Medicines Act 1968;

(j) a person employed or engaged in connection with a scheme for testing the quality or amount of the drugs, preparations and appliances supplied under the national Health Service Acts 1946 to 1973 or the National Health Service (Scotland) Acts 1947 to 1973 and the Regulations made thereunder;

(k) an inspector appointed by the Pharmaceutical Society of Great Britain under section 25 of the Pharmacy and Poisons Act 1933,

may, when acting in his capacity as such, supply or offer to supply any drug specified in Schedule 3 to any person who may lawfully have that drug in his possession:

Provided that nothing in this paragraph authorises—

(i) the matron or acting matron of a hospital or nursing home, having a pharmacist responsible for the dispensing and supply of medicines, to supply or offer to supply any drug;

(ii) a sister or acting sister for the time being in charge of a ward, theatre or other department to supply any drug otherwise than for administration to a patient in that ward, theatre or department in accordance with the directions of a doctor or dentist.

(3) Notwithstanding the provisions of section 4 (1) (b) of the Act, a person who is authorised as a member of a group may, under and in accordance with the terms of his group authority and in compliance with any conditions attached thereto, supply or offer to supply any drug specified in Schedule 3 to any person who may lawfully have that drug in his possession.

(4) Notwithstanding the provisions of section 4 (1) (b) of the Act—

(a) a person whose name is for the time being entered in the register kept for the purposes of this sub-paragraph by the Secretary of State may, at the premises in respect of which his name is so entered and in compliance with any conditions subject to which his name is so entered, supply or offer to supply any drug specified in Schedule 3 to any person who may lawfully have that drug in his possession;

(b) a person whose name is for the time being entered in the register kept for the purposes of paragraph (1) (c) by the Secretary of State may supply or offer to supply any drug which he may, by virtue of his name being so entered, lawfully produce to any person who may lawfully have that drug in his possession.

(5) Notwithstanding the provisions of section 4 (1) (b) of the Act—

(a) the owner of a ship, or the master of a ship which does not carry a doctor on board as part of her complement, may supply or offer to supply any drug specified in Schedule 3—
   (i) to any member of the crew; or
   (ii) to any person who may lawfully supply that drug;

(b) the installation manager of an offshore installation may supply or offer to supply any drug specified in Schedule 3—
   (i) to any person on that installation, whether present in the course of his employment or not; or
   (ii) to any person who may lawfully supply that drug.

10. Possession of drugs in Schedules 2 and 3 Notwithstanding the provisions of section 5 (1) of the Act—

(a) a person specified in Regulation 8 (2) may have in his possession any drug specified in Schedule 2;

(b) a person specified in Regulation 9 (2) may have in his possession any drug specified in Schedule 3,

for the purpose of acting in his capacity as such.

(2) Notwithstanding the provisions of section 5 (1) of the Act a person may have in his possession any drug specified in Schedule 2 or 3 for administration for medical, dental or veterinary purposes in accordance with the directions of a practitioner:

Provided that this paragraph shall not have effect in the case of a person to whom the drug has been supplied by or on the prescription of a doctor if—

(a) that person was then being supplied with any controlled drug by or on the prescription of another doctor and failed to disclose that fact to the first mentioned doctor before the supply by him or on his prescription; or

(b) that or any other person on his behalf made a declaration or statement, which was false in any particular, for the purpose of obtaining the supply or prescription.

(3) Notwithstanding the provisions of section 5 (1) of the Act, a person who is authorised as a member of a group may, under and in accordance with the terms of his group authority and in compliance with any conditions attached thereto, have any drug specified in Schedule 2 or 3 in his possession.

(4) Notwithstanding the provisions of section 5 (1) of the Act—

(a) a person whose name is for the time being entered in the register kept for the purposes of this sub-paragraph by the Secretary of State may, in compliance with any conditions subject to which his name is so entered, have in his possession any drug specified in Schedule 3;

(b) a person whose name is for the time being entered in the register kept for the purposes of Regulation 9 (1) (c) by the Secretary of State may have in his possession any drug which he may, by virtue of his name being so entered, lawfully produce;

(c) a person whose name is for the time being entered in the register kept for the purposes of Regulation 9 (4) (a) by the Secretary of State may have in his possession any drug which he may, by virtue of his name being so entered, lawfully supply or offer to supply.

(5) Notwithstanding the provisions of section 5 (1) of the Act—

(a) the owner of a ship, or the master of a ship which does not carry a doctor on board as part of her complement, may have in his possession any drug specified in Schedule 2 or 3 so far as necessary for the purpose of compliance with the Merchant Shipping Acts;

(b) the master of a foreign ship which is in a port in Great Britain may have in his possession any drug specified in Schedule 2 or 3 so far as necessary for the equipment of the ship;

(c) the installation manager of an offshore installation may have in his possession any drug specified in Schedule 2 or 3 so far as necessary for the purposes of compliance with the Mineral Workings (Offshore Installations) Act 1971.

11. Exemption for midwives in respect of pethidine   (1) Notwithstanding the provisions of section 4 (1) (b) and 5 (1) of the Act, a certified midwife, who has in accordance with the provisions of the Midwives Act 1951, or the Midwives (Scotland) Act 1951, notified to the local supervising authority her intention to practice, may, subject to the provision of this Regulation—

(a) so far as necessary for the practice of her profession or employment as a midwife, have pethidine in her possession;

(b) so far as necessary as aforesaid, administer pethidine; and

(c) surrender to the appropriate medical officer . . . any stocks of pethidine in her possession which are no longer required by her.

(2) Nothing in paragraph (1) authorises a midwife to have in her possession pethidine which has been obtained otherwise than on a midwife's supply order signed by the appropriate medical officer . . .

(3) In this Regulation, the expression—

'appropriate medical officer . . .' means—

(a) a doctor who is for the time being authorised in writing for the purposes of this Regulation by the local supervising authority for the region or area in which the pethidine was, or is to be, obtained;

(b) for the purposes of paragraph (2), a person appointed under section 17 of the Midwives Act 1951, or, as the case may be, section 18 of the Midwives (Scotland) Act 1951, by that authority to exercise supervision over certified midwives within their area, who is for the time being authorised as aforesaid;

'certified midwife' and 'local supervising authority' have the same meanings as in the Midwives Act 1951, or, in Scotland, the Midwives (Scotland) Act 1951;

'midwive's supply order' means an order in writing specifying the name and occupation of the midwife obtaining the pethidine, the purpose for which it is required and the total quantity to be obtained.

12. Cultivation under licence of Cannabis plant   Where any person is authorised by a licence of the Secretary of State issued under this Regulation and for the time being in force to cultivate plants of the genus *Cannabis*, it shall not by virtue of section 6 of the Act be unlawful for that person to cultivate any such plant in accordance with the terms of the licence and in compliance with any conditions attached to the licence.

13. Approval of premises for cannabis smoking for research purposes   Section 8 of the Act ((which makes it an offence for the occupier of premises to permit certain activities there) shall not have effect in relation to the smoking of cannabis or cannabis resin for the purposes of research on any premises for the time being approved for the purposes by the Secretary of State.

Part III: Requirements as to Documentation and Record Keeping

14. Documents to be obtained by supplier of controlled drugs   (1) Where a person (hereafter in this paragraph referred to as 'the supplier'), not being a practitioner, supplies a controlled drug otherwise than on a prescription, the supplier shall not deliver the drug to a person who—

(a) purports to be sent by or on behalf of the person to whom it is supplied (hereafter in this paragraph referred to as 'the recipient'); and

(b) is not authorised by any provision of these regulations other than the provisions of Regulation 6 (f) to have that drug in his possession, unless that person produces to the supplier a statement in writing signed by the recipient to the effect that he is empowered by the recipient to receive that drug on behalf of the recipient, and the supplier is reasonably satisfied that the document is a genuine document.

(2) Where a person (hereafter in this paragraph referred to as 'the supplier') supplied a controlled drug, otherwise than on a prescription or by way of administration, to any of the persons specified in paragraph (4), the supplier shall not deliver the drug—

(a) until he has obtained a requisition in writing which—
   (i)   is signed by the person to whom the drug is supplied (hereafter in this paragraph referred to as 'the recipient');
   (ii) states the name, address and profession or occupation of the recipient;
   (iii) specifies the purpose for which the drug supplied is required and the total quantity to be supplied; and
   (iv) where appropriate, satisfies the requirements of paragraph (5);
(b) unless he is reasonably satisfied that the signature is that of the person purporting to have signed the requisition and that that person is engaged in the profession or occupation specified in the requisition:

Provided that where the recipient is a practitioner and he represents that he urgently requires a controlled drug for the purpose of his profession, the supplier may, if he is reasonably satisfied that the recipient so requires the drug and is, by reason of some emergency, unable before delivery to furnish within the twenty-four hours next following.

(3) A person who has given such an undertaking as aforesaid shall deliver to the person by whom the controlled drug was supplied a signed requisition in accordance with the undertaking.

(4) The persons referred to in paragraph (2) are—
(a) a practitioner;
(b) the matron or acting matron of a hospital or nursing home;
(c) a person who is in charge of a laboratory the recognised activities of which consist in, or include, the conduct of scientific education or research;
(d) the owner of a ship, or the master of a ship which does not carry a doctor on board as part of her complement;
(e) the master of a foreign ship in a port in Great Britain;
(f) the installation manager of an offshore installation.

(5) a requisition furnished for the purposes of paragraph (2) shall—
(a) where furnished by the matron or acting matron of a hospital or nursing home, be signed by a doctor or dentist employed or engaged in that hospital or nursing home;
(b) where furnished by the master of a foreign ship, contain a statement signed by the proper officer of the port health authority, or, in Scotland, the medical officer designated under section 21 of the National Health Service (Scotland) Act 1972 by the Health Board within whose jurisdiction the ship is, that the quantity of the drug to be supplied is the quantity necessary for the equipment of the ship.

(6) Where the person responsible for the dispensing and supply of medicines at any hospital or nursing home supplies a controlled drug to

the sister or acting sister for the time being in charge of any ward, theatre or other department in that hospital or nursing home (hereafter in this paragraph referred to as 'the recipient') he shall—

(a) obtain a requisition in writing, signed by the recipient, which specifies the total quantity of the drug to be supplied; and

(b) mark the requisition in such manner as to show that it has been complied with,

and any requisition obtained for the purposes of this paragraph shall be retained in the dispensary at which the drug was supplied and a copy of the requisition or a note of it shall be retained or kept by the recipient.

(7) Nothing in this Regulation shall have effect in relation to the drugs specified in Schedule 1 or poppy-straw.

15. Form of prescriptions   (1) Subject to the provisions of this Regulation, a person shall not issue a prescription containing a controlled drug other than a drug specified in Schedule 1 unless the prescription complies with the following requirements, that is to say, it shall—

(a) be in ink or otherwise so as to be indelible and be signed by the person issuing it with his usual signature and dated by him;

(b) insofar as it specifies the information required by sub-paragraphs (e) and (f) below to be specified, be written by the person issuing it in his own handwriting;

(c) except in the case of a health prescription, specify the address of the person issuing it;

(d) have written thereon, if issues by a dentist, the words 'for dental treatment only' and, if issued by a veterinary surgeon or a veterinary practitioner, the words 'for animal treatment only';

(e) specify the name and address of the person for whose treatment it is issued or, if it is issued by a veterinary surgeon or veterinary practitioner, of the person to whom the controlled drug prescribed is to be delivered;

(f) specify the dose to be taken and—

(i) in the case of a prescription containing a controlled drug which is a preparation, the form and, where appropriate, the strength of the preparation, and either the total quantity (in both words and figures) of the preparation or the number (in both words and figures) of dosage units, as appropriate, to be supplied;

(ii) in any other case, the total quantity (in both words and figures) of the controlled drug to be supplied;

(g) in the case of a prescription for a total quantity intended to be dispensed by instalments, contain a direction specifying the amount of the instalments of the total amount which may be dispensed and the intervals to be observed when dispensing.

(2) Paragraph (1) (b) shall not have effect in relation to a prescription issued by a person approved (whether personally or as a member of a class) for the purposes of this paragraph by the Secretary of State.

(3) In the case of a prescription issued for the treatment of a patient in a hospital or nursing home, it shall be a sufficient compliance with paragraph (1) (e) if the prescription is written on the patient's bed card or case sheet.

16. Provisions as to supply on prescription (1) A person shall not supply a controlled drug other than a drug specified in Schedule 1 on a prescription—

(a) unless the prescription complies with the provisions of Regulation 15;

(b) unless the address specified in the prescription as the address of the person issuing it is an address within the United Kingdom;

(c) unless he either is acquainted with the signature of the person by whom it purports to be issued and has no reason to suppose that it is not genuine, or has taken reasonably sufficient steps to satisfy himself that it is genuine;

(d) before the date specified in the prescription;

(e) subject to paragraph (3), later than thirteen weeks after the date specified in the prescription.

(2) Subject to paragraph (3), a person dispensing a prescription containing a controlled drug other than a drug specified in Schedule 1 shall, at the time of dispensing it, mark thereon the date on which it is dispensed and, unless it is a health prescription, shall retain it on the premises on which it was dispensed.

(3) In the case of a prescription containing a controlled drug other than a drug specified in Schedule 1, which contains a direction that specified instalments of the total amount may be dispensed at stated intervals, the person dispensing it shall not supply the drug otherwise than in accordance with that direction and—

(a) paragraph (1) shall have effect as if for the requirement contained in sub-paragraph (e) thereof there were substituted a requirement that the occasion on which the first instalment is dispensed shall not be later than thirteen weeks after the date specified in the prescription;

(b) paragraph (2) shall have effect as if for the words 'at the time of dispensing it' there were substituted the words 'on each occasion on which an instalment is dispensed'.

17. Exemption for certain prescriptions Nothing in Regulations 15 and 16 shall have effect in relation to a prescription issued for the purposes of a sheme for testing the quality and amount of the drugs, preparations and appliances supplied under the [National Health Services Acts 1946 to 1973] or the [National Health Service (Scotland) Acts 1947 to 1973] and the Regulations made thereunder or to any prescriptions issued for the purposes of the Food and Drugs Act 1955 or, in Scotland, the Food and Drugs (Scotland) Act 1956 to a sampling officer within the meaning of those Acts or for the purposes of the Medicines Act 1968 to a sampling officer within the meaning of that Act.

18. Marking of bottles and other containers (1) Subject to paragraph (2), no person shall supply a controlled drug otherwise than in a bottle, package or other container which is plainly marked—

(a) in the case of a controlled drug other than a preparation, with the amount of the drug contained therein;

(b) in the case of a controlled drug which is a preparation—

(i) made up into tablets, capsules or other dosage units, with the amount of each component (being a controlled drug) of the preparation in each dosage unit and the number of dosage units in the bottle, package or other container;

(ii) not made up as aforesaid, with the total amount of the preparation in the bottle, package or other container and the percentage of each of its components which is a controlled drug.

(2) Nothing in this Regulation shall have effect in relation to the drugs specified in Schedule 1 or poppy-straw or in relation to the supply of a controlled drug by or on the prescription or a practitioner.

19. Keeping of registers   (1) Subject to paragraph (3) and Regulation 21, every person authorised by or under Regulation 5 or 8 to supply any drug specified in Schedule 2 or 4 shall comply with the following requirements, that is to say—

(a) he shall, in accordance with the provisions of this Regulation and of Regulation 20, keep a register and shall enter therein in chronological sequence in the form specified in Part I or Part II of Schedule 5, as the case may require, particulars of every quantity of a drug specified in Schedule 2 or 4 obtained by him and of every quantity of such a drug supplied (whether by way of administration or otherwise) by him whether to persons within or outside Great Britain;

(b) he shall use a separate register or separate part of the register for entries made in respect of each class of drugs, and each of the drugs specified in paragraghs 1, 3 and 6 of Schedule 2 and paragraphs 1 and 3 of Schedule 4 together with its salts and any preparation or other product containing it or any of its salts shall be treated as a separate class, so however that any stereoisomeric form of a drug or its salts shall be classed with that drug.

(2) Nothing in paragraph (1) shall be taken as preventing the use of a separate section within a register or separate part of a register in respect of different drugs or strengths of drugs comprised within the class of drugs to which that register or separate part relates.

(3) The foregoing provisions of this Regulation shall not have effect in relation to—

(a) a person licensed under Regulation 5 to supply any drug, where the licence so directs; or

(b) the sister or acting sister for the time being in charge of a ward, theatre or other department in a hospital or nursing home.

20. Requirements as to registers   Any person required to keep a register under Regulation 19 shall comply with the following requirements, that is to say—

(a) the class of drugs to which the entries on any page of any such register relate shall be specified at the head of that page;

(b) every entry required to be made under Regulation 19 in such a register shall be made on the day on which the drug is obtained or, as the case may be, on which the transaction in respect of the supply of the drug by the person required to make the entry takes place or, if that is not reasonably practicable, on the day next following that day;

    (c) no cancellation, obliteration or alteration of any such entry shall be made, and a correction of such an entry shall be made only by way of marginal note or footnote which shall specify the date on which the correction is made;

    (d) every such entry and every correction of such an entry shall be made in ink or otherwise so as to be indelible;

    (e) such a register shall not be used for any purpose other than the purposes of these Regulations;

21. Record-keeping requirements in particular cases (1) Where a drug specified in Schedule 2 is supplied in accordance with Regulation 8 (5) (a) (i) to a member of the crew of a ship, an entry in the official log book required to be kept under the Merchant Shipping Acts or, in the case of a ship which is not required to carry such an official log book, a report signed by the master of the ship, shall, notwithstanding anything in these Regulations, be a sufficient record of the supply if the entry or report specifies the drug supplied and, in the case of a report, it is delivered as soon as may be to the superintendent of a mercantile marine office established and maintained under the Merchant Shipping Acts.

    (2) Where a drug specified in Schedule 2 is supplied in accordance with Regulation 8 (5) (b) (i) to a person on an offshore installation, an entry in the installation logbook required to be maintained under the Offshore Installations (Logbooks and Registration of Death) Regulations 1972 which specifies the drug supplied shall, notwithstanding anything in these Regulations, be a sufficient record of the supply.

    (3) A midwife authorised by Regulation 11 (1) to have pethidine in her possession shall—

    (a) on each occasion on which she obtains a supply of pethidine, enter in a book kept by her and used solely for the purposes of this paragraph the date, the name and address of the person from whom the drug was obtained, the amount obtained and the form in which it was obtained; and

    (b) on administering pethidine to a patient, enter in the said book as soon as practicable the name and address of the patient, the amount administered and the form in which it was administered.

22. Preservation of registers, books and other documents (1) All registers and books kept in pursuance of Regulation 19 or 21 (3) shall be preserved for a period of two years from the date on which the last entry therein is made.

    (2) Every requisition, order or prescription (other than a health prescription) on which a controlled drug is supplied in pursuance of these Regulations shall be preserved for a period of two years from the date on which the last delivery under it was made.

23. Preservation of records relating to drugs in Schedule 1 (1) A producer of any drug specified in Schedule 1 and a wholesale dealer in any such drug shall keep every invoice or other like record issued in respect of each quantity of such a drug obtained by him and in respect of each quantity of such a drug supplied by him.

(2) A retail dealer in any drug specified in Schedule 1 shall keep every invoice or other like record issued in respect of each quantity of such a drug obtained by him.

(3) Every document kept in pursuance of this Regulation shall be preserved for a period of two years from the date on which it is issued:

Provided that the keeping of a copy of the document made at any time during the said period of two years shall be treated for the purposes of this paragraph as if it were the keeping of the original document.

PART IV: MISCELLANEOUS

24. Destruction of controlled drugs (1) No person who is required by any provision of, or by any term or condition of a licence having effect under, these Regulations to keep records with respect to a drug specified in Schedule 2 or 4 shall destroy such a drug or cause such a drug to be destroyed except in the presence of and in accordance with any direections given by a person authorised (whether personally or as a member of a class) for the purposes of this paragraph by the Secretary of State (hereafter in this Regulation referred to as an 'authorised person').

(2) An authorised person may, for the purpose of analysis, take a sample of a drug specified in Schedule 2 or 4 which is to be destroyed.

(3) Where a drug specified in Schedule 2 or 4 is destroyed in pursuance of paragraph (1) by or at the instance of a person who is required by any provision of, or by any term or condition of a licence having effect under, these Regulations to keep a record in respect of the obtaining or supply of that drug, that record shall include particulars of the date of destruction and the quantity destroyed and shall be signed by the authorised person in whose presence the drug is destroyed.

(4) Where the master or owner of a ship or installation manager of an offshore installation has in his possession a drug specified in Schedule 2 which he no longer requires, he shall not destroy the drug or cause it to be destroyed but shall dispose of it to a constable or to a person who may lawfully supply it.

25. Transitional provisions (1) Any licence issued for the purposes of section 6 (1) of the Dangerous Drugs Act 1965 (which makes it an offence to cultivate any cannabis plant except under licence) and in force immediately before the repeal of that Act shall continue in force for the same period of time as if that Act had not been repealed and shall have effect as if it had been issued for the purposes of Regulation 12.

(2) Any licence issued for the purposes of any provision of the Dangerous Drugs (No 2) Regulations 1964 and in force immediately before the repeal of the said Act of 1965 shall, insofar as it authorises any person to do anything which could be authorised by a licence issued under Regulation 5, continue in force for the same period of time as if that Act had not been repealed and shall have effect as if it had been issued for the purposes of Rcgulation 5.

(3) Any authority granted in respect of any class for the purposes of any provision of the said Regulations of 1964 and in force immediately before the repeal of the said Act of 1965 shall, insofar as it authorises any class of

persons to do anything which could be authorised by an authority granted for the purposes of Regulation 8 (3) or 10 (3), continue in force as if that Act had not been repealed and shall have effect as if granted for the purposes of Regulation 8 (3) or 10 (3) as the case may be.

(4) Any register, record, book, prescription or other document required to be preserved under Regulation 26 of the said Regulations of 1964 shall, notwithstanding the repeal of the said Act of 1965, be preserved for the same period of time as if that Act had not been repealed.

(5) In the case of a prescription issued before the coming into operation of these Regulations, Regulation 16 (1) shall have effect as if—

(a) in the case of a prescription containing a controlled drug specified in the Schedule to the Drugs (Prevention of Misuse) Act 1964 immediately before the repeal of that Act, sub-paragraphs (a) and (b) of that paragraph were omitted; and

(b) in any other case, for the said sub-paragraphs (a) and (b) there were substituted the words 'unless the prescription complies with the provisions of the Dangerous Drugs (No 2) Regulations 1964 relating to prescriptions'.

(6) In this Regulation, any reference to the repeal of the Dangerous Drugs Act 1965 or the Drugs (Prevention of Misuse) Act 1964 shall be construed as a reference to its repeal by section 39 (2) of and Schedule 6 to the Act.

SCHEDULE 1

Regulations 4, 7, 8, 14, 15, 16, 18 and 23

CONTROLLED DRUGS EXCEPTED FROM THE PROHIBITION ON IMPORTATION, EXPORTATION AND POSSESSION AND SUBJECT TO THE REQUIREMENTS OF REGULATION 23

1. (1) Any preparations of one or more of the substances to which this paragraph applies, not being a preparation designed for administration by injection, when compounded with one or more other active or inert ingredients and containing a total of not more than 100 milligrammes of the substance or substances (calculated as base) per dosage unit and with a total concentration of not more than 2.5 per cent (calculated as base) in undivided preparations.

(2) The substances to which this paragraph applies are acetyldihydrocodeine, codeine, dihydrocodeine, ethylmorphine, nicocodine, nicodicodine (6-nicotinoyl-dihydrocodeine), norcodeine, pholcodine and their respective salts.

2. Any preparation of cocaine containing not more than 0.1 per cent of cocaine calculated as cocaine base, being a preparation compounded with one or more other active or inert ingredients in such a way that the cocaine cannot be recovered by readily applicable means or in a yield which would constitute a risk to health.

3. Any preparation of medicinal opium or of morphine containing (in either case) not more than 0.2 per cent of morphine calculated as anhydrous morphine base, being a preparation compounded with one or more other active or inert ingredients in such a way that the opium or, as the case may be, the morphine, cannot be recovered by readily applicable means or in a yield which would constitute a risk to health.

[3A. Any preparation of difenoxin (1-(3-cyano-3,3-diphenylpropyl)-4-phenylpiperidine-4-carboxylic acid) containing, per dosage unit, not more than 0.5

milligrammes of difenoxin and a quantity of atropine sulphate equivalent to at least 5 per cent of the dose of difenoxin.];

4. Any preparation of diphenoxylate containing, per dosage unit, not more than 2.5 milligrammes of diphenoxylate calculated as base, and quantity of atropine sulphate equivalent to at least 1 per cent of the dose of diphenoxylate.

[4A. Any preparation of propiram containing, per dosage unit, not more than 100 milligrammes of propiram calculated as base and compounded with at least the same amount (by weight) of methylcellulose.];

5. Any powder of epecacuanha and opium comprising—
    10 per cent opium, in powder,
    10 per cent ipecacuanha root, in powder,
      well mixed with
    80 per cent of any other powdered ingredient containing no controlled drug.

6. Any mixture containing one or more of the preparations specified in paragraphs 1 to 5 [(including paragraphs 3A and 4A)] being a mixture of which none of the other ingredients is a controlled drug.

SCHEDULE 2

Regulations 7, 8, 10, 19, 21 and 24

CONTROLLED DRUGS SUBJECT TO THE REQUIREMENTS OF REGULATIONS 14, 15, 16, 18, 19, 20, 21 AND 24

1. The following substances and products, namely:

Acetorphine.
Allylprodine.
Alphacetylmethadol.
Alphameprodine.
Alphamethadol.
Alphaprodine.
Anileridine.
Benzethidine.
Benzylmorphine (3-benzylmorphine).
Betacetylmethadol.
Betameprodine.
Betamethadol.
Betaprodine.
Bezitramide.
Clonitazene.
Cocaine.
Desomorphine.
Dextromoramide.
Diamorphine.
Diampromide.
Diethylthiambutene.
Dihydrocodeinone
   O-carboxymethyloxime.
Dihydromorphine.
Dimenoxadole.
Dimepheptanol.
Dimethylthiambutene.
[Difenoxin (1-(3-cyano-3,3-diphenyl-
   propyl)-4-phenylpiperidine-4-
   carboxylic acid].
Dioxaphetyl butyrate.

Diphenoxylate.
Dipipanone.
Drotebanol (3,4-dimethoxy-17-
   methylmorphinan-6β,14-diol).
Ecgonine, and any derivative of
   ecgonine which is convertible to
   ecgonine or to cocaine.
Ethylmethylthiambutene
Etonitazene.
Etorphine.
Etoxeridine.
Fentanyl.
Furethidine.
Hydrocodone.
Hydromorphinol.
Hydroxypethidine.
Isomethadone.
Ketobemidone.
Levomethorphan.
Levomoramide.
Levophenacylmorphan.
Levorphanol.
Medicinal opium.
Metazocine.
Methadone.
Methadyl acetate.
Methyldesorphine.
Methyldihydromorphine
   (6-methyldihydromorphine).
Metopon.
Morpheridine.

Morphine.
Morphine methobromide, morphine *N*-oxide and other pentavalent nitrogen morphine derivatives.
Myrophine.
Nicomorphine.
Noracymethadol.
Norlevorphanol.
Normethadone.
Normorphine.
Norpipanone.
Oxycodone.
Oxymorphone.
Pethidine.
Phenadoxone.
Phenampromide.
Phenazocine.
[Phencyclidine]
Phenomorphan.
Phenoperidine.

Piminodine.
Piritramide.
Proheptazine.
Properidine.
Racemethorphan.
Racemoramide.
Racemorphan.
Thebacon.
Thebaine.
Trimeperidine.
4-Cyano-2-dimethylamino-4,4-diphenylbutane.
4-Cyano-1-methyl-4-phenylpiperidine.
1-Methyl-4-phenylpiperidine-4-carboxylic acid.
2-Methyl-3-morpholino-1,1-diphenylpropanecarboxylic acid.
4-Phenylpiperidone-4-carboxylic acid ethyl ester.

2. Any stereoisomeric form of a substance specified in paragraph 1 not being dextromethorphan or dextrorphan.

3. Any ester or ether of a substance specified in paragraph 1 or 2, not being a substance specified in paragraph 6.

4. Any salt of a substance specified in any of paragraphs 1 to 3.

5. Any preparation or other product containing a substance or product specified in any of paragraphs 1 to 4, not being a preparation specified in Schedule 1.

6. The following substances and products, namely:

Acetyldihydrocodeine.
Amphetamine.
Codeine.
Dexamphetamine.
Dihydrocodeine.
Ethylmorphine (3-ethylmorphine).
Methaqualone.
Methylamphetamine.

Methylphenidate.
Nicocodine.
Nicodicodine
(6-nicotinoyldihydrocodeine).
Norcodeine.
Phenmetrazine.
Pholcodine.
Propiram.

7. Any stereoisomeric form of a substance specified in paragraph 6.

8. Any salt of a substance specified in paragraph 6 or 7.

9. Any preparation or other product containing a substance or product specified in any of paragraphs 6 to 8, not being a preparation specified in Schedule 1.

SCHEDULE 3

Regulations 7, 9 and 10

CONTROLLED DRUGS SUBJECT TO THE REQUIREMENTS OF REGULATIONS 14, 15, 16 AND 18

1. The following substances, namely:

Benzphetamine.
Chlorphentermine.
Mephentermine.

Phendimetrazine.
Pipradol.

2. Any stereoisomeric form of a substance specified in paragraph 1.

3. Any salt of a substance specified in paragraph 1 or 2.

4. Any preparation or other product containing a substance specified in any of paragraphs 1 to 3, not being a preparation specified in Schedule 1.

[SCHEDULE 4

Regulations 19 and 24

CONTROLLED DRUGS SUBJECT TO THE REQUIREMENTS OF REGULATIONS 14, 15, 16, 18, 19, 20 AND 24

The following substances and products, namely:

(a) Bufotenine
Cannabinol
Cannabinol derivatives
Cannabis and cannabis resin
Coca leaf
Concentrate of poppy-straw
Lysergamide
Lysergide and other N-alkyl derivatives of lysergamide
Mescaline
Psilocin
Raw opium
4-Bromo-2,5-dimethoxy-α-methylphenethylamine
N,N-Diethyltryptamine
N,N-Dimethyltryptamine
2,5-Dimethoxy-α,4-dimethylphenethylamine

(b) any compound (not being a compound for the time being specified in sub-paragraph (a) above) structurally derived from tryptamine or from a ring-hydroxy tryptamine by substitution at the nitrogen atom of the sidechain with one or more alkyl substituents but no other substituent;

(c) any compound (not being methoxyphenamine or a compound for the time being specified in sub-paragraph (a) above) structurally derived from phenethylamine, an N-alkylphenethylamine, α-methylphenethylamine, an N-alkyl-α-methylphenethylamine, α-ethylphenethylamine, or an N-alkyl-α-ethylphenethylamine by substitution in the ring to any extent with alkyl, alkoxy, alkylenedioxy or halide substituents, whether or not further substituted in the ring by one or more other univalent substituents.

2. Any stereoisomeric form of a substance specified in paragraph 1.

3. Any ester or ether of a substance specified in paragraph 1 or 2.

4. Any salt of a substance specified in any of paragraphs 1 to 3.

5. Any preparation or other product containing a substance or product specified in any of paragraphs 1 to 4, not being a preparation specified in Schedule 1.]

Misuse of Drugs (Safe Custody) Regulations 1973 SI 1973/798

1. These regulations may be cited as the Misuse of Drugs (Safe Custody) Regulations 1973 and (with the exception of Regulations 3 and 4 and Schedule 2 which shall come into operation on [1st April 1975]) shall come into operation on 1st July 1973.

2. (1) In these Regulations, unless the context otherwise requires, the expression—

'the Act' means the Misuse of Drugs Act 1971;

'retail dealer' means a person lawfully conducting a retail pharmacy business or a pharmacist engaged in supplying drugs to the public at a health centre within the meaning of the Medicines Act 1968.

(2) In these Regulations any reference to any enactment shall be construed as a reference to that enactment as amended, and as including a reference thereto as extended or applied, by or under any other enactment.

(3) The Interpretation Act 1889 shall apply for the interpretation of these Regulations as it applies for the interpretation of an Act of Parliament.

3. (1) This Regulation applies to the following premises, that is to say:
   (a) any premises occupied by a retail dealer for the purposes of his business;
   (b) any nursing home within the meaning of Part VI of the Public Health Act 1936. . .
   (c) . . .
   (d) any mental nursing home within the meaning of Part III of the Mental Health Act 1959;
   (e) . . .

(2) Subject to paragraph (4) of this Regulation, the occupier and every person concerned in the management of any premises to which this Regulation applies shall ensure that all controlled drugs (other than those specified in Schedule 1 to these Regulations) on the premises are, so far as circumstances permit, kept in a locked safe, cabinet or room which is so constructed and maintained as to prevent unauthorised access to the drugs.

(3) Subject to Regulation 4 of these Regulations, the relevant requirements of Schedule 2 to these Regulations shall be complied with in relation to every safe, cabinet or room in which controlled drugs are kept in pursuance of paragraph (2) of this Regulation.

(4) It shall not be necessary to comply with the requirements of paragraph (2) of this Regulation in respect of any controlled drug which is for the time being under the direct personal supervision of—
   (a) in the case of any premises falling within paragraph (1) (a) of this Regulation, a pharmacist in respect of whom no direction under section 12 (2) of the Act is for the time being in force; or
   (b) in the case of premises falling within paragraph 1 (b) to (e) of this Regulation, the person in charge of the premises or any member of his staff designated by him for the purpose.

4. (1) Paragraph (3) of Regulation 3 of these Regulations shall not have effect in relation to a safe, cabinet or room situated on any premises occupied for the purposes of his business by a person lawfully conducting a retail pharmacy business (hereafter in this Regulation referred to as 'the occupier') if a certificate has been issued in pursuance of paragraph (2) of this Regulation (hereafter in this Regulation referred to as a 'certificate') in respect of that safe, cabinet or room and the certificate is for the time being in force.

(2) On receiving written application in that behalf from the occupier, the chief officer of police for the police area in which the premises in question are situated may—

(a) cause the said premises and, in particular, any safe, cabinet or room in which controlled drugs are to be kept, to be inspected; and

(b) if satisfied that, in all the circumstances of the case, the safes, cabinets or rooms in which controlled drugs (other than those specified in Schedule 1 to these Regulations) are to be kept provide an adequate degree of security, issue a certificate in respect of those safes, cabinets or rooms.

(3) Every certificate shall specify—

(a) every safe, cabinet or room to which the certificate relates; and

(b) any conditions necessary to be observed if the safes, cabinets and rooms to which the certificate relates are to provide an adequate degree of security.

(4) Where a certificate is in force in respect of any safe, cabinet or room on any premises, the chief officer of police may cause the premises to be inspected at any reasonable time for the purpose of ascertaining whether any conditions specified in the certificate are being observed and whether as a result of any change of circumstances the safes, cabinets and rooms to which the certificate relates have ceased to provide an adequate degree of security.

(5) A certificate may be cancelled by the chief officer of police if it appears to him that—

(a) there has been a breach of any condition specified in the certificate; or

(b) as a result of any change of circumstances, the safes, cabinets and rooms to which the certificate relates no longer provide an adequate degree of security; or

(c) the occupier has refused entry to any police officer acting in pursuance of paragraph (4) of this Regulation.

(6) A certificate shall, unless previously cancelled in pursuance of paragraph (5) of this Regulation, remain in force for a period of one year from the date of issue thereof, but may from time to time be renewed for a further period of one year.

5. (1) Where any controlled drug (other than a drug specified in Schedule 1 to these Regulations) is kept otherwise than in a locked safe, cabinet or room which is so constructed and maintained as to prevent unauthorised access to the drug, any person to whom this Regulation applies having possession of the drug shall ensure that, so far as circumstances permit, it is kept in a locked receptacle which can be opened only by him or by a person authorised by him.

(2) Paragraph (1) of this Regulation applies to any person other than—

(a) a person to whom the drug has been supplied by or on the prescription of a practitioner for his own treatment or that of another person or an animal; or

(b) a person engaged in the business of a carrier when acting in the course of that business; or

(c) a person engaged in the business of the Post Office when acting in the course of that business.

SCHEDULE 1

Regulations 3 (2), 4 (2) (b), 5

EXEMPTED DRUGS

1. Any controlled drug specified in Schedule 1 to the Misuse of Drugs Regulations 1973.

2. Any liquid preparation designed for administration otherwise than by injection which contains any of the following substances and products, that is to say:

- (a) Amphetamine; dexamphetamine; levamphetamine
- (b) Benzphetamine
- (c) Chlorphentermine
- (d) Mephentermine
- (e) Methaqualone
- (f) Methylamphetamine
- (g) Methylphenidate
- (h) Phendimetrazine
- (i) Phenmetrazine
- (j) Pipradrol
- (k) Any stereoisomeric form of a substance specified in any of paragraphs (b) to (j) above.
- (l) Any salt of a substance specified in any of paragraphs (a) to (k) above.

SCHEDULE 2

(Deals with technical specification.)

Misuse of Drugs (Notification of and Supply to Addicts) Regulations 1973
SI 1973/799

1. These Regulations may be cited as the Misuse of Drugs (Notification of and Supply to Addicts) Regulations 1973 and shall come into operation on 1st July 1973.

2. (1) In these Regulations, the expression—

'drug' means a controlled drug specified in the Schedule to these Regulations;

'hospital'—

- (a) as respects England and Wales, has the same meaning as in the National Health Service Act 1946 and includes a nursing home within the meaning of Part VI of the Public Health Act 1936, a mental nursing home within the meaning of Part III of the Mental Health Act 1959 and a special hospital within the meaning of that Act;
- (b) *(Applies to Scotland.)*

(2) For the purposes of these Regulations, a person shall be regarded as being addicted to a drug if, and only if, he has as a result of repeated administration become so dependent upon the drug that he has an overpowering desire for the administration of it to be continued.

(3) In these Regulations any reference to any enactment shall be construed as a reference to that enactment as amended, and as including a reference thereto as extended or applied, by or under any other enactment.

(4) The Interpretation Act 1889 shall apply for the interpretation of these Regulations as it applies for the interpretation of an Act of Parliament.

3. (1) Subject to paragraph (2) of this Regulation, any doctor who attends a person who he considers, or has reasonable grounds to suspect, is addicted to any drug shall, within seven days of the attendance, furnish in writing to the Chief Medical Officer at the Home Office such of the following particulars with respect to that person as are known to the doctor, that is to say, the name, address, sex, date of birth and national health service number of that person, the date of the attendance and the name of the drug or drugs concerned.

(2) It shall not be necessary for a doctor who attends a person to comply with the provisions of paragraph (1) of this Regulation in respect of that person if—

(a) the doctor is of the opinion, formed in good faith, that the continued administration of the drug or drugs concerned is required for the purpose of treating organic disease or injury; or

(b) the particulars which, apart from this paragraph, would have been required under those provisions to be furnished have, during the period of twelve months ending with the date of the attendance, been furnished in compliance with those provisions—

(i) by the doctor; or

(ii) if the doctor is a partner in or employed by a firm of general practitioners, by a doctor who is a partner in or employed by that firm; or

(iii) if the attendance is on behalf of another doctor, whether for payment or otherwise, by that doctor; or

(iv) if the attendance is at a hospital, by a doctor on the staff of that hospital.

4. (1) Subject to paragraph (2) of this Regulation, a doctor shall not administer or supply to a person who he considers, or has reasonable grounds to suspect, is addicted to any drug, or authorise the administration or supply to such a person of, any substance specified in paragraph (3) below, or prescribe for such a person any such substance, except—

(a) for the purpose of treating organic disease or injury; or

(b) under and in accordance with the terms of a licence issued by the Secretary of State in pursuance of these Regulations.

(2) Paragraph (1) of this Regulation shall not apply to the administration or supply by a doctor of a substance specified in paragraph (3) below if the administration or supply is authorised by another doctor under and in accordance with the terms of a licence issued to him in pursuance of these Regulations.

(3) The substances referred to in paragraphs (1) and (2) above are—

(a) cocaine, its salts and any preparation or other product containing cocaine or its salts other than a preparation falling within paragraph 2 of Schedule 1 to the Misuse of Drugs Regulations 1973;

(b) diamorphine, its salts and any preparation or other product containing diamorphine or its salts;

(c) Dipipanone, its salts and any preparation or other product containing dipipanone or its salts.

5. These Regulations and, in relation only to the requirements of these Regulations, sections 13 (1) and (3), 14, 16, 19 and 25 of and Schedule 4 to the Misuse of Drugs Act 1971 (which relate to their enforcement) shall apply to servants and agents of the Crown.

6. (1) The Dangerous Drugs (Notification of Addicts) Regulations 1968 and the Dangerous Drugs (Supply to Addicts) Regulations 1968 are hereby revoked.

(2) For the purposes of paragraph 2 (b) of Regulation 3 of these Regulations, any particulars furnished, before the coming into operation of these Regulations, in compliance with the provisions of paragraph (1) of Regulation 1 of the Dangerous Drugs (Notification of Addicts) Regulations 1968 shall be deemed to have been furnished in compliance with paragraph (1) of Regulation 3 of these Regulations.

(3) Notwithstanding anything in paragraph (1) of this Regulation, any licence issued by the Secretary of State in pursuance of the Dangerous Drugs (Supply to Addicts) Regulations 1968 before the coming into operation of these Regulations shall continue in force for the same time as if these Regulations had not been made and shall be deemed to have been issued in pursuance of these Regulations.

SCHEDULE

Regulation 2 (1)

CONTROLLED DRUGS TO WHICH THESE REGULATIONS APPLY

1. The following substances and products, namely:

Cocaine	Hydromorphone	Oxycodone
Dextromoramide	Levorphanol	Pethidine
Diamorphine	Methadone	Phenazocine
Dipipanone	Morphine	Piritramide
Hydrocodone	Opium	

2. Any stereoisomeric form of a substance specified in paragraph 1 above, not being dextrorphan.

3. Any ester or ether of a substance specified in paragraph 1 or 2 above not being a substance for the time being specified in Part II of Schedule 2 to the Misuse of Drugs Act 1971.

4. Any salt of a substance specified in any of paragraphs 1 to 3 above.

5. Any preparation or other product containing a substance or product specified in any of paragraphs 1 to 4 above.

Misuse of Drugs Tribunal (England and Wales) Rules 1974
SI 1974/85

1. Citation and commencement   These Rules may be cited as the Misuse of Drugs Tribunal (England and Wales) Rules 1974 and shall come into operation on 1st March 1974.

2. Interpretation   (1) In these Rules, unless the context otherwise requires—

'the Act' means the Misuse of Drugs Act 1971;

'the chairman' means the person appointed by the Lord Chancellor to be the chairman of the tribunal;

'hearing' means the hearing by the tribunal of a case referred to it under section 14 of the Act;

'the respondent' has the same meaning as in section 14 (2) of the Act;

'the secretary' means, in relation to any proceedings, the person whose services are made available by the Secretary of State to act as secretary to the tribunal either generally or in relation to those proceedings;

'the solicitor' means, in relation to any proceedings, the solicitor nominated for the purposes of these Rules by the Secretary of State either generally or in relation to those proceedings;

'the tribunal' means a tribunal in England and Wales constituted under Part I of Schedule 3 to the Act.

(2) In these Rules a form referred to by number means the form so numbered in the Appendix to these Rules, or a form substantially to the like effect, with such variations as the circumstances of the particular case require.

(3) The Interpretation Act 1889 shall apply to the interpretation of these Rules as it applies to the interpretation of an Act of Parliament.

3. Terms of reference and parties   (1) As soon as the Secretary of State has referred a case to the tribunal under section 14 (1) of the Act, he shall serve on the solicitor and on the respondent a notice in writing specifying the terms of the reference, and the names and addresses of the secretary and of the solicitor.

(2) The solicitor shall thereafter be responsible for the preparation and presentation before the tribunal of the case against the respondent and shall be a party to the proceedings on the reference.

(3) No person other than the solicitor and the respondent shall be a party to the proceedings on the reference.

4. Notice of proceedings   (1) Within twenty-eight days after service on him of the notice of the terms of reference the solicitor shall serve on the respondent a notice of proceedings in Form 1, together with a copy of the Act and of these Rules (and of any instrument amending these Rules) and shall send a copy of the notice of proceedings to the tribunal.

(2) The notice of proceedings may be amended—
(a) before the hearing, with the leave of the chairman on an *ex parte* application (which may be disposed of if the chairman thinks fit without a hearing of the application), or
(b) at any time during the hearing, with the leave of the tribunal,
and where the notice of proceedings is amended before the hearing, the solicitor shall forthwith serve notice in writing of the amendement on the respondent and send a copy of the notice to the tribunal.

5. Notice of hearing The chairman shall fix a date, time and place at which the proceedings are to be held, and, not less than twenty-eight days before the date so fixed, the secretary shall serve a notice in Form 2 on the solicitor and on the respondent.

6. Inspection of documents (1) The solicitor shall within fourteen days after the issue of the notice of proceedings and the respondent may at any time serve on the other party a list of the documents on which he proposes to rely, and the solicitor and the respondent shall send to the tribunal a copy of any list served under this paragraph.

(2) A list under paragraph (1) shall specify a reasonable period (commencing not earlier than seven days and ending not later than fourteen days after the date of the list) during which, and a reasonable place at which, the other party may inspect and take copies of the documents contained in the list.

(3) A party shall be entitled to inspect and take copies of any document set out in the list of documents served by the other party during the period and at the place specified by such other party in his list of documents or during such period and at such place as the tribunal may direct.

(4) Unless the tribunal otherwise directs, a party shall produce any document set out in his list of documents at the hearing of the case when called upon to do so by the other party.

7. Interlocutory applications (1) An application for directions of an interlocutory nature in connection with the proceedings may be made by the solicitor or the respondent to the chairman.

(2) The appliction shall be in writing and shall state the matters on which directions are sought and the grounds upon which the application is made.

(3) Notice of the application shall be served on the respondent or on the solicitor, as the case may be, who may send to the chairman and serve on the other party written notice of objection.

(4) Where written notice of objection is sent the chairman shall, before giving any direction on the application, consider such objection and, if he considers it necessary for the proper determination of the application, shall give the parties an opportunity of appearing before him.

(5) The chairman shall serve notice in writing of his decision on the solicitor and on the respondent.

(6) If at any stage the chairman decides that an application involves a question which ought to be decided by the tribunal, he shall fix a date, time and place for a hearing of the application by the tribunal and the

secretary shall serve notice thereof on the solicitor and on the respondent not less than fourteen days before the date fixed.

8. Right of audience At the hearing and at the hearing of an application under rule 7 the parties shall be entitled to appear and be heard either in person or by counsel or a solicitor.

9. Default of appearance (1) Where, on the date fixed for the hearing, the solicitor does not appear, then, whether or not the respondent appears, the tribunal shall adjourn the proceedings on such terms (if any) as it thinks fit.

(2) Where, on the date fixed for the hearing, the respondent does not appear, it shall be the duty of the solicitor to satisfy the tribunal that the notice of proceedings and the notice of hearing have been served on the respondent in accordance with rule 18 and, if so satisfied, the tribunal may proceed, if it thinks fit, in the absence of the respondent.

(3) Where, on the date fixed for the hearing of an application under rule 7, the solicitor or the respondent does, or both of them do, not appear, the tribunal may make such order as it thinks fit.

10. Procedure at hearing (1) Where the respondent appears at the hearing the following order of proceedings shall, unless the tribunal otherwise directs, be observed, that is to say—

(a) the solicitor shall read out the allegations in the notice of proceedings;

(b) the chairman shall ask the respondent whether he admits each such allegation, and if the respondent admits any allegation there shall be recorded a finding that there has been such a contravention or such conduct as is alleged therein;

(c) in respect of any allegation which is not admitted the chairman may ask the respondent whether he is willing to admits any of the facts stated in the allegation;

(d) the solicitor may, in relation to any allegation which is not admitted, address the tribunal and adduce evidence in respect of any fact which has not been admitted;

(e) the respondent may address the tribunal and adduce evidence in relation to any allegation still undisposed of;

(f) on the application of either party the tribunal may then allow evidence in reply or rebuttal if it considers it to be in the interests of the fair disposal of any such allegation to do so;

(g) the solicitor may then address the tribunal;

(h) the respondent may then address the tribunal.

(2) Where the respondent does not appear at the hearing and the tribunal proceeds in his absence, the solicitor may address the tribunal both before and after he has adduced evidence.

11. Evidence (1) Any witness called by a party to the proceedings shall be liable to cross-examination by the other party and, if cross-examined, to re-examination by the party calling him.

(2) The tribunal may accept without proof any matter admitted by a party to the proceedings.

(3) Where any document is put in evidence at the hearing it shall not be necessary to prove its authenticity unless the tribunal otherwise directs.

(4) The tribunal shall not be bound to reject evidence on the gound only that it would be inadmissible in a court of law.

12. Findings of tribunal   In respect of each allegation, other than one in respect of which a finding has been recorded under rule 10 (1) (b), the tribunal shall make and record a finding either—
(a) that there has been such a contravention or such conduct as is alleged; or
(b) that there has been no such contravention or conduct.

13. Submissions and evidence with reference to recommendation   Where there has been recorded any such finding as is mentioned in rule 10 (1) (b) or 12 (a) the solicitor and, if he appears, the respondent may address the tribunal and adduce evidence with reference to the recommendation to be made in respect of the respondent.

14. Majority decision, etc.   In the event of disagreement between the members of the tribunal any decision of the tribunal may be taken by a majority thereof and, if the members are equally divided, the chairman shall have a second and casting vote.

15. Report of tribunal   (1) At the conclusion of the hearing the tribunal may adjourn in order to consider its report to the Secretary of State.
(2) The report shall contain a statement—
(a) of the findings of the tribunal;
(b) of the reasons for the findings;
(c) (in the event of a finding under rule 10 (1) (b) or 12 (a))
  (i) of the recommendation of the tribunal, or, as the case may be, of the fact that the tribunal considers that a direction should not be given, and
  (ii) of the reasons for the recommendation, or, as the case may be, for so considering; and
(d) (in the event of a disagreement between the members of the tribunal) of the names of the majority and of the minority, and of the latter's reasons, so far as at variance with those of the majority, on—
  (i) the findings, or, as the case may be,
  (ii) the question whether a recommendation should be made, or
  (iii) the terms of any recommendation.
(3) The chairman shall sign the report on behalf of the tribunal and the secretary shall serve a copy of the report on the solicitor and on the respondent.
(4) Where the hearing has taken place in private the tribunal shall ensure that the report does not disclose the identity of any person, other than the respondent, about whom an adverse finding of fact has been made, or of any person referred to in the report as being addicted to or having taken controlled drugs of any description.

16. Reference back to or to another tribunal (1) When the Secretary of State has referred a case to the tribunal under section 14 (7) (b) of the Act he shall serve on the solicitor and on the respondent notice in writing of the terms of the reference under that paragraph, and subject to paragraph (2) of this rule, the provisions of these Rules shall apply to the proceedings on that reference as they apply to proceedings on a reference under section 14 (1) of the Act.

(2) Where the notice of proceedings served under paragraph (1) is the same, or substantially the same, as that on the previous reference under section 14 (1) or, as the case may be, under section 14 (7) (b) of the Act (in this paragraph alike referred to as the 'previous reference') an order may be made on an application under rule 7 that the list or lists of documents supplied under rule 6 and any order made under rule 7 or under this paragraph for the purposes of the previous reference shall be deemed to have been supplied or made in the proceedings on the reference (or latest reference) under section 14 (7) (b) of the Act.

17. Application for consent of tribunal under section 15 (6) of the Act (1) An application by the Secretary of State for the consent of the tribunal under section 15 (6) of the Act to the extension of a direction may be made by sending to the chairman a notice of application in writing, together with a copy of the report of the professional panel, and an application for consent under that subsection to a further extension may be made by sending to him a notice of application in writing.

(2) The Secretary of State shall serve a copy of the notice of application, and, as the case may be, of the report, on the respondent and shall at the same time inform the respondent that he may, within five days of service upon him, send to the chairman written representations relating to the proposed extension or further extension.

(3) On the expiration of the time limit for the sending of representations the chairman shall consider the application and any representations and may give or withhold the consent of the tribunal.

(4) The secretary shall as soon as may be inform the Secretary of State and serve notice on the respondent of the consent or of the withholding of the consent of the tribunal.

18. Service of notice (1) Any notice or document required to be served on the respondent under these Rules shall be deemed to have been duly served if it is sent or given to a solicitor acting on behalf of the respondent or is delivered to the respondent personally or left at his proper address or sent to him there—

   (a) in the case of notices under rules 3, 4 and 5, by registered post or by recorded delivery service, or
   (b) in any other case, by post.

(2) Any notice or document required to be served on the solicitor may be sent to the address for service specified in the notice of the terms of reference.

(3) Any notice or document to be sent to the tribunal or to the chairman may be sent to the address of the secretary specified in the notice of the terms of reference.

(4) In this rule 'proper address' means the address of the respondent for the time being registered in the Register kept by the relevant body within the meaning of paragraph 1 of Schedule 3 to the Act, and where, in the opinion of the person serving the document or notice, a letter addressed to the respondent at that address appears unlikely to reach him, the last-known residential or professional address of the respondent, or any other address at or through which he may be found.

19. Extension of time   The time appointed by or under these Rules for doing any act or taking any step in connection with any proceedings may be extended by the chairman, whether or not the period has expired, on such terms and conditions, if any, as appear to him just.

20. Failure to comply with rules   Any failure on the part of any person to comply with the provisions of these Rules shall not render the proceedings, or anything done in pursuance thereof, invalid unless the chairman or the tribunal so directs, but the chairman or the tribunal may give such directions for the purpose of mitigating the consequences of the irregularity as the justice of the case may require.

21. Power to regulate procedure   Subject to the provisions of the Act and of these Rules the tribunal shall have power to regulate its own procedure, and may adjourn or postpone the proceedings as it thinks fit.

APPENDIX
(Sets out two forms referred to in rr. 4 and 5)

Misuse of Drugs (Designation) Order 1977 SI 1977/1379

CONTROLLED DRUGS TO WHICH SECTION 7 (4) OF THE MISUSE OF DRUGS ACT 1971 APPLIES

1. The following substances and products, namely;

(a)   Bufotenine   Lysergide and other *N*-alkyl derivatives
      Cannabinol   of lysergamide
      Cannabinol derivatives   Mescaline
      Cannabis   Psilocin
      Cannabis resin   Raw opium
      Coca leaf   4-Bromo-2,5-dimethoxy-α-methylphenethylamine
      Concentrate of   *N,N*-Diethyltryptamine
         poppy-straw   *N,N*-Dimethyltryptamine
      Lysergamide   2,5-Dimethoxy-α-4-dimethylphenethylamine

(b)   any compound (not being a compound for the time being specified in sub-paragraph (a) above) structurally derived from tryptamine or from a ring-hydroxy tryptamine by substitution at the nitrogen atom of the sidechain with one or more alkyl substituents but no other substituent;

(c)   any compound (not being methoxyphenamine or a compound for the time being specified in sub-paragraph (a) above) structurally derived from phenethylamine, an *N*-alkylphenethylamine, α-methylphenethylamine, an *N*-alkyl-α-methylphenethylamine α-ethylphenethylamine, or an *N*-alkyl-α-ethylphenethylamine by substitution in the ring to any extent with alkyl, alkoxy, alkylenedioxy or halide substituents, whether or not further substituted in the ring by one or more other univalent substituents.

2. Any stereoisomeric form of a substance specified in paragraph 1 above.

3. Any ester or ether of a substance specified in paragraph 1 or 2 above.

4. Any salt of a substance specified in any of paragraphs 1 to 3 above.

5. Any preparation or other product containing a substance or product specified in any of paragraphs 1 to 4 above.

4 Specimen Indictments, Search Warrant and Licence to Produce, Supply and Possess

This appendix contains some specimen indictments for drug offences and also a specimen search warrant and the 'information which is required to obtain it'.

1 Specimen Indictments

1 Possession

Statement of offence
Unlawful possession of a controlled drug contrary to section 5 (2) of the Misuse of Drugs Act 1971.

Particulars of offence
A.B. on 12 August 1983 was unlawfully in possession of a Class B controlled drug namely 4 kilograms of cannabis resin.

2 Possession with intent to supply

Statement of offence
Unlawful possession of a controlled drug with intent to supply contrary to section 5 (3) of the Misuse of Drugs Act 1971.

Particulars of offence
C.D. on 15 July 1983 was unlawfully in possession of a Class B drug, namely 10 kilograms of cannabis resin, with intent to supply the said controlled drug to another.

3 Permitting premises

Statement of offence
Permitting premises to be used for the production of a controlled drug contrary to section 8 (a) of the Misuse of Drugs Act 1971.

Particulars of offence
A.B. on 9 September 1983 at (*address*) in the county of .... being the occupier of the said premises knowingly permitted the

production of a Class A controlled drug, namely lysergide, at the said premises.

4 Importation

Statement of offence
Being knowingly concerned in the fraudulent evasion of the prohibition on importation of a controlled drug contrary to section 170(2) of the Customs and Excise Management Act 1979.

Particulars of offence
A.B. on 12 August 1983 was knowingly concerned in the fraudulent evasion of the prohibition on importation of a Class B controlled drug, namely 100 grammes of amphetamine, imposed by section 3(1) of the Misuse of Drugs Act 1971.

5 Conspiracy

Statement of offence
Conspiracy to possess a controlled drug contrary to section 1(1) of the Criminal Law Act 1977.

Particulars of offence
A.B., C.D. and E.F. between 1 April and 31 May 1983 conspired together to possess a quantity of a class A drug namely cocaine.

2 Specimen search warrant

In the County of

In the Petty Sessional Division of

SEARCH WARRANT

To each and all of the constables of the .... Police.

WHEREAS I, the undersigned Justice of the Peace, am satisfied by information on oath laid this day

by

of the   Police.

that there is reasonable ground for suspecting

> *that controlled drugs are, in contravention of the Misuse of Drugs Act, 1971 or Regulations made thereunder,
> *(and) that a document directly or indirectly relating to, or connected with a transaction or dealing, which was, or an intended transaction or dealing which would if carried out be, an offence under the Misuse of Drugs Act, 1971, or in the

case of a transaction or dealing carried out or intended to be carried out in a place outside the United Kingdom, an offence against the corresponding law in that place, is

in the possession of

on certain premises situate at

YOU ARE THEREFORE HEREBY COMMANDED, at any time or times within one month from the date of this warrant, to enter, if need be by force, the above-mentioned premises and to search the premises and any persons found therein and, if there is reasonable ground for suspecting that an offence under the Misuse of Drugs Act, 1971 has been committed in relation to any controlled drugs found on the premises or in the possession of any such persons, or that a document so found is such a document as is mentioned in paragraph (b) sub-section 23(3) of the said Act, to seize and detain those drugs or that document.

DATED this   day of   19

Justice of the Peace for the

Search Warrant
Misuse of Drugs Act 1971.

(*Delete where inappropriate)

THE INFORMATION

of
of the   Police, who upon oath states that he has reasonable ground for suspecting and does suspect

*that controlled drugs are, in contravention of the Misuse of Drugs Act, 1971 or Regulations made thereunder,
*(and) that a document directly or indirectly relating to, or connected with a transaction or dealing which was, or an intended transaction or dealing which would if carried out be, an offence under the Misuse of Drugs Act, 1971, or in the case of a transaction or dealing carried out or intended to be carried out in a place outside the United Kingdom, an offence against the corresponding law in that place, is

in the possession of

on certain premises situate at

TAKEN AND SWORN

before me this   day of   19 .

Justice of the Peace for the

Information for
Search Warrant.
Misuse of Drugs Act 1971.

(*Delete where inappropriate)

3 Specimen licence to produce, supply and possess

MISUSE OF DRUGS ACT 1971
LICENCE TO PRODUCE, SUPPLY AND POSSESS

HOME OFFICE   Licence No.
Form M.D.12   File No.

In pursuance of the Misuse of Drugs Act 1971 (hereinafter called 'the Act'), the Secretary of State hereby grants to

(hereinafter called 'the licensee') at

a licence to produce any preparation or other product (hereinafter called the 'preparation(s)'), containing any proportion of the following drug(s), including any stereoisomeric forms, and the salts thereof

(hereinafter called the 'drug(s)'), and to supply, offer to supply and to have in his possession the drug(s) and preparation(s) subject to the following conditions.

1. All stocks of the drug(s) and preparation(s) shall at all times be in the charge of the licensee himself or some responsible servant appointed by him for the purpose.
2. The licensee shall furnish to the Secretary of State such returns of the amounts of the drug(s) obtained, the amounts of the preparation(s) produced and the amounts of the drug(s) and preparation(s) supplied by him and held in his possession as may from time to time be required.
3. The licensee shall inform the Secretary of State in writing as soon as practicable of any thefts or losses of the drug(s) or preparations(s) from the address named above or during transit.
4. The licensee shall supply the drug(s) and preparation(s) only to such persons as may lawfully have the drug(s) or preparation(s) in their possession.
5. The licence is valid only for the licensee, and in respect of the address named above. In the event of the licensee ceasing to carry on business or to be employed or otherwise engaged at this address or if the authority of the licence is revoked by the Secretary of State he shall return the licence immediately to the address below.

This licence, unless sooner revoked, shall continue in force until

NOTES: *1.* *Under section 18 of the Act it is an offence for the licensee to contravene a condition of this licence.*
  2. *Under section 23 of the Act this licence and any stocks of the drug(s) and preparation(s) shall be produced for inspection when required by any person duly authorised.*
  3. *Regulation 24 of the Misuse of Drugs Regulations 1973 imposes requirements regarding the destruction of drugs.*

HOME OFFICE
  50 QUEEN ANNE'S GATE
    LONDON SW1H 9AT

Date   Assistant Secretary

5   Sentencing Table

Section creating offence	Nature of offence	Class A	Class B
CEMA 1979, s. 170(2)	'...evasion of prohibition on importation...'	Heroin etc. up to £100,000, 7 years and up appropriately to £1m, 12–14 years. Seldom less than 4 years for appreciable amount.[1] Not necessarily less for cocaine or LSD.[2]	Small amounts, as for possession. Less than 20 kgs, 1½–3 years. Medium quantities, 3– years. Large scale, up to 10 years.
MDA, s. 4(2)	Production	(Usually applies to LSD), 7–13 years if large scale.[3]	(Usually amphetamine analogous to importation.[4]
MDA, s. 4(3)	Supply/Offer to supply	Seldom less than 3 years. May incur sentences similar to importers.[1]	Large quantities up to 10 years. Otherwise 1–4 years.
MDA, s. 5(2)	Possession	No general rule. Prison often appropriate.[1]	Fine often sufficient. Persistent flouting ma lead to imprisonment.
MDA, s. 5(3)	Possession with intent to supply	As for supplier.	As for supplier.[5]
MDA, s. 6	Cultivation of cannabis	If commercial motive or distribution, as for supplier. If not, as for possession.[6]	
MDA, s. 8	'...Permitting premises...'	Depends on activity permitted.[7]	
MDS, s. 20	Involvement in foreign offences	Depends on nature of offence.	

[1] *Aramah* (1983) 76 Cr App Rep 190. [2] *Virgin* (1983) 5 Cr App Rep (S) 148. [3] *Bott* (1979) 1 Cr App R (S) 218; *McCulloch* (1982) 4 Cr App Rep (S) 98. [4] *Rubinstein & Grandison* (1982) 4 Cr App Rep (S) 202. [5] If a defendant is acquitted of a charge under section 5(3) or if the prosecution accept a not guilty plea to such a charge, he must not be sentenced on the basis that he is a supplier: *Spires* (infra). [6] See *Stearn* (1982) 4 Cr App Rep (S) 195; *Lawrence* (1981) 3 Cr App Rep (S) 49. [7] Even permitting premise to be used for smoking cannabis, the least serious section 8 offence, will usually merit a custodial sentence: *Spires*, 17 November 1983, CA (unreported).

6 Selected Statistics

The following tables provide statistics on various aspects of drug abuse. The source of these statistics is the Home Office statistical department, with whose kind permission those tables are reproduced.

Table 1 Quantity¹ of controlled drugs seized by the police by drug type

United Kingdom   *Kilogrammes*

Drug type	1973	1974	1975	1976	1977	1978	1979	1980	1981	1982
CLASS A DRUGS										
Cocaine	2.8	1.4	0.8	0.5	1.7	1.5	2.4	4.2	5.4	6.6
Dextromoramide	0.110	0.014	0.017	0.018	0.025	0.033	0.028	0.028	0.022	0.027
Dipipanone	0.260	0.044	0.012	0.006	0.046	0.019	0.026	0.010	0.011	0.008
Heroin	1.7	0.5	2.7	4.2	2.6	2.2	1.6	1.8	7.6	10.3
Methadone	0.041	0.064	0.075	0.036	0.532	0.038	0.358	0.047	0.952	0.061
Morphine	1.6	0.7	5.1	0.7	1.1	0.8	1.5	1.4	1.3	0.3
Opium	0.4	5.8	12.2	0.5	2.5	10.4	4.5	5.9	7.2	4.3
Pethidine	1.4	1.0	0.9	0.6	0.6	0.5	0.6	0.5	0.3	0.2
LSD	0.182	0.059	0.041	0.015	1.488	0.006	0.102	0.003	0.013	0.086
Other Class A drugs	1.2	0.5	0.7	0.8	0.8	0.3	0.1	0.1	0.2	1.5
CLASS B DRUGS										
Cannabis	107.0	366.0	376.9	253.5	215.9	156.3	145.1	476.4	247.0	419.5
Cannabis plants²	6,932	5,616	5,298	9,718	10,580	8,467	22,306	34,654	21,175	18,086
Cannabis resin	768.4	399.4	466.8	270.5	309.7	290.8	207.0	312.2	300.4	410.4
Cannabis liquid	–	0.1	0.3	26.4	3.4	0.2	1.9	7.3	7.8	2.6
Amphetamine } Dexamphetamine Levamphetamine	1.7	2.4	19.3	6.6	7.6	1.6	3.8	4.9	10.7	10.2
Methylamphetamine	0.1	–³	0.7	0.3	3.5	0.2	4.7	0.1	0.1	1.1
Other Class B drugs	0.9	0.9	3.9	0.5	0.1	0.1	0.1	0.1	0.1	0.7
CLASS C DRUGS										
Methaqualone	6.4	24.6	3.2	1.5	2.3	2.5	3.3	2.0	0.8	0.2
Other Class C drugs	0.008	0.013	0.007	0.013	0.011	0.019	0.018	0.013	0.004	0.030

¹ Seizures of unspecified quantities are not included.   ² Number of plants seized.   ³ Less than 50 grammes.

Table 2 Quantity[1] of controlled drugs seized by HM Customs and Excise by drug type

United Kingdom

Kilogrammes

Drug type	1973	1974	1975	1976	1977	1978	1979	1980	1981	1982
CLASS A DRUGS										
Cocaine	3.6	9.0	6.3	9.4	12.0	14.6	21.6	36.0	15.7	12.1
Dextromoramide	–	–	–[3]	0.001	–[3]	–[3]	0.005	–	–[3]	–
Dipipanone	–	–	–	–	–	–[3]	–	–	–	–
Heroin	1.6	2.3	4.2	16.0	24.0	58.6	43.3	36.4	85.8	185.1
Methadone	0.003	–[3]	–[3]	–[3]	–[3]	–[3]	0.001	0.004	0.001	0.001
Morphine	–[4]	–[4]	2.3	0.7	0.9	3.1	2.9	6.6	5.2	1.7
Opium	5.1	14.2	7.1	2.2	16.0	10.0	58.7	30.3	9.3	17.2
Pethidine	–[4]	–[4]	–[4]	–[4]	2.0	0.4	–[4]	–[4]	–[4]	–[4]
LSD	0.035	0.003	–[3]	0.001	–[3]	0.001	0.241	0.002	0.011	0.005
Other Class A drugs	–[4]	–[4]	0.1	–[4]	0.4	0.4	0.1	1.0	0.4	0.1
CLASS B DRUGS										
Cannabis	3140.9	1613.6	2734.5	2915.3	1729.4	3005.2	6299.9	17942.8	16627.4	12575.9
Cannabis plants[2]	–	–	–	–	–	–[1]	–	–	3	5
Cannabis resin	5248.5	5382.3	1645.0	1652.3	2068.9	3188.8	5247.5	7440.3	7517.1	4002.6
Cannabis liquid	29.1	2.9	84.3	41.4	25.1	55.0	39.5	120.7	73.8	31.6
Amphetamine ⎫ Dexamphetamine ⎬ Levamphetamine ⎭	–[4]	1.4	0.9	1.0	10.8	0.1	0.1	0.2	7.3	2.2
Methylamphetamine	–[4]	–[4]	0.5	0.5	13.7	0.1	–[4]	–[4]	–[4]	–
Other Class B drugs	0.4	25.7	–[4]	–[4]	0.1	0.2	0.1	0.1	0.1	0.2
CLASS C DRUGS										
Methaqualone	0.1	0.3	5.3	0.4	4.0	0.7	0.2	1.3	0.4	12.8
Other Class C drugs	–[3]	0.001	0.001	0.001	0.002	0.002	0.033	0.001	0.001	–

[1] Seizures of unspecified quantities are not included. [2] Number of plants seized. [3] Less than ½ gramme. [4] Less than 50 grammes.

Table 3 Persons¹ found guilty of or cautioned for drugs offences by offence type and age group
United Kingdom

Number of persons

Offence type and age group	1973	1974	1975	1976	1977	1978	1979	1980	1981	1982
DRUGS ACTS OFFENCES²										
Under 17	614	325	194	169	180	142	213	279	289	453
17 and under 21	5,973	4,264	3,312	3,138	2,929	3,043	3,088	3,594	3,945	4,898
21 and under 25	4,828	4,175	4,195	4,320	4,111	4,132	4,039	4,541	4,568	5,307
25 and under 30	1,907	1,992	2,281	2,930	3,142	3,391	3,629	4,259	4,279	4,455
30 and over	1,029	1,055	1,164	1,384	1,632	1,938	2,257	3,179	3,390	3,997
All ages	14,351	11,811	11,146	11,941	11,994	12,646	13,226	15,852	16,471	19,110
OFFENCES OF UNLAWFUL IMPORT OR EXPORT										
Under 17	–	–	1	1	1	2	–	2	4	2
17 and under 21	59	60	63	63	93	69	61	81	104	97
21 and under 25	128	118	176	195	203	181	228	256	271	231
25 and under 30	82	103	139	196	276	242	289	358	398	323
30 and over	96	124	138	174	242	306	404	489	580	481
All ages	365	405	517	629	815	800	982	1,186	1,357	1,134
OTHER OFFENCES INVOLVING DRUGS										
Under 17	27	16	12	5	4	7	3	1	2	4
17 and under 21	237	307	274	208	103	101	82	56	50	44
21 and under 25	227	292	258	211	188	170	140	127	122	88
25 and under 30	107	120	131	137	137	152	120	138	128	100
30 and over	114	92	89	80	67	69	71	79	98	86
All ages	712	827	764	641	499	499	416	401	400	322
ALL DRUGS OFFENCES										
Under 17	622	335	203	171	185	149	214	282	293	459
17 and under 21	6,109	4,446	3,470	3,273	3,044	3,163	3,185	3,691	4,068	5,004
21 and under 25	5,030	4,410	4,416	4,564	4,354	4,364	4,319	4,846	4,886	5,560
25 and under 30	2,033	2,129	2,441	3,168	3,442	3,674	3,952	4,665	4,709	4,808
30 and over	1,183	1,212	1,316	1,578	1,882	2,254	2,669	3,674	3,965	4,488
All ages	14,977	12,532	11,846	12,754	12,907	13,604	14,339	17,158	17,921	20,319

¹ As a person found guilty or cautioned for offences of different types will appear in more than one section of the table, sections cannot be added together to produce totals. ² Drugs Act offences prior to 1 July 1973 were offences against the Dangerous Drugs Act 1965 and the Drugs (Prevention of Misuse) Act 1964. Drugs Act offences from 1 July 1973 are offences against the Misuse of Drugs Act 1971.

Table 4 Persons[1] found guilty of or cautioned for drugs offences by type of drug

United Kingdom

Number of persons

Type of drug	1973	1974	1975	1976	1977	1978	1979	1980	1981	1982
FOUND GUILTY										
Cocaine	175	372	377	327	307	348	330	475	565	425
Heroin	427	443	392	460	392	483	517	749	806	963
Methadone	344	463	480	414	346	366	295	362	445	402
Dipipanone	196	367	405	360	377	491	451	439	496	564
LSD	1,243	824	789	624	277	291	203	245	344	460
Cannabis	11,113	9,235	8,834	9,744	10,440	11,389	12,155	14,690	15,153	16,958
Amphetamines	1,733	1,460	1,480	1,882	1,772	1,081	755	821	1,065	1,500
Other drugs	1,598	1,626	1,600	1,266	1,283	1,249	1,149	1,281	1,130	995
All drugs	14,446	12,138	11,603	12,482	12,704	13,394	14,054	16,919	17,667	19,833
CAUTIONED										
Cocaine	6	3	2	—	2	—	1	1	1	1
Heroin	8	1	1	4	1	—	3	2	2	3
Methadone	3	1	4	2	1	3	3	1	—	2
Dipipanone	2	2	4	1	—	2	2	—	2	2
LSD	80	81	37	23	2	—	5	1	1	6
Cannabis	363	282	153	202	167	183	254	220	235	452
Amphetamines	44	22	21	27	16	12	5	6	9	21
Other drugs	74	28	42	27	15	13	16	11	11	13
All drugs	531	394	243	272	203	210	285	239	254	486
FOUND GUILTY OR CAUTIONED										
Cocaine	181	375	379	327	309	348	331	476	566	426
Heroin	435	444	393	464	393	483	520	751	808	966
Methadone	347	464	484	416	347	369	298	363	445	404
Dipipanone	198	369	409	361	378	493	453	440	498	566
LSD	1,323	905	826	647	279	291	208	246	345	466
Cannabis	11,476	9,517	8,987	9,946	10,607	11,572	12,409	14,910	15,388	17,410
Amphetamines	1,777	1,482	1,501	1,909	1,788	1,093	760	827	1,074	1,521
Other drugs	1,672	1,654	1,642	1,293	1,298	1,262	1,165	1,292	1,141	1,008
All drugs	14,977	12,532	11,846	12,754	12,907	13,604	14,339	17,158	17,921	20,319[2]

[1] As the same person may be found guilty or cautioned for offences involving more than one drug, rows cannot be added together to produce totals for all drugs.

[2] The figure for 1983 is 23,341, an increase on 1982 of approximately 15%.

Table 5 Persons under sentence[1] in prison department establishments on 30 June for drugs offences by length of sentence, previous convictions, previous custodial sentences and sex

England and Wales

Number of persons and percentages

	30 June 1980				30 June 1981				30 June 1982			
	Number of persons			Percentage of total	Number of persons			Percentage of total	Number of persons			Percentage of total
	Males	Females	Total		Males	Females	Total		Males	Females	Total	
LENGTH OF SENTENCE												
Up to and including 1 month	11	—	11	1	10	—	10	1	13	1	14	1
Over 1 month up to and including 3 months	17	—	17	2	19	5	24	3	16	1	17	1
Over 3 months up to and including 6 months	43	5	48	6	48	5	53	6	45	6	51	5
Over 6 months up to and including 12 months	69	7	76	9	100	6	106	12	91	11	102	10
Over 1 year up to and including 2 years	172	18	190	23	189	30	219	25	228	26	254	25
Over 2 years up to and including 5 years	318	21	339	41	298	20	318	37	356	36	392	39
Over 5 years up to and including 7 years	75	4	79	10	68	4	72	8	97	3	100	10
Over 7 years	57	3	60	7	52	3	55	6	74	4	78	8
Borstal training	6	2	8	1	8	2	10	1	8	4	12	1
	768	60	828	100	792	75	867	100	928	92	1,020	100
NUMBER OF PREVIOUS CONVICTIONS												
0	202	27	229	28	215	36	251	29	203	31	234	23
1–2	116	7	123	15	114	7	121	14	154	17	171	17
3–5	116	6	122	15	108	4	112	13	125	3	128	13
6–10	97	1	98	12	101	3	104	12	120	6	126	12
11 and over	64	1	65	8	61	—	61	7	84	2	86	2
Not available	173	18	191	23	193	25	218	25	242	33	275	27
	768	60	828	100	792	75	867	100	928	92	1,020	100
NUMBER OF PREVIOUS CUSTODIAL SENTENCES												
0	377	37	414	50	378	43	321	49	543	56	599	59
1–2	133	4	137	16	140	6	146	17	95	2	97	10
3–5	58	1	59	7	59	1	60	7	32	1	33	3
6–10	22	—	22	3	17	—	17	2	14	—	14	1
11 and over	5	—	5	1	5	—	5	1	2	—	2	—[2]
Not available	173	18	191	23	193	25	218	25	242	33	275	27
	768	60	828	100	792	75	867	100	928	92	1,020	100

[1] Including fine defaulters and person serving partly suspended sentences. [2] Less than 1 per cent.

Table 6 New narcotic drug addicts notified to the Home Office during the year by age (total)

United Kingdom

Age	1973	1974	1975	1976	1977	1978	1979	1980	1981	*Number of persons* 1982
				Total addicts						
Under 16	–	4	–	–	–	–	–	1	2	4
16	11	6	2	5	4	3	5	10	8	11
17	33	34	23	21	12	22	16	27	38	42
18	65	61	40	27	31	34	44	41	77	105
19	81	85	56	48	62	61	64	80	107	148
20	120	91	70	63	74	88	77	98	125	179
21	99	77	96	97	93	95	103	99	163	179
22	70	100	95	87	82	134	117	110	150	229
23	66	65	74	92	94	100	141	117	167	173
24	58	68	87	76	85	103	125	133	164	187
25	35	51	64	99	91	102	124	115	143	186
26	30	38	61	70	73	111	119	123	140	184
27	19	31	46	60	64	65	111	101	147	179
28	14	15	33	42	37	85	83	81	133	130
29	11	11	28	35	40	55	79	84	134	147
30 and under 35	30	39	46	70	96	141	186	213	353	436
35 and under 50	28	29	46	45	59	74	101	74	96	159
50 or over	32	53	24	32	36	38	59	27	29	28
Not recorded	5	12	31	15	76	36	43	66	72	87
Total	807	870	922	984	1,109	1,347	1,597	1,600	2,248	2,793[1]

[1] The 1983 figure is 4,186, an increase on 1982 of approximately 50%. The total number of addicts notified to the Home Office (new addicts plus former addicts) was 5,864, an increase of 42% on the 1982 figure of 4,200. A total of 5,156 persons were no longer recorded as addicts during 1983.

Table 7 Narcotic drug addicts recorded by the Home Office as receiving notifiable drugs in treatment of their addiction at 31 December by age
United Kingdom

Total addicts

Number of persons

Age	1972	1973	1974	1975	1976	1977	1978	1979	1980	1981	1982
Under 16	—	—	—	—	—	—	—	—	—	2	—
16	3	2	1	—	—	—	—	—	1	1	2
17	12	9	7	4	3	1	5	2	—	10	5
18	24	24	15	10	3	7	9	12	7	24	26
19	56	49	41	25	12	13	22	20	26	47	50
20	98	96	72	44	33	29	39	38	44	74	79
21	119	139	110	80	44	53	67	53	45	103	106
22	169	157	141	120	89	68	88	76	76	137	142
23	177	186	175	145	112	116	115	123	99	136	165
24	167	173	195	173	134	123	129	138	132	175	166
25	132	164	189	188	163	148	167	160	151	204	198
26	92	146	173	184	162	174	182	188	182	207	258
27	65	93	149	157	186	175	217	205	192	276	269
28	52	75	103	144	153	176	193	233	212	248	295
29	37	52	70	83	145	152	186	230	245	297	319
30	119	35	50	77	84	127	165	193	239	304	313
31	}	28	35	49	66	85	141	169	202	299	321
32		28	28	36	44	62	94	153	187	244	315
33		22	29	32	31	48	68	87	134	194	244
34		21	21	25	25	35	43	70	90	144	202
35 and under 50	121	136	165	171	189	209	255	288	326	439	604
50 and over	173	180	196	194	189	201	205	206	209	216	237
Not recorded	1	1	2	8	7	14	12	22	47	63	55
Total	1,617	1,816	1,967	1,949	1,874	2,016	2,402	2,666	2,846	3,844	4,371[2]

[1] There figures only show those addicts receiving treatment, which is but a fraction of the total number. The total number of narcotic addicts in the UK is estimated variously at between 20,000 and 40,000.
[2] The figure for 1983 is 5,079, an increase on 1982 of approximately 16%.

7 Profits at Various Stages of the Supply Chain

The following table is intended to give an approximate indication of the prices paid at various stages in the drug distribution chain. It must be emphasised that such figures are only guidelines. They will vary from one transaction to another and many factors will affect the market prices at any given time.

South West Asian Heroin	Cocaine	High grade Cannabis resin[1]	Home grown herbal cannabis[2]
Producer[3]	Producer	Producer	Producer
↓ £3,000/kg[4]	↓ £6,000–£8,000/kg	↓ £250/kg	
Importer	Importer	Importer	
↓ £15,000–£20,000/kg	↓ £20,000–£25,000/kg	↓ £1,000–£1,200/kg	
Wholesaler	Wholesaler	Wholesaler	£500/kg
↓ £20,000–£25,000/kg	↓ £40,000/kg	↓ £1,750/kg	
Secondary Wholesaler			
↓ £30,000–£40,000/kg			
Retailer	Retailer	Retailer	
↓ £70,000/kg	↓ £60,000–£70,000/kg	↓ £2,500/kg	↓
Consumer	Consumer	Consumer	Consumer

All figures are expressed in £ sterling per kilogram for convenient comparison, although at 'street level' prices are normally expressed in £ per gram, or in the case of cannabis, £ per ounce.

[1] The price of resin varies with its origin and quantity. The figures given are for high grade resin such as 'black' resin from Afghanistan. Moroccan resin is normally of lower quality, with that of Middle Eastern origin being somewhere in the middle.

[2] Most home-grown cannabis is in fact given away by the grower to friends.

[3] The term producer in this table refers not to the farmer or grower but to the first person in the chain who is in possession of the finished product in commercially saleable form.

[4] As a general rule, large-scale dealers in heroin are very rarely users of the drug, although cocaine traffickers frequently are. At the bottom end of the chain, however, almost all 'retail' dealers in heroin are themselves addicts.

8 Further Information

One of the greatest obstacles encountered in attempting to overcome drug-related problems is ignorance. Many of 'society's' attitudes to drugs and drug use are based on inaccurate information. Often there is a basic lack of knowledge about drugs on the part of those who come into contact with them in a professional capacity. On a more practical level those who experience problems with drugs and those who wish to help them may not know about the various options available to them in the way of treatment, rehabilitation, counselling and so on. This book does not attempt to deal with the more general aspects of drug abuse, but the following list of organisations may be of assistance to those seeking further information.

General information

Institute for the Study of Drug Dependence (ISDD)   Kingsbury House, 3 Blackburn Road, London NW6 1XA; tel 01-328 5541. A good starting point. The Institute has a large amount of material on drugs and drug use generally. The staff are friendly and knowledgeable, and if they cannot provide the answer they will know somebody who can.

Release   1 Elgin Avenue, London W9; tel 01-289 1123. This organisation gives advice on all aspects of drug use, including the state of the law, referral for those with drug problems and general educational information.

The Home Office   Advice on the application of the Misuse of Drugs Act 1971 and associated regulations can be obtained from one of the three Home Office Inspectorates. These are:
  South Eastern   01-637 2355
  Midlands, South West and Wales   0272-276736
  Northern   0274-727149
  This information will be of relevance principally to those involved with the legal use of controlled drugs such as doctors, pharmacists etc.

Advice/referral
Both Release and the ISDD can provide information on where to go to for help for those with drug problems. Also useful in this way are:

Standing Conference On Drug Abuse (SCODA)   3 Blackburn Road, London NW6; tel 01-328 6556.

Teachers Advisory Council on Alcohol and Drug Education (TACADE) 2 Mount Street, Manchester M2 5NG; tel 061-834 7210.

Rehabilitation, treatment, counselling

A list of hospitals in the UK which provide some treatment for drug addiction is available from SCODA. Specific projects include:

The Community Drug Project 7 New Church Road, London SE5; tel 01-703 0559. Help for those with drug-related problems in South London.

The Hungerford Project 26 Craven Street, London WC2; tel 01-930 4688. Advice, support, counselling and referral for those with drug-related problems.

Blenheim Project 7 Thorpe Close, London W10; tel 01-960 5590. Information, counselling and advice in West London.

Lifeline Project Day Centre Jodrell Street, Manchester M3 3HE. Day centre offering advice, support and practical help.

City Roads 358 City Road, London EC1; tel 01-278 8671. Treatment and crisis centre dealing mainly with barbiturate users.

Narcotics Anonymous PO Box 246, London SW10; tel 01-871 0505.

Families anonymous 88 Caledonian Road, London N1 9DN; 01-278 8805. Self-help group for addicts' relatives.

Index

Abuse of drugs
  general points about, 9–11
  impurities, 10
  indirect damage, 10
  means of administration, 9–10
  mixing of different drugs, 10
  responsibility for legal control, 24
  subjective reactions, 10
Addiction
  policy on treatment, 6
Addicts
  Home Office statistics, 215–216
  meaning, 136
Advisory bodies
  membership, 144
  procedure, 144
Advisory Council on Misuse of Drugs
  constitution, 8, 139
  consultation with, 8
  establishment, 7, 118
  general duty, 7, 118–119
  relationship with government, 7–8, 119
  specific areas for particular attention, 7
Aerosol sprays
  inhalation, 19–20
Aircraft
  constructed for concealing goods, forfeiture of, 156
  customs officer
    access, powers of, 152
    boarding, powers of, 152
    detention, powers of, 152–153
Alcohol
  effects, 19
  use, 19
Amphetamines
  appearance, 15
  dosage, 15
  effects, 15
  general information, 14
  method of administration, 15
  moves to counter growth in misuse, 5
  popularity with teenagers, 5

Amphetamines—*continued*
  price, 15
  slang names, 15
  some drugs in this category, 14
  source, 15
Armed forces
  detention, powers of, 29
  forfeiture by, 101
Arrest
  customs officers' powers, 29
  police powers, 25–28, 32–33, 133
  private citizen, powers of, 26
  warrant, without, 172–173
Attempt
  abolition of common law offence, 85
  cannabis, to procure, 85
  impossible, 85
  meaning, 84–85
  proximate test, 85

Barbiturates
  appearance, 17
  dosage, 17
  effects, 18
  general information, 17
  methods of administration, 17
  price, 17
  slang names, 17
  some drugs in this category, 17
  source, 17
Books
  preservation, 186
Bottles
  marking, 184–185
Box
  drug concealed from direct perception by, 55–56
Breach of peace
  glue sniffing, offences involving, 81

Cannabis
  admission of possession, 64
  appearance, 16
  attempt to procure, 85

Cannabis—*continued*
cultivation
  active process, as, 69
  Britain, in, 68
  defence of ignorance, 68
  increase in, 68
  licence, by, 109, 181
  meaning, 68–70
  prohibition, 68
  restriction, 122
  treated as offence of production,
    69
dosage, 16
effects, 16–17
general information, 16
general slang, 16
history, 3
increase in use, 5
meaning, 60–61, 137
methods of administration, 16
price, 16
resin
  meaning, 61
  possession of, 64
smoking for research purposes, 181
some drugs in this category, 15
source, 16
Cargo
ship jettisoning, forfeiture of, 156
Citizen, private. *See* PRIVATE CITIZEN
Cleaning fluids
inhalation, 19–20
Coca leaf. *See* COCAINE
Cocaine
appearance, 12
dosage, 13
drugs in this category, 12
effects, 13
general information, 12
history, 3
methods of administration, 13
price, 12
slang names, 12
source, 12
Condemnation. *See* FORFEITURE
Conspiracy
abroad, 83
acquiring possession of controlled
  drugs, 83
agreement to do something
  inherently impossible, 83
common law, 82
continuing nature of, 83
evading the prohibition, 82–83
exportation of controlled drugs, 82
importation of controlled drugs, 82

Conspiracy—*continued*
offence of, 173
specimen indictment, 205
statutory offence, 82–84
Consumption of drug
possession after, 57
Container
marking, 184–185
possession of contents of,
  55–56
Control of drugs
international. *See* INTERNATIONAL
  CONTROL OF DRUGS
Controlled drugs
administration, 176
amphetamines. *See* AMPHETAMINES
cannabis. *See* CANNABIS
categories, 106
Class A, 120, 139–141
Class B, 120, 141
Class C, 120, 141
classification, 120, 139–142
coca leaf. *See* COCAINE
cocaine. *See* COCAINE
designation, 202–203
destruction, 187
different forms, 62–63
hallucinogens. *See* HALLUCINOGENS
imperial system, 175
lawful use. *See* LAWFUL USE
meaning, 60–61, 119
metric system, 175
opioids. *See* OPIOIDS
overlap between medical and non-
  medical use, 105
production of. *See* PRODUCTION OF
  CONTROLLED DRUGS
safe custody, special precautions for, 124
supply of. *See* SUPPLY OF CONTROLLED
  DRUGS
Corporation
liability for offences, 79
meaning, 80
offences by, 79–80, 131
officers, liability of, 79
similar officer, meaning, 79
Criminals
drug trafficking, 6
Cultivation of cannabis. *See* CANNABIS
Customs and Excise
aircraft
  access, powers of, 152
  boarding, powers of, 152
  detention, powers of, 152–153
Commissioners' power to mitigate
  penalties, 163

Customs and Excise—*continued*
  forfeiture, 100–101
  legal control of abuse, 24
  obstruction of officer, 30, 151–152
  powers
    arrest, 29
    detention, 29, 156–157
    forfeiture, 29
    generally, 25, 28
    persons, to search, 166
    premises, to search, 165
    search, 28–29, 165–166
    vehicles, to search, 165–166
    vessels, to search, 165–166
  proceedings. *See* PROCEEDINGS
  proof
    certain other matters, 164
    documents, of, 163–164
  protection of officers, 160
  quantity of drugs seized by, 211
  ship
    access, powers of, 152
    boarding, powers of, 152
    detention, powers of, 152–153

Defence
  ignorance, 68
  lack of knowledge, 86
  possession, 65
  prescription, 65–66
  proof of lack of knowledge, 134
Detention
  customs officers' powers, 29, 156–
    157
Doctor. *See* MEDICAL PRACTITIONER
Documents
  obtained by supplier, 181–183
  preservation, 186
  proof of, 163–164
  service of, 134–135
  supply of controlled drugs, 109–110
Driving
  when unfit through drugs, 80–81
Drugs
  abuse of. *See* ABUSE OF DRUGS
  commonly abused, 9 *et seq*.
  controlled. *See* CONTROLLED DRUGS
  driving when unfit through, 80–81
  non-controlled. *See* NON-CONTROLLED
    DRUGS
Drunk
  meaning, 81
Duplicity
  possession and, 59

Duty
  penalty for fraudulent evasion, 166–
    167

Evidence
  police powers to search and obtain,
    131–132
  possession, and, 63–64
  tribunal, 199–200
Exportation
  activities amounting to being
    concerned in, 48
  conspiracy, 82
  exemptions from prohibition, 188–
    189
  prohibited or restricted goods,
    offences, 155–156
  prohibition of, 41
  restriction, 120
  time of, 42, 151
Extradition
  procedure, 36–37
  provisions, 136

Forfeiture
  aircraft, ship or vehicle constructed
    for concealing goods, 156
  armed forces, by, 101
  claim, notice of, 169
  condemnation
    certain claimants, special
      provisions, 171
    generally, 170
    proceedings for, 170
    seizures before, 171
  Customs and Excise Management
    Acts, under, 100–101
  customs officers' powers, 29, 101
  detention, seizure and condemnation
    of goods, 157–158
  discretionary, 101
  goods improperly imported, 153–154
  order, 99–100
  procedure, 102
  proof, 171
  provisions, 134
  purpose, 99
  seizure, notice of, 169
  ship. *See* SHIP
  smuggling, to deter, 101
  unfair, 101
Freud, Sigmund
  advocacy of beneficial effects of
    cocaine, 3

General practitioner. *See* MEDICAL
    PRACTITIONER
Glue sniffing
    increase in practice, 19–20
    offences involving breach of peace,
        81
Government
    relationship with Advisory Council,
        7–8

Hallucinogens
    appearance, 13
    dosage, 14
    effects, 14
    general information, 13
    methods of administration, 14
    price, 14
    some drugs in this category, 13
    source, 14
Health prescription
    meaning, 174
    See also PRESCRIPTION
Hearing. *See* TRIBUNAL
History
    legislation, 3–6
Hospital
    drug units, 97
    meaning, 194

Ignorance. *See* KNOWLEDGE
Importation
    concerned in, meaning, 44–46
    conspiracy, 82
    exemptions from prohibition, 188–
        189
    fraudulent, meaning, 46
    frequency of offences, 41
    improper
        forfeiture of goods, 153–154
        penalty, 154–155
    knowingly concerned, meaning, 42–
        44
    persons normally effecting, 41
    prohibition of, 41
    restriction, 120
    specimen indictment, 205
    time of, 42, 151
    treatment of cases involving, 41
Imprisonment
    maximum terms, 162
    persons under sentence, 214
Incitement
    offence, 84
Indictments
    drafting of, 35–36
    specimen, 204–205

Information
    power to obtain from doctors and
        pharmacists, 129–130
International control of drugs
    corresponding law, meaning, 78, 136
    penalty under foreign law, 93–94
    person assisting or inducing
        commission of offence outside
        UK, 78

Knowledge
    belief of entitlement to possess, 87
    general defence of lack of, 86
    ignorance of some other material
        fact, 87–88
    ignorance that substance was
        controlled drug, 86–87
    lack of case law, 86
    possession and, 54, 86–88
    proof of lack of as defence, 134

LSD
    slang name, 13
    spread of use, 5
Lawful use
    documentation, 109–110
    licence, 109
    notification, 111–114
    possession, 107–108
    production of controlled drugs, 108
    regulations. *See* REGULATIONS
    supply of controlled drugs, 108
Legal proceedings. *See* PROCEEDINGS
Legislation
    assessment of success of, 6
    history and policy, 3–6
    1914–18 war, effect of, 4
    technical aspect, 23
Licence
    cannabis cultivation, 109, 181
    offences, 114
    possession, manufacture and supply,
        109
    production of controlled drug, 176
    provisions, 135
    specimen, 207
Local byelaws
    convictions under, 81
Local enactments
    power to amend, 138

Magistrates
    limitation of powers, 38
Manufacture
    licence, 109

Medical practitioner
convicted of offence, prohibition of
prescription, 125
information, power to obtain, 129–
130
notification, 111–114, 194–196
overprescribing, problems of, 6
prohibition of prescription
directions, 125–126
investigation, 126–127
supplementary provisions, 129
temporary directions, 127–129
treatment of addict, 97–98
Midwives
pethidine, exemption in respect of,
180–181
Minor tranquillisers
appearance, 18
effects, 18–19
general information, 18
slang names, 18
some drugs in this category, 18
use, 18
Morphia
use in 1914–18 war, 4
Motor vehicle
customs officers' powers to search,
165–166
driving when unfit through drugs,
80–81
Mushrooms
magic, 62–63
peyote, 3

Non-controlled drugs
alcohol, 19
barbiturates. *See* BARBITURATES
minor stimulants, 19
minor tranquillisers. *See* MINOR
TRANQUILLISERS
solvents, 19–20
Non-statutory groups
assistance by, 98
Northern Ireland
special provisions, 138
Notice
seizure, of, 169
service of, 36
Notification
doctor, by, 111–114, 194–196

Obstruction
customs officer, 30, 151–152
Occupier of premises
concerned in management, meaning,
73–74

Occupier of premises—*continued*
facilitating production, supply or use
of drugs, 71
knowingly permits or suffers,
meaning, 73
meaning, 72
permitting activities to take place
there, 123
Offences
attempts to commit, 130
conspiracy, 173
customs officers' powers. *See*
CUSTOMS AND EXCISE
drop in prosecutions for, 5
drunken, extension to other drugs, 81
exportation of prohibited or
restricted goods, 155–156
general provisions, 167–168
licences, 114
miscellaneous, 130
person
against, 80, 172
assisting or inducing commission
outside UK, 78, 131
found guilty of or cautioned for,
212–213
under sentence, 214
police powers. *See* POLICE POWERS
problems
lack of direct victims, 23
size in numerical terms, 23
technical aspect of law, 23
procedure. *See* PROCEDURE
proceedings for, 37–38
prosecution and punishment, 133,
146–148
range of, 91–92
regulations, 114
substantive. *See* SUBSTANTIVE
OFFENCES
trial. *See* TRIAL
See also PENALTIES
Offender
age of, 93
degree of participation, 94
foreign, 93
motive of, 94
rehabilitation of, 95–97
sentencing. *See* SENTENCING
treatment. *See* TREATMENT
Opioids
appearance, 11
dependence on, 11*n*
dosage, 12
drugs in this category, 11
effects, 12

Opioids—*continued*
　general information, 11
　method of administration, 12
　price, 12
　slang names, 11
　source, 11
Opium
　growing awareness of abuse, 4
　history, 3
　meaning, 61
　medicinal, meaning, 61
　prohibition of certain activities, 123
　prohibition of use, 4
　smoking, 75–77

Package
　drug concealed from direct
　　perception by, 55–56
Penalties
　application of, 163
　Commissioners' power to mitigate,
　　163
　foreign law, under, 93–94
　forfeiture, in lieu of, 159–160
　fraudulent evasion of duty, 166–167
　general provisions, 167–168
　imprisonment, maximum terms, 162
　maximum, 34–35, 92
　non-payment, 162
　variation of, 168–169
Persons
　customs officers' powers to search,
　　166
　offences against, 80, 172
Pethidine
　midwives, exemption in respect of,
　　180–181
Peyote mushroom
　history, 3
Pharmacist
　convicted of offence, prohibition of
　　prescription, 125
　information, power to obtain, 129–
　　130
Police
　co-operation with, 94
　concentration of resources, 23–24
　evidence, power to search and
　　obtain, 131–132
　legal control of abuse, 24
　powers
　　arrest, 25–28, 32–33, 133
　　extra, 30–33
　　generally, 25
　　search, 25–28, 30–32
　　seizure, 25–28
　quantity of drugs seized by, 210

Poppy-straw
　exemption, 176
Possession
　actus reus of offence of, 67
　admission of, 64
　case of *Goodchild*, 61–62
　consumption, after, 57
　contents of container, of, 55–56
　controlled drug, meaning, 60–61
　defences, 65
　different forms of controlled drugs,
　　62–63
　drug concealed from direct
　　perception by package, box or
　　container, 55–56
　duplicity, and, 59
　evidence and, 63–64
　exemptions from prohibition, 188–
　　189
　extension back in time of offence, 60
　extension of notion, 53–54
　forensic precision required to prove,
　　63
　general authority, 176
　generally, 179–180
　ideal, 52
　illustrations of meaning, 52–53
　joint, 56–57
　knowledge, and, 54, 86–88
　lawful use, 107–108
　licence, 109
　meaning, 51–52
　minute quantities, of, 57–59
　miscellaneous cases on definition, 63
　miscellaneous points, 60
　offences, generally, 51
　prescription defence, 65–66
　provisions, 51
　restriction, 121
　specimen indictment, 204
　strict, 54–55
　with intent to supply, 48–50, 66–67,
　　204
Premises
　cannabis smoking for research
　　purposes, 181
　customs officers' powers to search,
　　165
　occupier of. *See* OCCUPIER OF PREMISES
　permitting, specimen indictment,
　　204–205
Prescription
　defence, 65–66
　exemption, 184
　form of, 183
　meaning, 174
　supply on, 184

Private citizen
arrest, search and seizure, powers of, 26
Probation service
helping drug users, 98
Procedure
Customs and Excise. *See* CUSTOMS AND EXCISE
drafting of indictments, 35–36
extradition, 36–37
forfeiture, 102
general, 37
generally, 23–24
maximum penalties, 34–35
miscellaneous provisions, 38
police. *See* POLICE
proceedings
institution of, 37
offences, for, 37–38
provisions peculiar to this branch of law, 34 *et seq.*
service of notices, 36
service of process, 37
trial
mode of, 34
place of, 38
tribunal. *See* TRIBUNAL
See also OFFENCES
Proceedings
condemnation, for, 170
incidental provisions, 162–163
institution, 160–161
offences, for, 37–38, 161
persons who may conduct, 164–165
tribunal. *See* TRIBUNAL
Process
service of, 37, 161
Production of controlled drugs
cultivation treated as, 69
generally, 176–179
lawful use, 108
licence, 176
meaning, 47–48
occupier of premises facilitating, 71–74
person assisting in, 48
produce, meaning, 47
restriction, 120–121
Professional panels
membership, 144
procedure, 144
Profits
forfeiture to eliminate, 99
various stages of supply chain, 217
Prohibited goods
offences in relation to exportation, 155–156

Records
preservation, 186–187
requirements in particular cases, 186
Registers
keeping of, 185
preservation, 186
requirements as to, 185
Regulations
authorisation of activities otherwise unlawful, 122–123
categories of drugs, 106
general provisions, 106–107, 135–136
generally, 105
notification, 111
offences, 114
prevention of misuse, 124
principal sets, 106
provisions, 135
safe custody, 110–111
Secretary of State's further power to make, 131
Rehabilitation. *See* TREATMENT
Research
cannabis smoking for purposes of, 181
Secretary of State's power to conduct, 136
Restricted goods
offences in relation to exportation, 155–156

Safe custody
special precautions, 124, 191–194
Search
customs officers' powers, 28–29, 165–166
police powers, 25–28, 30–32
private citizen, powers of, 26
warrant, specimen, 205–206
Seizure
Customs and Excise, by, quantity by drug type, 211
notice of, 169
police, by, quantity by drug type, 210
police powers, 25–28
private citizen, powers of, 26
Sentencing
basic principles, 91
Class A drugs, 92
Class B drugs, 92
factors affecting
age of person to whom drugs supplied, 93
co-operation with police, 94
offender
age of, 93

Sentencing—*continued*
  factors affecting—*continued*
    offender—*continued*
      degree of participation, 94
      foreign, 93
      motive of, 94
      personal circumstances, 94–95
      penalty under foreign law, 93–94
      quantities of drugs involved, 93
  forfeiture. *See* FORFEITURE
  general policy, 91–93
  guidelines, 92
  maximum terms of imprisonment,
    162
  persons under sentence in prison
    department establishments, 214
  range of offences, 91–92
  rehabilitation of offender, 95–97
  table, 208
  treatment. *See* TREATMENT
Service
  documents, of, 134–135
  process, of, 161
Ship
  customs officer
    access, powers of, 152
    boarding, powers of, 152
    detention, powers of, 152–153
    search, powers of, 165–166
  forfeiture
    constructed for concealing goods,
      156
    jettisoning cargo, 156
    larger ships, 158–160
    liability, 101
    penalty in lieu of, 159–160
    used in connection with goods
      liable to forfeiture, 158
Smoking
  cannabis, 181
  opium, 75–77
Smuggling
  forfeiture to deter, 101
Social problem
  doctors and pharmacists, power to
    obtain information from, 129–
    130
  existence of problem area, 114
  meaning, 114
Solvents
  effects, 20
  inhalation, 19–20
Statistics
  selected, 209–216
Stimulants
  minor, 19

Substantive offences
  attempts, 84–85
  conspiracy. *See* CONSPIRACY
  corporation, by. *See* CORPORATION
  cultivation of cannabis. *See* CANNABIS
  exportation. *See* EXPORTATION
  importation. *See* IMPORTATION
  incitement, 84
  meaning, 133
  occupier of premises, by. *See*
    OCCUPIER OF PREMISES
  opium smoking, 75–77
  other offences, 80–81
  person, offences against, 80
  possession. *See* POSSESSION
  production of controlled drugs, 47–
    48
  supply of controlled drugs, 48–50
Supplier
  documents to be obtained by, 181–
    183
Supply of controlled drugs
  constructive intent to supply, 67
  contravention of prohibition, 48
  documentation, 109–110
  generally, 176–179
  lawful use, 108
  licence, 109
  occupier of premises facilitating, 71–
    74
  pharmacist, by, 125
  possession with intent to supply,
    48–50, 66–67, 204
  prescription, on, 184
  profits at various stages of chain, 217
  restriction, 120–121
  specimen indictment, 204

Trafficking
  professional criminals, by, 6
Tranquillisers. *See* MINOR
    TRANQUILLISERS
Treatment
  general practitioners, 97–98
  Home Office statistics, 216
  hospitals, 97
  non-statutory groups, 98
  probation service, 98
  rehabilitation of offender, 95–97
  voluntary groups, 98
Trial
  mode of, 34
  place of, 38, 162
Tribunal
  consent, application for, 201
  constitution and procedure, 114

Tribunal—*continued*
default of appearance, 199
evidence, 199–200
extension of time, 202
failure to comply with rules, 202
financial provisions, 143
findings, 200
hearing
notice of, 198
procedure at, 199
inspection of documents, 198
interlocutory applications, 198–199
majority decision, 200
notice of proceedings, 197–198
membership, 142

Tribunal—*continued*
procedure, 142–143
recommendation, submissions and
evidence, 200
reference back to or to another, 201
regulation of procedure, 202
report, 200
right of audience, 199
service of notice, 201–202
supplementary provisions, 143
terms of reference and parties, 197
Vehicle. *See* MOTOR VEHICLE
Vessel. *See* SHIP
Voluntary groups
assistance by, 98